Alexandria, Virginia USA

STUDENTS TAKING ACTION TOGETHER

5 Teaching Techniques to Cultivate **SEL**, **Civic Engagement**, and a **Healthy Democracy**

Lauren M. **Fullmer**

Laura F. **Bond**

Crystal N. **Molyneaux**

Samuel J. **Nayman**

Maurice J. **Elias**

1703 N. Beauregard St. • Alexandria, VA 22311-1714 USA
Phone: 800-933-2723 or 703-578-9600 • Fax: 703-575-5400
Website: www.ascd.org • Email: member@ascd.org
Author guidelines: www.ascd.org/write

Ranjit Sidhu, *CEO & Executive Director*; Penny Reinart, *Chief Impact Officer*; Genny Ostertag, *Managing Director, Book Acquisitions & Editing*; Allison Scott, *Senior Acquisitions Editor*; Julie Houtz, *Director, Book Editing*; Katie Martin, *Editor*; Thomas Lytle, *Creative Director*; Donald Ely, *Art Director*; Mary Duran and Derrick Douglass, *Graphic Designers*; Keith Demmons, *Senior Production Designer*; Kelly Marshall, *Production Manager*; Shajuan Martin, *E-Publishing Specialist*; Christopher Logan, *Senior Production Specialist*

PAPERBACK ISBN: 978-1-4166-3097-5   ASCD product #122029   n4/22
PDF E-BOOK ISBN 978-1-4166-3098-2; see Books in Print for other formats.
Quantity discounts are available: email programteam@ascd.org or call 800-933-2723, ext. 5773, or 703-575-5773. For desk copies, go to www.ascd.org/deskcopy.

Library of Congress Cataloging-in-Publication Data

Names: Fullmer, Lauren M., author.
Title: Students taking action together : 5 teaching techniques to cultivate
  SEL, civic engagement, and a healthy democracy / Lauren M. Fullmer,
  Laura F. Bond, Crystal N. Molyneaux, Samuel J. Nayman, Maurice J. Elias.

Other titles: Five teaching techniques to cultivate social-emotional
  learning, civic engagement, and a healthy democracy
Description: Alexandria, Virginia USA : ASCD, [2022] | Includes
  bibliographical references and index.
Identifiers: LCCN 2021056251 (print) | LCCN 2021056252 (ebook) | ISBN
  9781416630975 (Paperback) | ISBN 9781416630982 (PDF)
Subjects: LCSH: Affective education--United States. | Democracy and
  education--United States. | Teachers--Training of--United States.
Classification: LCC LB1072 .F85 2022 (print) | LCC LB1072 (ebook) | DDC
  370.15/340973--dc23/eng/20220211
LC record available at https://lccn.loc.gov/2021056251
LC ebook record available at https://lccn.loc.gov/2021056252

31 30 29 28 27 26 25 24 23 22   1 2 3 4 5 6 7 8 9 10 11 12

This book is dedicated to our future citizens—the students of today and tomorrow who will feed the ecology of democracy and civic institutions in the years to come. We hope our book will make a positive contribution to your success.

STUDENTS TAKING ACTION TOGETHER

5 TEACHING TECHNIQUES TO CULTIVATE SEL, CIVIC ENGAGEMENT, AND A HEALTHY DEMOCRACY

Introduction: Democracy, Schools, and the Classroom

It's not an exaggeration to say that we are at an inflection point in our democracy. The teaching practices we use today—especially in social studies, but not limited to that area—will define our society tomorrow. Therefore, as educators we must adjust our practices to prepare students for their role as adults in a democracy. We need to adapt instruction to promote collaborative problem solving and youth leadership to address issues of race, gender, and socioeconomic status (SES), as well as the inclusion of individuals with varied abilities and heritages.

We are at a similar inflection point in education. Research and brain science have spoken: social, emotional, and academic development and accomplishment are inextricably interrelated. This means that we must imagine and create classrooms where students learn to build their muscles and skills for civility along with their social-emotional learning (SEL) competencies in service of a democratic society.

Both John Dewey and Martin Luther King Jr. insisted that democracy demands students acquire citizenship skills by *experiencing* them, not just by learning about them secondhand from historical and civics texts (Dewey, 2018; Goodloe, 2021). Their call has been picked up by advocates of whole child education, positive youth development, and moral and character education, as well as by other adherents to the importance of social-emotional learning (Elias & Yuan, 2020). Indeed, developing students' SEL competencies is now a focus both across the United States and internationally (see the Social Emotional

Learning Alliance for the United States [www.SEL4US.org] and the European Network for Social and Emotional Competence [www.enseceurope.com]).

It is deceptively simple to say to students, "Please understand that living in a democracy means you don't always get your way; when you don't, you work to gain support and make changes through the democratic process." The truth is, carrying out that advice relies on a number of SEL-related skills that education has not systematically attended to, despite general agreement on their extraordinary importance. Indeed, here is what we know:

- All aspects of academic and civic life require taking others' perspectives, both intellectually and emotionally.
- Everyone must master emotional regulation skills that enable them to deal with their own discomfort and resist temptations to act impulsively.
- SEL skills are necessary for the next stage of college and career access: graduation and job advancement.
- The workplaces of the present and future will be increasingly collaborative.
- Managing the complex and ongoing challenges of civic life in a multicultural democracy requires the same degree of competency in social-emotional learning as we demand in reading and other traditional academic areas.
- Advancing the cause of equity in all classrooms and schools, and dismantling the underlying maintainers of racism and other forms of discrimination, require a strong mastery of emotional awareness, empathy, compassion, perspective-taking, problem solving, and communication skills (among other SEL abilities) as well as a sense of positive purpose and an optimistic future-mindedness (among other character virtues).

Public Education's Moral Purpose: Fostering a Democratic Society

We are witnessing positive trends to which the work in this book is a powerful contributor. National events and student activism on key issues like gun safety and climate change have rejuvenated a focus on civics education. Over the past few years, state departments of education—including those in Tennessee, Massachusetts, Michigan, Florida, Washington, New York, Indiana, and California—have been leading a return to civics education by reconceptualizing or piloting revisions to state social studies learning standards. These revisions blend into the curriculum the active civics practice of appreciating diverse perspectives, the roles and responsibilities of citizenship, and methods of social action. In a promising sign for renewed interest in civics education at the federal level, the 116th Congress saw the introduction of the Civics Learning Act of 2019 (H.R. 849), which aimed to expand grant funding to innovate civics teaching and learning during and after the school day (Library of Congress, 2019), and the Educating for Democracy Act of 2020 (H.R. 8295), which *Education Week* described as having "a broad range of support from social studies and civics organizations and [eyeing] a much larger role for the feds in this neglected content area. It would authorize $1 billion in all toward the two subjects [social studies and civics]" (Sawchuk, 2020, para. 3). Both these bills acknowledged the responsibility of public schools to help students learn, engage in, and rehearse essential civics skills so they can effectively participate in the democratic processes as citizens in their communities, and the latter was reintroduced in the 117th Congress as the Civics Secures Democracy Act (H.R. 1814).

However, civics education efforts continue to be sporadic. They often fail to focus on all students and, instead, take the form of an elective course offered at the secondary level, an extracurricular activity, or an offering from an out-of-school organization open to only a small subset of the student population. This book reflects an alternative perspective. Social justice and student voice and activism must be defining features of every classroom and school; they are inherent parts of the definition of a positive learning environment in the 21st century. Progress toward dismantling the hidden curriculum requires that *all* students learn how to speak about the unspeakable—power, privilege, patriarchy, and passivity—without fear and with discernment and humility.

Among many sobering calls to step back and reflect on the purpose of public education in a democracy, Neil Postman's book, *The End of Education: Redefining the Value of School* (1996), has stood the test of time:

> The question is not, does or doesn't public schooling create a public? The question is, what kind of public does it create? A conglomerate of self-indulgent consumers? Angry, soulless, directionless masses? Indifferent, confused citizens? Or a public imbued with confidence, a sense of purpose, a respect for learning, and tolerance? The answer to this question has nothing whatever to do with computers, with testing, with teacher accountability, with class size, and with the

other details of managing schools. The right answer depends on two things, and two things alone: the existence of shared narratives and the capacity of such narratives to provide an inspired reason for schooling. (p. 18)

Postman's perspective has received an important recent addendum from Pedro Noguera (2019):

Anyone who works in public schools knows that students arrive with different needs. Some have experienced trauma, others are learning English for the first time, and others may be reading below grade level. It follows that our students will need different things in order to thrive and meet their full potential. Addressing the needs of all students is not easy, but that is the goal of equity in education: to treat our students the way we would want our own children to be treated. This is the true meaning of equity—acknowledging students' differences and giving them what they need to be successful. (para. 3)

This book reflects our deeper understanding of what all children need to be successful, as well as what our democracy needs from its citizens to be equitable and thrive. Our children and future citizens need to be able to do the following:

- Acknowledge emotions in themselves and in others.
- Manage and appropriately express strong emotions (not contain, suppress, or defuse them).
- Take the perspective of diverse others and experience empathy and compassion.
- Engage in the critical thinking, listening, reading, writing, and speaking skills needed for informed citizenship.
- Collectively solve problems and use their collaboration skills.
- See themselves as leaders in the change process and as social change agents in their classrooms, schools, communities, and the wider world.

The Challenge . . . and Our Solution

The key question is this: How can teachers promote deeper engagement with content, promote civil discourse, and exercise students' SEL muscles in the context of preparing students for their roles in improving classroom, school, and community life *without* adding more to their already full plate?

What's needed is an integrative, accessible, authentic approach that courageously addresses both easy and hard issues confronting our society. And this approach must apply to *all* students across such areas as race, socioeconomic status, gender, and ability. By doing so, we respect both students and educators and their capacity to embrace complexity.

The answer we offer is the Students Taking Action Together (STAT) program, a set of five instructional strategies designed to integrate SEL skills and civil discourse into existing curriculum content in grades 5–12. Although the strategies are intended to be used individually, they build on one another in an evidence-based way to foster students' competence and confidence in the areas of perspective-taking, empathy, problem solving, communication, emotion regulation, and civic engagement.

As you proceed through the chapters of this book, you will encounter detailed descriptions of the five instructional strategies, suggestions for how to use them, vignettes drawn from educators' applications of the strategies, teaching tips for implementing them in a variety of instructional contexts, and lesson plans to support you as you embark on your STAT journey. The STAT strategies will empower your students to become engaged citizens and change agents in solving real-world problems—including problems within our schools.

In addition, we complement the book's contents by directing you to additional materials on Rutgers University's Social-Emotional Character Development (SECD) Lab website (www.secdLab.org/STAT) and to professional development and networking opportunities through the university's Academy for SEL in Schools (SELinSchools.org/STAT).

To get you started, we will briefly describe each chapter so you can best determine how to navigate the book. But before you begin, please keep the following in mind:

- Although each strategy is stand-alone, we encourage you to read the chapters in order and implement the strategies in the sequence in which we present them.
- We have designed the lessons and materials so you can easily adapt them to meet the needs of your individual students.
- Take your time and feel free to read and reread sections to best address your instructional needs. If you like, write and draw on the

pages of this book and highlight sections as you begin to plan and implement the strategies with your students.

- Engaging teachers who share a grade level or discipline in a book study of this book is definitely recommended. This is best followed up by a professional learning community focus on developing and delivering lesson plans that incorporate STAT strategies.

A Walk Through the Chapters

Chapter 1. The Five STAT Strategies. This foundational chapter provides an overview of the five STAT teaching techniques: Norms, Yes-No-Maybe, Respectful Debate, Audience-Focused Communication, and PLAN. It describes how each is grounded in research and how all integrate the five competencies of the Collaborative for Academic, Social, and Emotional Learning (CASEL). You will learn how the STAT strategies can empower your students to discuss tragic and contentious events and equip them with the skills they need to become active citizens in our democracy.

Chapter 2. *Norms:* Creating the Climate for Civil Conversation. This chapter focuses on the first STAT strategy, Norms. It highlights the importance of taking the time to establish a relationship-centered learning environment in which your students feel like valued participants and are comfortable taking risks. We walk you through four steps for cocreating norms with your students and provide you with sample activities to use. Throughout the chapter, we highlight the iterative process of developing norms to ensure equitable learning spaces as you encourage your students to embrace new habits of mind and heart.

Chapter 3. *Yes-No-Maybe:* Building Skills for Social Awareness and Peer Listening. Here we describe how the second STAT strategy, Yes-No-Maybe, provides a structure for peer opinion sharing. Here and in the three chapters that follow, we introduce the strategy, describe the steps involved in planning and implementation, consider how to address obstacles you may encounter, suggest how to scale up your practice once you have developed confidence, and provide tools for formatively assessing your students' progress. We use an exemplar lesson on gangs to bring our discussion to life.

Chapter 4. *Respectful Debate:* Developing Empathy and Perspective-Taking. Here you will see how teachers can steward debates that promote understanding rather than competitive discord. We describe how the third STAT strategy, Respectful Debate, deviates from the typical classroom debate by having students engage in perspective-taking as they assume both pro and con stances. They will learn how to carefully listen to others' points of view, instead of just focusing on how to present their own arguments. Guided by empathy, students will deconstruct the dominant narratives that sustain social inequality to redefine truth for a more just society. Step-by-step, we walk you through how to select a topic and craft controversial statements, choose appropriate background sources, arrange students into groups and assign roles, and adapt a Respectful Debate lesson to the digital learning environment. We provide tools for formative assessment and use an exemplar lesson on racial equality to enliven our discussion.

Chapter 5. *Audience-Focused Communication:* **Creating Effective Presentations.** This chapter focuses on helping teachers navigate one of the most important civic and career readiness skills—presentation skills. Using the fourth STAT strategy, Audience-Focused Communication, we coach you through a series of steps in a lesson on presenting a project or book report in view of helping students build critical skills in presentation design, planning, rehearsal, and delivery. Students learn to tailor their language and speech to have the greatest effect on their audience (which includes their teachers!). During and at the end of the lesson, students reflect on their efforts to sharpen their presentation skills. Tools for formative assessment are included.

Chapter 6. *PLAN:* **A Problem-Solving Strategy for Historical Understanding and Social Action.** This chapter tackles the last of the STAT strategies, PLAN, which stands for **P**roblem description, **L**ist of options, **A**ction plan, and **N**otice successes. We guide you through the process of implementing this approach and describe in detail each of the three levels of the strategy: PLAN Basic, PLAN Comprehensive, and PLAN Integrative. We provide an exemplar lesson for each level: the Barking Dog Lesson (PLAN Basic), Women's Suffrage Lesson (PLAN Comprehensive), and Women's Rights Extension Lesson (PLAN Integrative). And, once again, we provide tools to help you formatively assess student progress.

Chapter 7. STAT Integration Across the Curriculum. Here we shed light on the versatility and transdisciplinary nature of the STAT strategies by showing their application in science, technology, engineering, and mathematics (STEM); English language arts (ELA); and the visual and performing arts (VPA) classrooms. We demonstrate how STAT can enrich the lived curriculum of your students and support the critical skills needed to help students reach their fullest potential. We show how STAT strategies support the STEM, ELA, and VPA standards and curricula, as well as provide examples of STAT in action in each instructional environment.

Chapter 8. STAT in the Inclusion Classroom. Chapter 8 details the adaptations required for seamless use of STAT to meet a range of student needs. Here, we encourage you to look beyond students' labels and perceive your students from a strengths-based approach. We underscore that cultivating an inclusive environment is an ongoing process that requires continuous change, support, and respect to remove barriers to learning for students with challenged abilities and offer them the best learning situations. Using tenets of Universal Design for Learning (UDL) and tiered assignments, we walk you through the steps of planning and executing an inclusive STAT lesson, as well as indicate technical and human support resources that may be of help along the way.

Chapter 9. Scaling up STAT. In this closing chapter, we provide a roadmap for school leaders and teacher leaders to scale up STAT in your school using a thoughtful approach to implementation that honors the hearts and minds of your educators. We end with a series of examples of educators, from Idaho, United States, to Johannesburg, South Africa, who have applied STAT to empower their students to take action in their community.

Resources to Guide You Along the Way

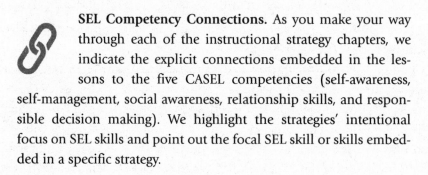

Teaching Tips. In addition to a comprehensive list of teaching tips included in Appendix C, we have embedded tips in each chapter to support you as you implement the STAT strategies. We crafted the tips on the basis of our own experiences integrating the strategies into our instruction, as well as from the feedback we received from grade 5–12 educators in diverse settings across the globe.

SEL Competency Connections. As you make your way through each of the instructional strategy chapters, we indicate the explicit connections embedded in the lessons to the five CASEL competencies (self-awareness, self-management, social awareness, relationship skills, and responsible decision making). We highlight the strategies' intentional focus on SEL skills and point out the focal SEL skill or skills embedded in a specific strategy.

Appendices. We have included a host of resources in five appendices. In Appendix A, we offer essential questions and statements for historical and current events for students in grades 5–8 and 9–12. Appendix B provides four sample STAT lessons, Appendix C includes a comprehensive list of teaching tips, and Appendix D provides lists of resources by topic for further reading. Finally, Appendix E includes elevator pitches for communicating to key stakeholders—teachers, parents, special services/school mental health professionals, and administrators—and shows you how to use STAT to strengthen the purpose of public school by turning schools into laboratories that forge connections among knowledge, social-emotional competence, and democracy.

Companion website. At the book's companion website (https://www .secdlab.org/stat/book/), we provide lesson plans for middle and high school students that emphasize the application of STAT strategies to issues of inequality related to race and ethnicity, gender, and socioeconomic status. They illustrate how you can apply STAT to historical and social issues that are difficult to discuss and how to plan lessons around these topics. Also included are several handouts and graphic organizers that will support you in your implementation of the instructional strategies.

For the Greater Good

We are confident that you will find this book to be a helpful and active resource as you begin to implement the STAT strategies. This will be a transformational professional journey for you as you empower your students and perhaps your school to shift away from the traditional hidden curriculum that all too often defines the culture of learning and schools. Because persistence is the key to social action and because privilege and power do not yield easily, in our lesson plans we share the stories of people who persisted in the face of obstacles to collaborate in the service of the ideas and ideals they believed in—such as Martin Luther King Jr., Cesar Chavez, Elizabeth Cady Stanton, Malala Yousafzai, and Alicia Garza. These leaders teach us that even when the fight seems won, it's not over forever and that vigilance in the service of one's goals is necessary. With the STAT model in hand, you will equip students to be active and powerful participants in a healthy democracy for the greater good of society.

The Five STAT Strategies

As history teacher Christine Chu drove to school, she realized that her lesson plan on the Great Depression was now going to compete with the breaking news of a school shooting that had just taken place the day before at Marjory Stoneman Douglas High School in Parkland, Florida. She anticipated that her 9th grade students would be angry and sad and would have strong views on the topic. Just thinking about the day ahead of her made her palms sweat. She hoped to connect with her department colleagues concerning how they planned to adjust their lessons to address the tragic news. She wondered if her students would feel safe. Her thinking teetered back and forth on how to navigate the conversation with the students, and her worries escalated. Then she bumped into four colleagues in the copy room—Julius, Sarah, Raul, and Keesha—and the following discussion transpired:

Julius: *I'm just going to teach and implement my planned lesson. You know how sensitive these parents are anytime you get into controversial topics. They call the principal immediately to complain.*

Sarah: *I feel like we should discuss this with students, but I'm worried that the discussion will descend into an argument and that feelings will be hurt. I don't know if some students can handle this topic. It's too controversial.*

Raul: *I agree with Sarah that we should talk about this with students. I plan to lead a small-group counseling session today with sophomores who I know have been recently affected by trauma. I'm going to comb through my counseling books to see if I can find a discussion protocol.*

Keesha: I don't know where you grew up, but I grew up in a community where we discussed politics all the time. We have to foster these discussions or students will never be ready. I just don't know how to begin the conversation, especially with an audience of students who get their political news from their social media news feeds.

Christine: I agree with Julius, but I also agree with Keesha. I feel as though we have no guidance on fostering the district's goal of 21st century citizenship, yet I'm the civics teacher! It gets me so frustrated. I'm at a loss.

Scenarios like this one are all too familiar for teachers. Politically contentious events that convulse our national imaginations can derail a lesson plan and catch teachers off guard. Many teachers don't feel confident to address traumatic school events or hot-button issues with their students or believe they don't have adequate time to do so. Consequently, teachers and schools often keep potentially divisive current events out of their classrooms in an effort to maintain order.

According to researcher Katrin Kello (2016), teachers feel underprepared and fearful about bringing sensitive and controversial issues into their classrooms because of their uncertainty about responding to their students' emotional reactions, pressures from the administration or community, and the ambivalent and conflicting feelings that may arise from their own beliefs and values. However, when we dismiss opportunities to discuss the nuances of such issues in our classrooms, we deprive students of the chance—indeed, the responsibility—to examine current and historically embedded narratives, especially those that sustain social inequality, and arrive at informed opinions about what they're seeing and hearing in the world around them.

In James Baldwin's 1962 *New York Times* article, "As Much Truth as One Can Bear," the novelist, poet, activist, and playwright wrote, "Not everything that is faced can be changed. But nothing can be changed until it is faced" (p. 38). As educators, we have a moral obligation to provide spaces in our public schools for students to process and discuss current events that affect them or that they experience in their lives and to integrate these discussions in classroom learning. Only this will prepare them to create the future they desire to see.

Moreover, depriving students of opportunities to process their emotions and thoughts can lead to unhealthy consequences and trauma. Students today are subject to a barrage of distressing images and live footage of tragic events; such media coverage is nearly inescapable. According to the Dart Center for Journalism & Trauma (2005), people who are indirectly exposed to tragedy through media coverage can develop symptoms akin to those associated with post-traumatic stress disorder.

So, although we can't control students' exposure to such media coverage, we must not underestimate our power to provide them with the space to process these shared experiences. This book, with its five Students Taking Action Together (STAT) strategies, will serve as a guide. The strategies will help teachers and students develop the skills to process and respond to tragic events in safe and secure learning environments. Students will learn the power of developing shared norms, expressing their opinions, listening respectfully and appreciating the perspectives of others, and generating plans for constructive social action, all while honing their public speaking skills. And teachers will learn how to prepare their students for life in a democracy by intentionally rehearsing democratic behaviors in their classrooms.

Social-Emotional Learning and Civil Discourse

The canvas of democracy is filled with emotion-laden discussion, debate, disagreement, and dissent. Naturally, these expressions are necessary for civil discourse and social justice work. Because emotions play such a large role in such interactions, effective civil discourse demands the development of effective social-emotional learning (SEL) skills. That's why the five research-based STAT strategies integrate the five competencies put forward by the Collaborative for Academic, Social, and Emotional Learning (CASEL), which are *self-awareness, self-regulation, social awareness, relationship skills,* and *responsible decision making.*

Emotions are the fuel for youth action. Placing emotions in the forefront of instructional planning values what many scholars, historians, and business leaders have noted—that the single most significant factor in transformational leadership is emotional intelligence (Goleman et al., 2002). Psychological theorists John Mayer and Peter Salovey (Mayer et al., 2004)—who influenced Daniel Goleman's 1994 bestseller, *Emotional Intelligence: Why It Can Matter More than IQ*—define emotional intelligence as one's ability to

- Reason about emotions to enhance thinking.
- Accurately perceive and read emotions.
- Access and generate emotions to assist thinking.

- Understand emotions and emotional knowledge.
- Regulate emotions to promote emotional and intellectual growth.

At this moment in education, teachers are eager to integrate social-emotional learning into their instruction without it being just another add-on intervention. To support such integration, as well as teacher awareness, vocabulary building, and knowledge construction in social-emotional learning, each STAT strategy lesson in this book features SEL Competency Connection boxes that show how a given competency can unleash deeper and more meaningful learning and prosocial behavior.

In her 1994 book, *Teaching to Transgress: Education as the Practice of Freedom*, author and activist bell hooks writes, "The classroom remains the most radical space of possibility in the academy" (p. 12). The more engaged students are in classroom discussions of oppression, justice, power, and equity, the greater the potential to raise student consciousness of how these constructs limit the rights, freedom, opportunities, and access of others in society. STAT strategies channel the enduring spirit of bell hooks and Paulo Freire's (1968) liberation pedagogy by empowering students to be cocreators of their learning and to interrogate power in the classroom.

According to the National Council for Social Studies (n.d.-a) in their *Guide to Civil Discourse for Students*, civil discourse is

> a conversation in which there is a mutual airing of views. It is not a contest; rather, it is intended to promote mutual understanding. Civil discourse follows general rules of polite behavior. This does not mean that you have to behave like Mr. or Ms. Manners, but it does mean that there are certain behaviors that make everyone uncomfortable and that indicate that a conversation has turned hostile and unproductive. (p. 1)

All too often, adolescents learn from the modeling of the adults around them to avoid sensitive conversations because they can boil over into conflicts. The STAT strategies can help normalize dissent, disagreement, and the discomfort associated with such challenging conversations while keeping the dialogue focused on the issues. They can help students engage with the content and facts rather than focus on personalities and who is "winning" in the discussion.

STAT strategies serve as the antidote for the vacuum of models that students are exposed to. "As a classroom community," bell hooks (1994) writes, "our capacity to generate excitement is deeply affected by our interest in one another, in hearing one another's voices, in recognizing one another's presence" (p. 8). Her point here reminds us that participating in social learning experiences and building connections with others generates a natural energy. To achieve hooks's vision, we need strategies that foster open and honest civil discourse.

Participating in STAT strategies-based learning gives students opportunities to

- Listen to opposing and diverse views.
- Wrestle with conflicting views, contradictions, and paradoxes.
- Come to understand that two things can be true but not match ethically.
- Learn to appreciate views they disagree with.
- Learn to express disagreement while respecting others' points of view.
- Come to appreciate their successes and also grasp what they might need to do differently in the future.

Everyone gains from experiencing productive struggle, dealing with the discomfort of uncertainty, and holding conflicting views in the mind. The journey through this social-emotional soup is a nonnegotiable path to nurture the muscles for civil discourse and civic engagement.

STAT and Social Justice Learning

On March 1, 2020, just months before his death, Congressman John Lewis spoke in front of the Edmund Pettus Bridge, the scene of the 1964 Selma March for voting rights, urging listeners to "get in trouble, good trouble and help redeem the soul of America" (Rashawn, 2020). Lewis's remark reminds us that a democracy demands responsible citizens, and it harks back to a warning from one of the Founding Fathers. In 1787, when Benjamin Franklin was asked what type of government the United States has, a republic or a monarchy, he replied, "a republic—if we can keep it" (Beeman, n.d.). A democratic republic requires a citizen's conscious choice to serve as an active agent of change in the ongoing struggle for human rights and justice for all. Thus, the spirit of active social justice—or, as Lewis put it, "good trouble"—is built into the foundation of the United States and is upheld in the Preamble to the U.S. Constitution.

STAT strategies provide rich academic social issues content and a pathway that give students the opportunity to practice social justice learning in the classroom rather than having to learn it by default when compelled to take action. In addition, STAT levels the traditional power dynamics of the classroom community from what Brené Brown (2020), in a recent conversation on leadership with then–presidential candidate Joe Biden, called "power over" to a more transformational learning space of "power with" that our democracy rests on.

For the purposes of this book, when we refer to social justice learning, it's helpful to consider Heather Hackman's (2005) five essential components of social justice learning (see Figure 1.1). Although we didn't develop our STAT lesson plans around Hackman's five components, we do see some natural alignment that can enhance your understanding.

FIGURE 1.1

Heather Hackman's Five Essential Components for Social Justice Education

1. Content mastery/factual information
2. Tools for critical analysis (systems of oppression)
3. Tools for action and social change
4. Tools for personal reflection
5. An awareness of multicultural group dynamics

Source: Hackman, 2005.

As you can see in Figure 1.2, we have structured our lesson plans to incorporate Hackman's five components of social justice learning. The lessons have a common structural approach to help you navigate your implementation of the strategies to support social justice learning.

In addition to featuring a focal social-emotional competency, each lesson harnesses social studies and English language arts academic standards. In the absence of national social studies standards, many states like Pennsylvania and New Jersey have recently revamped their standards, and this is getting teachers excited. In a *Washington Post* article, Shannon Salter, a high school social studies teacher and curriculum director in Allentown, Pennsylvania, shares that her state's new social studies standards help students learn "how to raise your voice in your community and advocate for your needs. [Students are] learning to collaborate to solve problems and challenge the way things are so that the country

FIGURE 1.2

The Five Essential Components for Social Justice Education in STAT Lesson Plans

Component	STAT Lesson Plan Feature
Content mastery/factual information	An inquiry-based problem-solving approach that drives deeper learning with topically relevant sources
Tools for critical analysis (systems of oppression)	Approaches to an analysis and evaluation of content sources that critique power systems and pursue the truth
Tools for action and social change	Strategy-driven activities that advance leadership and advocacy work to effect change for the common good
Tools for personal reflection	Thoughtful, reflective learning experiences at the end of each lesson
An awareness of multicultural group dynamics	Teacher supports that promote effective group processes for inclusive learning

continues to become that more perfect union that we envision" (Heim, 2021, para. 18).

The STAT lessons focus on three compelling and relevant topics: gender bias, racial injustice, and socioeconomic inequality. The lessons also explore transdisciplinary applications, such as inclusivity and equity focusing on neuro-abilities, as well as on lesbian, gay, bisexual, transgender, queer, intersex, and asexual (LGBTQIA+) identities, topics that students are currently questioning, exploring, and experiencing in their communities. (For more on social justice resources, see Appendix D.)

Promoting Active Citizenship for Social Change

By exploring historical and current issues, students will see how groups organize to bring about change in a democratic society. They will come to understand that fighting for human rights and against oppression is a long arc that often intersects with other groups' struggles and that these struggles are shared across generations.

Further, they will learn that change is not a linear and an immediate process, that many initial attempts are unsuccessful and incomplete. They will see that leaders pass the baton of inspiration to the next generation to continue the struggle—and that success depends on social-emotional awareness and persistence.

STAT lessons will help you deliver on the promise of active civics learning. With **Norms,** students develop working agreements for the good of the classroom. This social contract will foster safe and inclusive spaces for open expression and critical engagement of the issues. **Yes-No-Maybe** lessons will help students get comfortable with public speaking and active listening as they offer and consider differing opinions on an essential topic. In **Respectful Debate,** students will foster mutual understanding by drawing on multiple sources to debate public issues without diminishing opposing perspectives.

Audience-Focused Communication ensures that students are sensitive to the position and backgrounds of their intended audiences (which of course includes racial, socioeconomic, gender, disability status, and other factors) and the context in which the communication will take place. Finally, **PLAN** helps students transform their thinking into social action. Students will examine a problem from many sides, consider potential solutions, and draw up an action plan to redress the problem and then evaluate its effectiveness against actual historical examples. As small groups come together to problem solve, they engage with the structures of power to advocate for change.

Reflection is a core component of our approach. At the end of each lesson (Chapters 2–8), we include questions that provide opportunities for students to think about what they've learned. Instead of only building factual knowledge, students will reflect on the process and the skills needed for change. With the tools of STAT in hand, they are less likely to see themselves as passive and powerless in the experience of their learning; instead, they become active agents to direct, decide, and act on their learning for the common good.

Implementing the Five STAT Strategies

How do teachers implement academic lessons rich in social-emotional learning while, at the same time, cultivating civility and supporting their students' efforts to bring about social change? The five STAT strategies help answer this question in a manner that will blend with your unique approach to teaching. Instead of being an add-on to content-area curricula, they serve as a vehicle for teaching standards-driven content. For example, a 5th grade math teacher striving to teach her students about various methods to divide with fractions could engage her students in a Yes-No-Maybe about the efficacy of each method, whereas an

11th grade language arts teacher could facilitate a Respectful Debate about John Irving's portrayal of Owen Meany as a deity in *A Prayer for Owen Meany*. Teachers can use STAT strategies in limitless ways to support the academic curriculum.

We suggest that you teach the strategies in the order presented because we have designed them to build on one another in a spiraling fashion. For example, by teaching the Yes-No-Maybe strategy before Respectful Debate, your students will be competent in the areas of peer opinion sharing and taking a stand on an issue, both of which are necessary for their success with Respectful Debate. However, the progression is not linear by any means; we encourage teachers to revisit previously introduced strategies to provide students with opportunities for practice.

Further, some strategies lend themselves better than others to certain topics or content material. For example, if you are a biology teacher who wants your students to analyze the misconceptions surrounding race and genetics, a Yes-No-Maybe activity, with its focus on differing opinions, would be a better option than PLAN, which focuses more on social action. However, if you are a 6th grade social studies teacher instructing your students about the key events and outcomes of the American Revolutionary War, you might present a PLAN comprehensive lesson to analyze how the British and Colonial leaders dealt with the issues of the war to determine if there were more effective action plans each side might have taken. Beginning with the end in mind, consider the SEL skills and competencies you want to teach and practice with your students, and then choose the STAT strategy that best aligns with them. Of course, because you, too, are a learner, you should feel free to experiment and find your own comfort level with each of the strategies and how they best apply to the instructional situations you find yourself in.

Let's now look at each of the STAT strategies in more depth (see Figure 1.3).

Norms

Unlike classroom rules, which the teacher generally establishes to create an efficient and a safe environment, students cocreate the norms to make for a relationship-centered learning community in which they can openly communicate with one another. Through a discussion that the teacher facilitates, students decide on desirable and undesirable classroom behaviors. Ultimately, they develop a list of affirmatively stated norms and discuss the rationale behind each and its effect on students' well-being. Students also collectively determine ways to handle norm breaking. Norms lay the foundation for a successful

FIGURE 1.3

The Five STAT Strategies

The five STAT strategies allow teachers to plan instruction that promotes civil discourse, civic engagement, and social-emotional learning skills within the framework of existing curricula.

> **Norms** engage students in developing ethical standards that lay the groundwork for a relationship-centered classroom community.
>
> **Yes-No-Maybe (YNM)** offers students opportunities for peer opinion sharing in which they reflect on their views on an issue to take a stand and actively listen to the diverse perspectives of their classmates.
>
> **Respectful Debate (RD)** encourages students to practice the skill of perspective-taking by analyzing all sides of an issue to gain an appreciation for diverse viewpoints, and it promotes a level of comfort for revising one's original thinking.
>
> **Audience-Focused Communication (AFC)** gives students opportunities to tailor their language and style of presentation and the essential parts of their message to a specific audience or presentation context.
>
> **PLAN** involves students in action planning to change policies and practices for the greater good of society, implementation of STAT lessons by cultivating a climate that promotes respectful listening, peer opinion sharing, empathic debate, and collaborative problem solving.

implementation of STAT lessons by cultivating a climate that promotes respectful listening, peer opinion sharing, empathetic debate, and collaborative problem solving.

Yes-No-Maybe

Building off the work accomplished in developing norms, in which students establish a climate that fosters trust, participation, and equitable expectations, the Yes-No-Maybe strategy facilitates peer opinion sharing. It's a deceptively simple entry-level strategy that is easy to implement and that supports students in building the skills of perspective-taking and respectful listening. After the teacher presents a thought-provoking essential question that frames the controversial topic on which the lesson is focused, students reflect on several neutral statements related to the historical or current event and take a stance on each. They then practice respectful listening by discussing their opinions in small groups. Students can change their stance on an issue after hearing the diverse viewpoints of their peers. The instructor facilitates these conversations but does not seek to arrive at a consensus or firm conclusion.

Respectful Debate

With the skills of perspective-taking and respectful listening in place, Respectful Debate introduces students to the more complex skill of establishing and defending an informed position on a topic while empathically listening to opposing views. Respectful Debates provide ample opportunities for students to practice their emotional regulation skills. Students are assigned pro or con stances and must work in small groups. Using background sources, students collect evidence for their assigned stance. However, unlike traditional classroom debates, students must argue both sides of an issue, which enables them to analyze the question more objectively and broaden their perspectives. Yes, this does pose a challenge when students strongly disagree with one side of an issue; they must find ways to temper any strong emotions they're feeling in order to execute the task. At the same time, this presents instructional openings for teachers to teach emotional regulation techniques, such as deep breathing and positive self-talk.

Audience-Focused Communication

Teachers can use Audience-Focused Communication (AFC) as a stand-alone strategy when students present on smaller-scale classroom and school issues, such as making a report to classmates or at an assembly on how to respond to peer pressure. It can also serve as a natural extension of PLAN in that it provides students with detailed guidance on how to best present the solutions and action plans they've developed. The essence of AFC is that students identify their audience and the circumstances surrounding their presentation opportunity, determine the format of their presentation (be it a photo essay, video, song, commercial, etc.), and take into consideration their audience's views and prior knowledge in order to convey the information most effectively. AFC requires that students tap into skills from all five CASEL competencies, which the four other STAT strategies have helped to develop.

PLAN

The fifth and final strategy, PLAN, shifts the focus to social problem solving and prepares students to take civic action. PLAN stands for Problem definition, Listing options, Action plan, and Notice successes. Here, students work in small groups to collaboratively examine a historical or current problem that has no obvious solution, or perhaps they revisit a past situation to better understand how different decisions might have led to different actions and outcomes. They consider the options to address the problem and weigh the pros and cons of each.

Students then work together to develop a SMART goal and an action plan to solve the problem. They also engage in perspective-taking to consider the effect of their action plan on the various stakeholders involved, and they look to implement that plan when feasible, hence the program's (and this book's) title: *Students Taking Action Together*. The process culminates with a reflection, in which students notice successes with their plan and consider possible revisions to their thinking that might make them more successful the next time around. (See Chapter 6 for additional details about the three levels of PLAN.)

The five STAT strategies build on one another and share a common lesson design and structure, allowing for ease of implementation. Please see this book's companion website (https://www.secdlab.org/stat/book) for sample lesson plans.

STAT and 21st Century Skills

More than 20 years into the 21st century, our world is a place in which change is constant and the ability to adapt is of paramount importance. Just consider the arrival of COVID-19 in 2020. Within a year, students were faced with a global pandemic that forced them into virtual learning environments, grappled with navigating intense conversations about the resurgence of race-based ideologies and actions, and were confronted with radically opposing views on divisive political issues. Rapid advances in technology and media add another layer of adaptive complexity, as students must learn entirely new sets of skills to be successful.

Fortunately, the Partnership for 21st Century Learning (P21) has developed a framework to define the skills and knowledge students need to be successful in careers, in relationships, and as active citizens (Batelle for Kids, 2019). To ensure 21st century readiness, states and school districts have used this framework when developing standards and curricula. As you can see in Figure 1.4, the framework is based on the foundational literacy skills needed to fulfill everyday tasks; on the four competencies students need to address complex challenges; and on the character virtues that will empower young people to adapt to their changing environment (EdSurge, 2016).

Let's now examine the relationship between STAT strategies and 21st century skills by taking a deeper look at each of these areas.

FIGURE 1.4

The Components of 21st Century Skills

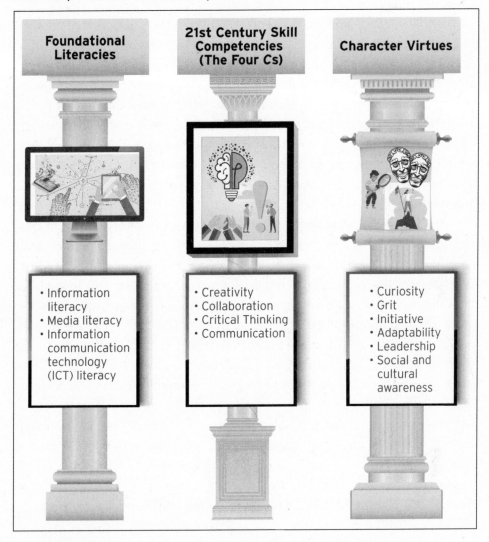

Source: EdSurge, 2016.

How STAT Supports Foundational Literacies

Our students live in an information society in which an overabundance of information is available at their fingertips; however, given the ease of publishing on the internet, much of that information is inaccurate or false (Burke, 2010). For full participation in our society, students must be able to access and critically evaluate factual information that presents all sides of an issue. This *information literacy* transcends all content areas and requires students not only to read and comprehend texts and articles, but also to analyze information presented in a variety of formats.

The STAT strategies of Yes-No-Maybe, Respectful Debate, and PLAN engage students in a critical reading of such background sources as podcasts, articles, speeches, and book excerpts. Students examine data presented in charts and tables, as well as artwork. If provided with multiple background sources, students must make meaning of what they have read or seen through synthesis. Finally, they decide how to use the information they've acquired in an ethical way by weighing any relevant social or economic issues (Emmons et al., 2009).

In addition, through the critical analysis of sources, students build their *media literacy*, which is the ability to access, evaluate, and create media for a given purpose.

STAT lessons ask students to analyze different types of media and to consider the message that a given source conveys and how it shapes an understanding of the world. For example, in a PLAN lesson on systemic racism, students review the guiding principles of the Black Lives Matter movement to consider the author's purpose in developing them. They consider the intended audience, examine the techniques used to convince that audience, and note details that were included or omitted, as well as the effect that piece of media has on the reader. In building these skills of *information communication technology (ICT) literacy*—the ability to use digital technology and communication tools purposefully and ethically—students not only develop a greater level of discernment in their consumption of media, but also a greater awareness of how, in our pluralistic society, media can significantly influence our views of different groups of individuals.

How STAT Supports the Standards—And the Four Cs of 21st Century Skills

All STAT lessons we explore in the implementation chapters are grounded in social studies standards; they also address one or more of the 10 thematic strands established by the National Council for the Social Studies (n.d.-b). Strands cover such topics as global connections; time, continuity, and change; and power, authority, and governance, to name a few.

Similarly, because all lessons build students' reading, listening, speaking, writing, and presentation skills, the English language arts standards drive the literacy elements of each lesson. The social studies and language arts standards blend together to support the four 21st century competencies (the Four Cs) of communication, collaboration, critical thinking, and creativity, which are, in essence, the expression of college and career readiness skills. Figure 1.5 shows how STAT lessons can offer students rich opportunities to practice skills that advance the aims of the Four Cs.

FIGURE 1.5

How STAT Strategies Support the Four Cs of 21st Century Learning

Creativity	Critical Thinking	Collaboration	Communication
In **PLAN** lessons, students engage in divergent thinking to brainstorm solutions to problems of inequality and human rights. With **Audience-Focused Communication**, students decide on the best type of presentation (e.g., a video collage, slideshow, song, or commercial) to deliver to a given audience.	With **all strategies**, students objectively analyze information and evaluate how to integrate it with other, possibly conflicting information. With **Respectful Debate**, students practice open-mindedness and perspective-taking by analyzing an issue from all sides.	Students begin establishing ground rules for collaboration with **Norms**. In **Yes-No-Maybe**, students meet in informal groups after taking a stance on a statement to discuss their views with others. In **Respectful Debate** and **PLAN**, students are arranged into formal groupings and with assigned roles to ensure equity.	With **all STAT strategies**, students engage in active listening, argumentative reasoning, deliberation, constructive disagreement, analysis, and learning to make decisions in and as a group.

How STAT Supports Character Development

One of the three main areas of the framework created by the Partnership for 21st Century Learning focuses on career and life skills, such as perseverance, leadership, and curiosity. Operating from a strengths-based approach, STAT strategies capitalize on the strengths of each student, as well as on other positive aspects, such as effort and the ability to work toward goals (Lopez & Louis, 2009). Each STAT strategy provides opportunities for students to develop character virtues. For example, the small-group structure enables students to practice *leadership* by summarizing and reporting on the group's work. Students exercise *curiosity* as they look to understand the perspectives of different groups and individuals involved in historical or current events. They need *perseverance* in the face of negative or discouraging feedback about their social action plans. And they learn to become more *adaptable* because they have agreed to abide by norms they might not fully accept.

More generally, students come to understand themselves better through reflective exercises that build their self-awareness; they learn to identify their strengths and how to tap into them to achieve specific goals. Through this collaborative experience, students come to see that the strengths of each individual contribute to the overall success of the group.

STAT lessons support students in developing nascent character virtues through explicit skill building. Consider a PLAN lesson designed to cultivate the character trait of initiative; here, students practice the skill of goal setting. The teacher might begin by explaining the relevance of goal setting, that it helps people effectively manage their time, stay focused, and gain confidence. The teacher might then model how to execute goal setting in terms of the issue in question using the SMART goal graphic organizer. Finally, students work in their groups to practice applying the skill and setting SMART goals of their own.

Further, implementing STAT strategies promotes another character trait that is essential for our times and in the decades to come—social and cultural awareness and responsiveness. As you will see, the lessons in this book focus on human rights, power, and injustice. We look at leaders who face ethical dilemmas framed around the topics of race, class, gender, and ability. These stories honor the array of human experiences in the struggle for advancing human rights and convey to students that all humans have dignity, despite perceived difference.

Nearly every lesson encourages students to deconstruct the dominant narratives that engender social inequality by

- Acknowledging any social or cultural biases of their own that may influence their views and decisions.
- Identifying social or cultural differences that characterize a given historical or current event (for example, the decision-making processes at work or the cultural norms or traditions prevalent at the time).
- Interpreting how the content of a historical or current event affects a specific group of people within a culture or society.

- Evaluating the effect of globalization on a specific cultural or social group.

A Better Approach

Let's now look at how the teachers we met at the beginning of this chapter might have used the STAT strategies to address the Parkland shooting with their students. What if Christine, Julius, Raul, Keesha, and Sarah had had the support of, and the experience working with, STAT strategies? Here's how that morning conversation in the copy room might have gone:

Julius: I'm going to conduct a Norms lesson with my students and then communicate to the parents that we'll be engaging in a Yes-No-Maybe lesson about the Marjory Stoneman Douglas school shooting. I'm being mindful of how sensitive the parents are anytime you get into controversial topics. My hope is that this will head off any concerns that parents may have and provide students a safe space to share their opinions on the event.

Sarah: I do worry that the discussion will descend into an argument and into outbursts of feelings, but I'm going to try a Respectful Debate to show how we can still have impassioned discussions without hurting others' feelings. With this strategy, I think that both my students and I can handle a safe and an inclusive conversation.

Raul: Like Julius, I'm going to draft a few neutral statements to use in a Yes-No-Maybe in my small-group counseling session today with sophomores who experienced trauma. I think this will help me surface their feelings in a safe group setting.

Keesha: I'm excited to launch a miniproject after our recent unit presentation. I'd like students to create a short TED Talk presentation on school safety using Audience-Focused Communication and tailor their speech to the school board.

Christine: I'm throwing out my lesson plan on the Great Depression to have students engage in a PLAN lesson for the next week on whether or not schools should have armed police officers in schools. I'm confident

that my students have learned civil discourse skills from using Norms,
Yes-No-Maybe, and Respectful Debate and that they can work in groups
to wrestle with this question.

Students need the space and opportunity to discuss their fears and experiences. Likewise, teachers need instructional strategies to meet their students
where they are at any moment in time. The STAT strategies can make this revised
scenario a reality.

More Than a Hope

As we close our introduction to the STAT strategies, let's review the purpose
of STAT. The five STAT strategies deliver a research-based instructional model
to integrate social-emotional learning, civil discourse, and social justice while
meeting academic standards. Envision a democratic classroom where students
have the skills to engage in civil discourse learning about relevant historical and
current issues and to effect change through social problem solving. Given the
complexities and dynamics of public education, this is often an unfulfilled hope
for student learning.

Now take a step back and imagine that you have the support you need, that
you're equipped with the instructional skills and guidance to facilitate students
as they engage in discussion, debate, and social problem solving with civility.
STAT can make this hope a reality for both you and your students.

Norms: Creating the Climate for Civil Conversation

The conversation in the teachers' room was pretty much the same as usual. Mr. Garcia was talking about how some students in his class talked over one another and didn't give other students a chance to finish a thought before responding. Ms. Rabinowitz looked beaten down. "I had to send Pat and Rey to the office again because they kept teasing students in the groups they were working in." Ms. Taylor wondered, and not for the first time, about the small group of students in her class who almost never spoke up and were so hesitant when she called on them that she felt bad doing so. Other teachers agreed. It was more and more rare to have all or even most students engaged in discussions, comfortable sharing their views, and working collaboratively as opposed to competitively.

For students to have authentic and meaningful learning experiences, they must be able to share their thoughts and feelings. Creating a climate for sharing is an ongoing task that requires educators' full attention, especially when they teach adolescents, an age group marked by sensitivity to social comparison and negative peer pressure and by a desire to avoid uncomplimentary labeling. Being a member of a marginalized group can amplify these complications—and students' reticence—even more.

Typically, creating a context in which all students feel they can honestly express themselves is a multistage process. First, you need to get a clear conception of the purpose and importance of norms within your classroom. Next, you need to arrange the physical environment of the classroom in a way that fosters positive relationships with and among your students. At that point, students can be engaging students in the active development of class norms through reflective exercises and collaboration. And once classroom norms are established, they must be revisited with students periodically and continually adjusted to maintain a positive, productive, and dynamic class climate.

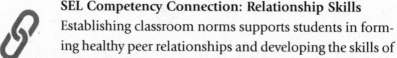

SEL Competency Connection: Relationship Skills
Establishing classroom norms supports students in forming healthy peer relationships and developing the skills of active listening, effective communication, constructively navigating conflicts, and appreciating the differences of others. The goal is for the teacher to support the application of these skills in a whole-class setting so students can then transfer those same skills to working with others in small groups, in partnerships, and on teams.

Start with Norms

Participating in meaningful conversations about important topics requires that certain norms are in place that will allow those conversations to occur productively, with all students feeling empowered to contribute. Like other areas of instruction, STAT thrives when students are in a trusting, caring environment where they feel close, supportive relationships with their teachers, other adult mentors, and one another. If you didn't establish such a positive climate at the start of the school year, you don't have to wait until next year to do so; conversely, if you *did* create this kind of climate at the outset, it's not guaranteed to last through the ensuing months without ongoing work on your part.

Teaching Tip
When getting started with norms, establish some checkpoints for revisiting them as a group and making necessary changes. Some natural checkpoints include the end of each marking period, after holiday breaks, and any time students are exhibiting problematic behaviors and struggling to adhere to the current norms.

When you take those first steps in developing norms for a relationship-centered classroom community, in essence you're working to answer this student question: *What will it feel like to be in this setting?* Your response will unfold over time. Arranging the environment and creating comfort are things you can do before students enter the classroom, while they enter the classroom, and as they get started on their activities. See Figure 2.1 for initial steps you can take.

FIGURE 2.1

Creating Norms for a Relationship-Centered Learning Community

1. **Consider the arrangement and tone of the classroom environment:**
   - Arrange seating so students can see one another.
   - Make sure bulletin boards and displays reflect the rich diversity of your students.
   - Be welcoming and greet students as they enter your room.
   - Have regular routines for how activities will start, including sharing circle moments or the equivalent if desired.

2. **Consider how you create a comfortable learning environment:**
   - Use students' names often.
   - Establish and enforce ground rules and agreements consistently with the help of students, and revisit periodically.
   - Model the behaviors of respect, caring, self-control, and fair decision making.
   - Use energetic, enthusiastic, and receptive body language and words to convey interest and respect.
   - Use a respectful "get quiet" signal to refocus students during group work.
   - Focus on all students' positive qualities and praise their efforts.

3. **Consider how you manage collaborative or group work:**
   - Give students time before they begin work to set academic and social goals for the activity.
   - Provide periodic mindful moments for students to take a break. Have them engage in a one-minute breathing or focusing activity to help relieve stress before they continue their work.
   - Allow students time to reflect after lessons, sessions, or units, ideally in a reflection journal.
   - Take time at the conclusion of group work to debrief the activity so students can identify successful experiences and partner skills, as well as set goals for improving future group work.

4. **Consider how you manage discipline:**
   - Encourage students to discuss solutions rather than blame others for problems.
   - Frequently discuss classroom and group agreements with students, and work with them to make changes when things are not going well.
   - Handle problems quickly and discreetly, treating students with respect and fairness.
   - Share your reactions to inappropriate behaviors and actions, and explain why the behaviors are unacceptable.
   - Talk outside class with students who continue to disregard the group agreements.
   - Monitor your own tendencies to ensure discipline is consistent, fair, and not reflective of any bias due to student race, ethnicity, gender, socioeconomic status, family circumstance, sexual orientation, or differing student attributes or abilities.

How the room looks and how you greet students are powerful tone setters, as is the practice of calling students by name, your own appearance of enthusiasm to see them, and clarity about what typically happens in the room and what will happen today. Students want to know that their teacher will be considerate of their feelings and fair in their treatment of all students. They may challenge you at times, but this is more to *find* the limits—to be sure you have guardrails up that will protect them—than to break those limits. Of course, some students may relentlessly test the limits, which may require you to consult with school support staff, but typically such students are exceptions to the rule.

Developing Classroom Behavioral Norms

STAT encourages students to take an active, participatory approach to learning and problem solving, to be respectful and curious, and to question their own preconceptions and ideas as well as those of classmates. In STAT discussions and projects, it's helpful to be optimistic about possibilities for the future and forgiving of classmates who may not use the "right" words the first couple of times they try to express their complicated ideas and feelings. When you consider problems and issues, whether past, present, or future, it's important to be generous about all ideas—both yours and others—and to be constructively creative in finding new ways to think about problems. For this to take place as effectively as possible, norms must align with these aspirations.

Following are some techniques that will guide teachers and students in creating empathic and inclusive spaces for true exchange and understanding and that will enable students to feel both a sense of connection to and ownership of their learning. If you already have norms or if you have not touched on them in a while, revisit them before starting a STAT activity. It never hurts to remind students of how to be civil, respectful, and engaged in class discussion. When you do revisit established norms, consider giving the new norms a different name, such as Classroom Constitution or Group Agreement.

Focusing on the Value of Norms

Start class with an activity that highlights the importance of norms. Here are some to consider.

Do-Now Activity 1: Free Response

Ask students to respond to the following prompts:

- What is your favorite sport or game? Pick three rules you would remove from it. How would the game differ? Would it be easier or harder to play? Would it be more or less enjoyable? Why?

- Think of classes or groups you've been in that you enjoyed, as well as those that made you uncomfortable. Write down five reasons that made the class or group enjoyable and five reasons that made it uncomfortable.

Do-Now Activity 2: Picture Projection

Project the image displayed in Figure 2.2—an illustration called "My Wife and My Mother-in-Law" by early-20th century cartoonist W. E. Hill, which is in the public domain and widely available online.

Ask students what they see. Are they sure of what they're seeing? How do they know? What else could the image be depicting? What might someone else be seeing? Next, have students share their answers and reflect on how people can see the same thing in different ways. Ask what they think the artist intended for them to see. (Students might see either a young or an old woman; both faces are there.) Make the point that we can't always be sure about what we're seeing and hearing, so it's important to follow up before making judgments.

FIGURE 2.2

Perspective-Taking: *What Do You See in This Picture?*

Do-Now Activity 3: Collaborative Exploration

Divide students into small groups. Provide several index cards; two plastic straws; a deck of cards; tokens of some kind; and a pen, pencil, or marker. When all the materials are distributed, ask students to create a game with rules that everyone agrees on. After 5 to 10 minutes, check in with the groups and ask them what it was like to develop rules and if they had difficulty deciding on norms. If so, what made it difficult?

Through this activity, groups begin to understand that the nature of a game and our enjoyment of a game are tied to its norms. Games like Scrabble, Mancala, or Monopoly wouldn't be what they are without the rules and norms that give them a framework and an identity. Having students collaboratively create their own games with norms emphasizes that participation, learning, and respect are important because they provide clarity, direction, and engagement.

 Teaching Tip

These do-now activities are great to use when introducing the concept of developing norms in small groups or teams. Although each group's norms may differ, they can all successfully clarify the behavior of group members, the role that each member will play, and the consequences that will ensue if students violate the norms. Also, remind students that they may need to revise the norms throughout the process as the group evolves over time.

Engaging Students in Norm Development

The two activities that follow can help students get started on developing their own classroom norms.

Specific Norm Development: Activity 1

1. *Small-group list generation.* Divide the class into groups of three to five and ask students to generate a short list of desirable and undesirable classroom behaviors—those that support the well-being of everyone in the class and those that undermine class well-being.

2. *List sharing and consolidation.* After about 5 minutes, ask groups to take turns sharing their lists and providing the rationales behind their choices. Encourage contrasting viewpoints, but stress that the objective is to work toward consensus: a set of norms that

everyone agrees will benefit all. If your students would benefit from more guidance, you might also explicitly structure norms in a list of "shoulds" and "should nots" (e.g., *We should* listen to one another; we *should not* interrupt someone who has the floor.)

3. *Norm (and consequence) setting.* Work with students to engage in perspective-taking by asking how breaking a norm might affect others in the class and why the person breaking the norm might have done so. Facilitate a conversation on how to respond if a student departs from the norms. Discuss sanctions or consequences (both positive and negative) for following and departing from the norms.

4. *Rule alignment.* Your school may have buildingwide policies concerning the consequences for certain actions (for example, harassment, intimidation, and bullying); if so, discuss these and align the norms accordingly.

5. *STAT connections.* Underscore the purpose of norm setting and its link to the upcoming STAT lessons. You want them to understand that the point of this work is to create a climate that will promote responsible listening, respectful empathic debate, peer sharing, and collaborative creativity.

Specific Norm Development: Activity 2

1. *Think-pair-share.* Ask students about the classrooms or groups in which they felt the most successful. Why did they feel this way? Have students report out ideas and create a list.

2. *Idea rating.* Have students use thumbs up (yes), thumbs to the side (maybe), and thumbs down (no) to share their views on the ideas put forward. Create a list of the top seven ideas, combining ideas as needed.

3. *Group list refinement.* Have students meet in small teams to focus on two to three activities or actions that would make the classroom or group more effective in carrying out each idea. For example, if "being listened to" is on the list, an associated action might be ensuring students don't interrupt or talk over others. Have teams share and come to a consensus on actions related to each of the ideas.

4. *Revisiting existing norms.* Review your current norms and consider how to integrate these new ideas. Model for students the courage to revise or replace existing norms if needed.

5. *Reviewing consequences.* Discuss with students how norms can help the class work more effectively, and encourage everyone's participation. Let students know that you will routinely review the ideas, actions, and consequences contained in the norms and adjust as necessary.

For a sample set of norms for a STAT class, see Figure 2.3.

FIGURE 2.3

Sample Norms for a STAT Lesson

1. Be a careful and considerate listener by paying attention to the speaker's words, tone, and body language, and avoid interrupting, yelling, and name calling.

2. Treat your classmates the way you would like to be treated.

3. Help everyone participate, because everyone's contributions and ideas matter.

4. Work to understand other points of view. Ask yourself, *Why might they have that opinion?*

5. Be a builder of ideas! Think how you can contribute to someone else's idea.

6. Respect one another even if you disagree. When you disagree with a classmate, ask a question to try and understand the other student's perspective. You can disagree without being disagreeable.

7. Have a strategy for dealing with strong emotions, especially negative ones. For example, you might draw what you're feeling; write in a journal; express emotions using an "I feel" statement; take five deep breaths with slow exhales; close your eyes and visualize a calm scene; or repeat to yourself, *Stay calm, stay calm.*

Creating Instructional Norms

STAT asks students to think differently. They're going to revisit history and imagine it happening in different ways. They're going to look at current problems in their school, their community, and beyond to find creative and effective solutions to long-standing difficulties. We want to encourage new habits of mind and heart and turn those into new norms for students.

Research has identified the kind of pedagogical strategies that are most likely to create respectful, safe, supportive, and intellectually challenging classroom environments (Durlak et al., 2015; Zins et al., 2004). Figure 2.4 captures a number of strategies you can use to foster such a climate that are effective in both live and virtual environments.

Review the strategies you already use in each of the four areas depicted earlier in Figure 2.1—the physical arrangement of the room, how you create a comfortable learning environment, how group work plays out, and how you manage discipline. Then pick one new strategy you will use in each of the four areas. Work to implement your chosen strategies over the next marking period, evaluating your progress at the end. Create a plan to improve for the next marking period or add another area to focus on. This clearly is an ongoing, personal process of professional development.

FIGURE 2.4

How to Foster a Positive Classroom Environment

---

1. **Prepare students to learn, practice, and apply new skills (including cognitive strategies) and information:**
   - State the purpose of the guided practice and the skill that students need to demonstrate.
   - Assure students that it's OK to make mistakes as they learn a new skill or apply a skill to new situations. Help them review these situations and extract a constructive takeaway.
   - Model guided practice before asking students to practice and apply new skills and knowledge.
   - Give timely, supportive, and clear feedback immediately after guided practice.
   - Ask students questions to help them reflect on their learning and imagine ways they might put the new skill or information to use in their own lives.
   - Assign follow-up activities that are essential to the practice and application of the new skills and information, and continue emphasizing the new skills with students to provide a continuous thread of learning beyond formal sessions.

2. **Introduce material and present new information in ways that are likely to increase student buy-in and connection:**
   - Connect new skills and information to students' interests.
   - Give clear instructions; model tasks when appropriate.
   - Respond respectfully to a wide variety of student responses to show openness to divergent thinking—for example, "Thank you, that's a new idea"; "You added an interesting point to what was just said"; "I appreciate your sharing your perspective"; "What do others think of that?"; and "Who would like to share a different idea? A similar one?"
   - Share personal experiences from time to time to create deeper connection, and model and encourage appropriate and authentic student disclosure.

continued

FIGURE 2.4 (*continued*)

---

3. Encourage student participation in learning activities:
- Ask open-ended questions to discover what students already know and to review retention from previous sessions.

4. How to Foster a Positive Classroom Environment
- Use "What do you think?" rather than "Why?" questions to stimulate divergent thinking.
- Invite students to participate in a nonthreatening way by posing a question to individuals, pairs, or small groups to consider a moment on their own, to respond to in writing, and to discuss as appropriate, and then encourage volunteers to share their responses in pairs or groups.
- Use a generous wait time of 7–10 seconds before asking for responses to a question.

5. Encourage safety, caring, and responsiveness:
- Encourage a service orientation. Help all students understand what it means to be responsible, involved citizens of the class, group, and school and how success for each depends on many others.
- Pursue social, emotional, and character development by integrating SEL skills into the curriculum.
- Promote an environment where students appreciate differences by teaching them to understand issues of diversity.
- Help students feel safe expressing their feelings, and build a "feelings vocabulary" in the classroom. Recognize, honor, and talk about your own feelings and the feelings of your students.

But What If . . . ?

Several questions will arise as you implement these new practices. Let's take a look at some of them.

What happens if there's a conflict in a discussion?

- Acknowledge the feelings in the room.
- Take a break, and have the class quickly write down or draw what they may be feeling, thinking, or experiencing.
- Reorient students to the class norms and values, such as respectful empathetic debate and responsible listening. Help students use the tools to communicate their experiences in a way that encourages understanding.
- Help students focus on solutions, not problems, in conflicts.

How do I ensure that students will buy into the norms?

- Keep ground rules or class discussion norms visible at all times.
- At the end of each marking period, have students rate themselves on how well they followed the rules, and have them create a PLAN on how to better follow them.
- Refer to norms when things go well. For example, "That was a great discussion. Let's reflect on what made it so good. Which norms did we follow?" You can use the same approach for small-group work, pair shares, and so on.

How do I respond when behaviors violate the norms?

Part of any discussion about norms includes how to handle situations when norms are not kept: Do we mention the departure when it happens or wait until later and discuss it with the student in private? Of course, we need to do both at various times. It's best to defer comment when a student has been the object of a negative remark, teasing, or other disparagement; even constructive correction will likely add to the student's separation from peers. In those cases, hold a conversation with the student in private as soon as you can arrange it. At the next opportunity, have a discussion with the class or group about how peers should respond to behavior that goes against the classroom norms. Here's one guideline directed to students, based on "I" messages: When someone is violating the norms, start by saying what you saw and heard. Whether it was directed at you or to another student, say, "I feel X when you say or do Y. That behavior is not something we do in our class."

By teaching this explicitly, you're creating a climate where upstanding is expected, not heroic. That is, you communicate clearly to students that they have come together for a reason—to learn and accomplish—and that you expect them to help one another participate and succeed. Students need to know that the norms are not there to control them or make them compliant; rather, they define ethical standards of how people relate to one another, an essential element of character development (Lickona, 2004).

The expectation is that students will be *upstanders*—that is, that they will stand up for these norms and not watch or support norm violation without acting. Indeed, the norms help everyone learn how to act toward others even when conflicts or strong feelings are involved. That's the spirit in which comments about violations of norms should be delivered and taken.

SEL Competency Connection: Self-Management

Although norms lay the groundwork for effective self-management, it's often necessary to explicitly teach self-management skills. For example, if you notice that students are struggling to manage their emotions, you can certainly support them in developing a related norm, but it's also helpful to teach them skills that can help them succeed in this area, such as 5-2-5 breathing (a five-count inhale, two-count hold, and five-count exhale) and grounding techniques. (Additional techniques are available in the "Handouts" section of the book's companion website: https://www.secdlab.org/stat/book.) When teaching these skills, explain why the skill is purposeful, clearly model the skill, provide a prompt so students know when to implement the skill, and offer many opportunities for practice.

Assessing—and Adjusting—Norms

As you sense the climate in the classroom is shifting, revisit the agreed-on norms. Remind students what *norms* are: shared working agreements that need to be continually reviewed and adjusted.

Have students reassess the norms using the Norms Check-In Assessment shown in Figure 2.5. The check-in presents five questions for students to address with their peers in small groups and then debrief as a whole class. Underscore with your students that their honesty and candid views will help improve the classroom norms. Walk around the room to monitor the discussions, and encourage students to voice their observations and experiences. You can debrief as a whole class after each question or after students have completed all five questions.

FIGURE 2.5

Norms Check-In Assessment: Questions for a Student-Driven Discussion

1. Does our current list of norms still encourage everyone to get along and learn together as a classroom community?
2. Which norms are helping you work with one another and get along in the classroom community? How do you know?

3. Have you had any experiences that indicate a need to change or revise the norms?

4. Which norms do you think we need to revise, and why?

5. Do we need to add any new norms to encourage everyone to continue to work together and get along as a classroom community?

Post the suggested revisions publicly so the entire class can see them. Wait a day or two before officially revising the original norms document to allow for any additional thoughts to surface in class. When the class is ready to finalize their new list of working norms, review the suggested revisions, write them down on chart paper, and have every student sign off on the chart paper that they agree to these norms for the good of the group. Post the signed norms in a visible location. Express your appreciation for the students' collective and brave efforts, and let them know you will all return to the document when the times call for it.

Creating Norms: Some Forward Reflections

As you conclude your planning on implementing the norms strategy, contemplate the following:

- What norms have you already established in your class? How do you feel about modifying them in light of any current polarization or lack of decorum?

- What are the benefits of adding a social-emotional learning focus to your norms?

- What challenges do you think your students might have adhering to the norms while discussing difficult issues?

- How might you leverage the support of other school personnel to help you implement your norms and enhance your practice?

Yes-No-Maybe: Building Skills for Social Awareness and Peer Listening

You launch a statement for the class to respond to: "Poor people are the victims of their own decisions." Your volley is met with wide-eyed expressions that convey shock . . . and silence. The silence surprises you; you know your students have no shortage of opinions about social issues, because you've heard them talking in the hallway and lunchroom. You throw out another statement: "Government policies contribute to economic disparities in wealth." A lone student volunteers a response. The others remain silent, smirking or look down at their desks or exchanging glances with one another. All that preparation, you think, and students are still reluctant to openly share their opinions. Why are they so unwilling to express their views on issues that have such a profound effect on their communities and home lives? You take a deep breath to quell your mounting frustration. Then you abandon the conversation and announce your "Plan B" lesson option: students will write about how and why people should share their opinions and then discuss this issue in small groups.

The Yes-No-Maybe Strategy

The experience of developing a whole-class set of norms lays the foundation for peer opinion sharing. Asking each student to agree to those commitments fosters safety and the opportunity to learn how to get along with others and work as a healthy, functioning group. Although students may snicker at agreeing to a class social contract, remind them that approaching others' views with generosity, curiosity, nonjudgment, and an open mind sets the table for a free discourse. Getting adolescents to jump into open and free discourse *without* asking them to put on the training wheels would be foolhardy. Yes-No-Maybe serves as an entry-level structured lesson where students can learn to express their opinions and regulate their emotions on controversial topics.

Yes-No-Maybe is easy to implement and helps encourage perspective-taking and respectful listening. Figure 3.1 shows the strategy's five sequenced steps for guiding students through the process of sharing opinions with peers.

FIGURE 3.1

The Five Steps of Yes-No-Maybe

---

1. **Introduction and Initial Reflection**
   - The teacher introduces the Yes-No-Maybe strategy and one or more statements.
   - Students engage in free writing to reflect on each statement.

2. **Yes-No-Maybe: Round One**
   This step repeats for each statement.
   - The teacher reads a statement, and students reflect on whether they agree with it (yes), disagree with it (no), or are unsure about it (maybe).
   - Students move to groups on the basis of their Yes-No-Maybe response.
   - Students engage in peer opinion sharing within their Yes-No-Maybe group and explain their reasons for agreeing, disagreeing, or taking a neutral stance.

3. **Background Source Analysis**
   - Students critically read and analyze background sources related to the topic of the lesson.

4. **Yes-No-Maybe: Round Two**
   - Given the knowledge gleaned from background sources and from peer opinion sharing, students reflect on whether their stance on each statement has changed.
   - Students repeat the steps from Round One—that is, they move to groups that express their current opinion about that issue, and they explain their reasons for holding that opinion.

5. **Reflection and Assessment**
   - Students respond in writing to questions about the experience.
   - Students debrief as a whole class as to whether or not their perspectives have changed.

In Step 1, teachers introduce the strategy and provide students with a set of neutral statements related to either a historical or current event for them to free write about.

In Step 2, students must decide if they *agree* with each statement, *disagree* with it, or *are not sure* what they think about it. After students reflect on their opinions related to the issue, they move to one of three designated areas of the room—"Yes" (agree), "No" (disagree), or "Maybe" (not sure)—to discuss their views in triads or quartets.

During this dialogue, students practice *social awareness skills* by engaging in respectful listening, making eye contact with the speaker, and asking clarifying questions or paraphrasing what the speaker said to check for understanding. Students tap into their *emotional regulation skills* to inhibit their own reactions as their peers share their opinions on an issue, and they practice connecting with their peers' feelings and thoughts. Practice with these two social-emotional skill sets helps students broaden their perspectives and understand that their peers can have opinions that are very similar to and very different from their own. They also learn that when trying to better understand others' perspectives, it's preferable to reserve judgment and ask questions, as opposed to making assumptions based on one's own experiences. Step 2 is repeated for as many neutral statements as were presented in Step 1.

SEL Competency Connection: Self- and Social Awareness
The combination of self- and social awareness skills involved in Yes-No-Maybe strategy helps students recognize and accurately account for their own emotional state while interacting with their peers. Students come to understand that their peers are experiencing their own set of emotions; this understanding creates a willingness to hear others' perspectives, as well as an openness to the emotional resonance of others' opinions. Some discomfort and awkwardness are to be expected at first. This is no easy skill to build; it requires immense courage and repeated practice.

In Step 3, students engage in a critical reading of background sources. Through coaching, teachers cultivate students' abilities to bring their outside knowledge and values to the reading and combine them with the information in the text to develop new ideas. Through inquiry, teachers support students in reflecting on what the text says, and by doing so, they might arrive at an inference about the text as a whole (Yu, 2015). This analysis either leads students to refute their previous stance on the issue or provides them with additional evidence to support their initial position.

Step 4 is the second round of Yes-No-Maybe, in which students determine whether their stance on each of the statements presented during the first round has changed. This provides the perfect opportunity to convey to students that shifting their opinions and beliefs is natural and acceptable. In fact, taking part in engaged dialogue and perspective-taking with an open mind are fundamental habits for building empathy and taking democratic action.

When students hear the perspectives of their peers and read background sources to broaden their understanding of the issue at hand, it's only natural that their opinions might shift. However, be aware that changing one's opinion on an issue can be perceived as a sign of weakness, particularly among those in leadership positions ("flip-flopping"). From a young age, children are taught the importance of sticking to their moral beliefs and virtues—no matter what. However, people and circumstances evolve over time, as do their beliefs, which is the point we must drive home to our students.

Finally, during Step 5, students respond in writing to several reflection questions that prompt them to consider what they learned about the topic and how their views may have changed as a result. The lesson culminates in a whole-class discussion to debrief on those changes in perspective and clarify what students learned from engaging in peer opinion sharing.

Planning for a Yes-No-Maybe Lesson

The versatility of Yes-No-Maybe lessons is practically limitless. You can use them to meet academic content standards, you can apply them to historical or current events, you can implement them to resolve contentious disagreements that arise in student learning or in guidance or school discipline issues, and you can embed them in professional development and cocurricular activities.

Although you can integrate Yes-No-Maybe across the curriculum, we will situate our discussion around using the strategy in the social studies classroom. This content area's necessary consideration of conflict, inequality, human rights, technological developments, and human interactions with the environment provides fodder for students to exercise their skills of peer opinion sharing. Moreover, the inequality and injustice that are featured daily in the news are the hot topics students engage with on social media platforms, in school hallways, and at lunch tables with their peers. Yes-No-Maybe is a safe and an equitable entry-level discussion strategy teachers can use to help students express their views, listen to multiple perspectives, and learn how information can play a role in modifying opinions.

Integrating this strategy into your curricular content can be exciting, but knowing where to start can be vexing. Figure 3.2 shows the steps to take when planning a Yes-No-Maybe lesson.

FIGURE 3.2

How to Plan a Yes-No-Maybe Lesson

---

1. **Select a topic for the lesson.**
   - Review the curriculum for controversial social issues that have no clear solution.
   - Consider current events that your students have expressed an interest in discussing.
   - Consult with a colleague or media center specialist for guidance and support.
   - Enlist your students in the process by sharing a copy of the curricular unit with them and having them brainstorm possible topics.

2. **Develop an essential question related to the topic.**
   - Phrase the question in a way that provokes inquiry.
   - Connect the question to content standards and desired learning outcomes.

3. **Craft four to five neutral statements related to the topic.**
   - Phrase statements in a way that does not express support for any side.
   - Refer to any curricular documents and potential background sources.

4. **Select background sources that present all sides of the issue.**
   - Consider a variety of sources (podcasts, articles, excerpts from speeches, photographs, and so on).
   - Tap into the expertise of the media center specialist to fine-tune your selections.

Selecting a Topic

Start by taking time to survey your curriculum for issues that have no clear solution. Look at natural points in the curriculum that reflect divisiveness, debate, and conflict, as well as social issues that are commonly misunderstood, like poverty, racism, and gender inequality. Similarly, choose a topic that's been in the news that relates to your curriculum and that students have expressed an interest in discussing. For example, if your class is studying the Great Depression's 1933 Agricultural Adjustment Act's Food Stamp Program, you might develop a Yes-No-Maybe lesson on how the Trump Administration's budget reductions affected the Supplemental Nutrition Assistance Program from 2016 to 2020. This does take time on your end to research, so don't hesitate to work with a colleague or your media center specialist. The juice will be worth the squeeze when you find a topic that will engage your students.

Enlisting your students in this process can elevate student voice and ownership of their learning. Share a copy of the unit of study with students, and have them work in small groups to brainstorm potential current events connections to the unit's topic or theme. Encourage researching the topics if appropriate. Facilitate a whole-class debriefing of suggested current events to explore. Make a list of the topics, and have students vote on their top three choices. Note that students will likely need guidance to figure out how to effectively read the unit of study document.

Developing an Essential Question

Once you've agreed on a topic, you'll need to develop a compelling essential question to frame the lesson and inspire your students. The question should be written in such a way that it guides students to a more thorough understanding of the conceptual underpinnings and allows them to grasp connections between the past and the present. Each question should provoke deeper thinking and consideration of different perspectives and should be phrased to frame content objectives and promote enduring understanding. Here's an example: *"Does racism backfire on the people it intends to privilege?"* Note how the phrasing frames the content objectives of analyzing the impact of racism—socially, politically, and economically—on the lives of Brown, Black, and white people.

Keep in mind that the essential question you develop here will be the foundation for all the neutral statements you will craft. Notice how the essential question *"Are gangs trying to do good for society?"* offers an entry point for neutral statements about the sense of purpose that people might derive from joining gangs, as well as the impact that gangs have on society as a whole.

Crafting Neutral Statements

Once you have set an essential question, you can begin the process of writing four to five neutral statements that will help guide the lesson. The goal here is to phrase the statements in a way that does not lead students' thinking in one direction or another. Be sure to reflect on your own biases on the topic to ensure they don't influence the content of the statements. Collaborating with a colleague or supervisor can be a valuable check-and-balance to this process.

Let's use the "Yes-No-Maybe: Gangs Doing Good for Society" lesson as an example. You can find this lesson on our companion website (https://www.secdlab.org/stat/book) and in Appendix B (see p. 174). As mentioned, proceeding from the essential question *"Are gangs trying to do good for society?"* you might ask students to contemplate the neutral statement *"There is a link between gangs and drugs, violence, and crime."* Compare that to something like *"People in gangs are dangerous individuals."* Notice how the first statement focuses on potential connections, whereas the second focuses on the all-too-common perceptions held about people in gangs.

Here are three other neutral statements that might follow from this essential question:

- *People can be motivated to join gangs to make money and gain power.*
- *Gangs can give people a sense of purpose.*
- *Young people who live in an area where gangs are prevalent are often pressured to join.*

Crafting neutral statements does take repeated practice to develop a level of comfort with the process. However, it will heighten your awareness of how the language you use might foster implicit biases in the classroom.

Selecting Background Sources

Before selecting background sources, it is first helpful to recognize any of your own biases about an issue. Awareness of your own biases will support you in making wise, objective choices when picking background sources. Do not limit yourself to just text-based sources. Instead, consider using podcasts, recorded speeches, TED Talks, photographs, political cartoons, and songs. Enlist the support of your media center specialist to help cull sources, as well.

It's essential that the sources reflect all perspectives on the issue. For example, for a lesson on COVID-19 and anti-Chinese sentiment, you may want to present firsthand accounts of Asian Americans sharing their experience of living in the United States during the COVID-19 pandemic, along with a collection of current and historical political cartoons reflecting xenophobic attitudes toward Asian immigrants.

Finally, to accommodate the needs of the diverse learners in your classroom, ensure that your background sources are in accessible formats and at appropriate reading levels. Websites like Newsela and Scholastic will adjust the same source to a higher or lower Lexile level. Consult with the literary experts in your building to determine what the appropriate levels for your students would be.

When you have come up with a set of neutral statements and selected a background source or sources for students to read between Round One and Round Two of the Yes-No-Maybe, you are ready to begin. To prepare students for the strategy, design a small anchor chart that lists the steps of the strategy, or project the steps on a slide and review with students (see Figure 3.3).

FIGURE 3.3

Yes-No-Maybe: Student Anchor Document

---

1. **Introduction and Initial Reflection**
   - Reflect and free write about your opinions related to each of the statements the teacher shares.

2. **Yes-No-Maybe: Round One**
   - For each statement, in the small group that reflects your opinion about the statement shared ("Yes" for "I agree," "No" for "I disagree," or "Maybe" for "I'm not sure yet if I agree or disagree"), share your initial opinions about each statement with peers through discussion.

3. **Background Source Analysis**
   - Closely read the background source(s) provided.

4. **Yes-No-Maybe: Round Two**
   - Reflect on whether your opinion on each statement has changed, and move to the group ("Yes," "No," or "Maybe") that expresses your current opinion to discuss your reasoning.

5. **Reflection and Assessment**
   - Engage in a whole-class reflective discussion of the issue.

For teachers, flexibility is key; you must be willing to pivot and deliver instruction in a moment's notice using a different platform or with different materials. Although it may be challenging, you can adapt any lesson to the digital learning environment, and Yes-No-Maybe lessons are no exception. Figure 3.4 provides some suggestions on how to do so.

Not only is Yes-No-Maybe a vehicle through which to address academic content standards, but the teaching strategy also reinforces many social-emotional learning skills. In particular, Yes-No-Maybe is designed to help students become aware of and learn to identify the feelings, thoughts, and perspectives of others; they come to exhibit an acceptance for and an understanding of the diversity of other people and groups. Students will call on these skills when applying other STAT strategies, including Respectful Debate and PLAN, so repeated practice and reinforcement are key.

FIGURE 3.4

Tips for Yes-No-Maybe in a Virtual Environment

- Establish new classroom norms for the remote learning environment. For example, "Turn your camera on, and mute your microphone unless you are speaking."
- Digitize and organize any written student materials in the learning management system.
- Use a program like Jamboard or Google Slides, and have each student create a selfie or marker with their name to move in Rounds One and Two.
- Post each statement on a single frame or slide, using virtual sticky notes or text boxes to indicate "Yes," "No," and "Maybe," similar to how you would post signs in the classroom.
- Use breakout rooms or links to individual virtual meetings for each of the respective stances.

Implementing Yes-No-Maybe

Before implementing a Yes-No-Maybe, teachers need to create space for and model active listening skills. Students must be able to listen closely to their peers and pay attention to not only their words, but also their body language and tone so they can "read between the lines and hear between the words" (Cook, 2013, p. 50). Teachers can support students by paraphrasing what their peers shared or by asking clarifying questions. All members of the group should be prepared to report out to the whole class and respectfully restate the reasoning of their peers.

During Yes-No-Maybe lessons, teachers need to make their students comfortable with the feeling of standing apart from the group and taking a different stance on an issue; they also need to prepare students for the possibility that they might change their stance after receiving additional information. The current social norms of our culture don't reward these actions. We teach and praise compliance in school, and students learn early on the benefits of conforming to the majority. Yes-No-Maybe provides students with the first step in learning how to lead instead of how to follow.

To get started, model a Yes-No-Maybe lesson with a small group of students in front of the rest of the class. Using a topic that all students can connect to, like the quality of school lunches or cell phone use in the classroom, walk through Steps 1–3 of the strategy, showing students what the steps look like. This can be a novel learning experience, so expect some reluctance, uncertainty, and even a bit of resistance. Remember that sharing opinions publicly in front of one's peers requires courage and confidence. To ease into this, students might clarify their thinking by writing down their thoughts on the issue in question.

Given the sensitive nature of many of the topics that students will discuss, be prepared for emotions to flow. Pay attention to your students' body language and facial expressions to gauge their comfort level with the topic at hand. This is a prime opportunity to review the classroom norms and reorient students to the skills of showing respect and empathy and engaging in respectful dialogue. When necessary, take a step back to model and reinforce these skills. Don't steer away from discussing difficult topics; you want to convey to your students that they can talk about any topic at all as long as they respect the opinions of others. Further, as the teacher, you must remain neutral and facilitate the class discussions. Allow students to have their opinions, no matter how radical, and underscore that all opinions are welcome.

SEL Competency Connection: Self-Management
Speaking one's opinions and listening to a diversity of opinions stretches the self-management subcompetencies of impulse control, stress management, and self-discipline. Openly acknowledge that the intensity of emotions associated with controversial topics is very human and will create discomfort for deeper learning to occur. Remind students to draw on their self-awareness skills to support impulse control—they should breathe deeply and withhold judgment—and emphasize that the goal of this strategy is to learn how to share opinions on contentious topics in a productive manner.

Preparing for Controversy and Discord

As you tackle controversial issues, be prepared for students to express politically charged views. For example, during the lesson on gangs, a student might comment, "Gang members should all be arrested or deported like President Trump suggested," in reference to taking down the leaders of the international criminal gang MS-13. Don't ban this conversation from your classroom or dissuade students from discussing politics. However, always lead with the content of the lesson first and politics second. If you notice that students are veering off topic, get them back on track by relating the focus of the political discussion to the lesson.

For instance, if the aforementioned statement leads to a discussion about who should have won the 2020 U.S. presidential election, remind students that the goal of the discussion is to grapple with whether gangs do good for society. Share that like each of your students, presidential candidates possess their own stance on gangs, as well as a plan for how they would address the issue. However, part of being a respected leader and a democratic citizen is being open to and exploring new ideas, critically examining one's own beliefs and attitudes, and being prepared to change one's stance on an issue.

As with any lesson, it's essential to anticipate various directions a lesson might take as well as any potential obstacles you may face. This way, you will not be caught off guard. Figure 3.5 identifies several possible obstacles that you may encounter during your implementation of the Yes-No-Maybe strategy and suggestions for troubleshooting them.

FIGURE 3.5

Troubleshooting Obstacles During a Yes-No-Maybe Lesson

If . . .	Then . . .
Only one student moves to the "Yes," "No," or "Maybe" space in the room	Commend this student for having the courage to stand apart from their peers and remain true to their beliefs. Engage in a partner discussion with the student, posing questions that encourage them to share their views on the statement.
A student refuses to share their stance on an issue	Don't force the student to share. After Round One is complete, pull the student aside and encourage them to explain why they would rather not share. If it's an issue that stirs up uncomfortable emotions for them, consider consulting your school's mental health professional to offer support. If the student believes that the statement should not be open to discussion, address their point of view with care and concern. Remind them of the need to be open-minded throughout the learning process. Invite the student to share evidence with you in support of their belief.
Students change their stance on the basis of where their friends are standing	Don't condemn students for doing this, but do remind them of the objective of the activity—to get in touch with *their* views on the issue. If you feel it's helpful, engage students in thinking more deeply about their values and the principles they hope to live by. For example, have them think about a person they admire and the traits of that person or the qualities they value in a teacher, friend, or parent (Elias, 2017).

A student puts down another student for their view or uses disrespectful language	Intervene to stop this behavior immediately, being careful not to make a spectacle of the students involved. Pull the offending student aside and remind them of the classroom norm that requires them to use respectful language when engaging in discussion. If needed, provide examples and nonexamples of respectful language.
A majority of students do not change their views between Round One and Round Two	Consider presenting additional background sources that present the issue from a different point of view. Also, after the lesson is over, debrief with a colleague about the framing of each neutral statement to see if it was phrased to invite multiple stances on the issue.

Although this list is certainly not exhaustive, it does reflect many of the issues that teachers, school mental health professionals, and administrators have faced. The key is to remain calm and to consider the source of the issue. Oftentimes you'll find that revisiting classroom norms or explicitly teaching a specific skill, such as active listening, will remedy the situation. In more extreme circumstances, you might enlist the support of your school's mental health professional. However, even when a lesson seems to veer off track, it's important to maintain your own growth mindset and positive attitude and seize the opportunity as a teachable moment from which your students can learn.

Each Yes-No-Maybe lesson is followed by the rich opportunity to forge deep learning by reinforcing a connection between this strategy and democratic citizenship. Emphasize how sharing opinions, engaging in research to craft informed opinions, and making informed decisions are crucial components of effective citizenship. Further, as students share their reflections, ask them how listening actively to their peers' points of view influenced their original thinking. Ask them to notice how the strategy revealed the diversity of opinions in just a small classroom community. Listening to others express their views and regulating your emotions while hearing views you might not agree with are foundational skills in building the muscle for civility.

Extending Your Practice

Too often, the loud and most vocal voices dominate a discussion, or only a few students feel comfortable to speak openly in front of their peers. The Yes-No-Maybe strategy can upend this status quo. As you launch a unit, you can use Yes-No-Maybe to prime students' thinking and surface impressions. You can share a variety of background articles to foster a more nuanced, research-based understanding of the topic. Yes-No-Maybe can also enhance project-based learning as students initially explore concepts and subsequently move toward developing a solution to the problem.

Moreover, Yes-No-Maybe can also be applied in collegial discussions to promote a culture of creative expression over compliance discussions. We have sat through plenty of meetings in which some of our colleagues were reluctant to share because a "stay in your lane" culture prevailed as the norm. Yes-No-Maybe can easily surface diverse opinions on issues of practice, such as how to increase student engagement in the remote learning classroom, how to enhance formative assessment practices, or, more sensitive yet, how to address implicit bias in the school community.

Further, to better leverage the strategy, consider implementing a Yes-No-Maybe with a professional learning community, especially if members are digging into a curricular initiative that has no clear path forward. Remember to conduct a Yes-No-Maybe on key statements *before* exposing teachers to a research-based reading and then again *after* that reading has taken place to help assess where the group stands and to contemplate next steps.

SEL Competency Connection: Relationship Skills
Engaging this competency with adult colleagues will no doubt surface their emotions publicly. Normalizing speaking and listening to a diversity of opinions will demand the self-management skills of impulse control and self-discipline, the doorways to authentic connection and empathy for others. The rewards are great because adults have the chance to practice relationship-building skills that effectively resist inappropriate social pressure and conflict as the group engages in collaborative work.

Students can also harness the power of Yes-No-Maybe to foster safe and inclusive environments for student expression. Student government, cocurricular clubs, and even guidance groups can use Yes-No-Maybe to support democratic conversations on school-based issues. Counselors, advisors, or coaches can first model this strategy to strengthen dialogue on a problem confronting the group and then have students lead this process on their own. Encouraging student use of Yes-No-Maybe beyond the classroom can energize student leadership and provide opportunities for introverted, shy, and reluctant students to lead, be heard, and contribute to the group process.

Formative Assessment Tools and Peer Opinion Sharing

We have designed three tools that teachers and students can use to evaluate a student's ability to reflect on their opinion on an issue and respectfully share it with others. Teachers and students can use the first tool (Figure 3.6) to evaluate the student's ability to initially give an opinion on a given statement and then reflect on whether the background sources and the opinions of peers ultimately influenced that opinion. Teachers can use the second tool (Figure 3.7) to assess the student's peer opinion–sharing abilities. Finally, students can use a comparable student-facing checklist (Figure 3.8) to reflect on how well they engage in active listening, accurately share the group's opinions during Rounds One and Two, confidently express their opinion in the small group, and respectfully react to their peers' opinions. Use these formative assessment tools to improve students' peer opinion–sharing abilities and empower them to take charge of their learning through self-assessment.

FIGURE 3.6

Yes-No-Maybe Formative Assessment Checklist: Informed Opinion

- ☐ Student contributes to discussion by sharing an opinion on a given statement or statements.
- ☐ Student references their thinking or quotes from the article(s) provided for background reading.
- ☐ Student communicates that the background reading has prompted a reevaluation or revision of their original opinion.
- ☐ Student expresses that hearing peers' opinions about the issue has influenced their own opinion.

FIGURE 3.7

Yes-No-Maybe Formative Assessment Checklist: Peer Opinion Sharing

- ☐ Student volunteers to summarize the small group's opinion.
- ☐ Student accurately summarizes the small group's opinion.
- ☐ Student contributes by sharing opinions on the statement(s) in Round One.
- ☐ Student reacts to peers' shared views on the topic or article content within small groups.
- ☐ Student's written or oral reflection indicates that they have integrated the thoughts, feelings, or perspectives of peers into their own revised opinion.

FIGURE 3.8

Yes-No-Maybe Student Self-Assessment: Peer Opinion Sharing

> ☐ I volunteered to summarize the small group's opinion.
> ☐ I accurately summarized the small group's opinion.
> ☐ I contributed to Round One by sharing my opinion(s) on the statement(s).
> ☐ I share my response to my peers' shared views on the topic or article content within small groups.
> ☐ I used statements such as "I never thought of seeing it this way," "I learned from ___ that___," "I felt moved by _____'s contributions," and "I learned a lot from _____."

Getting Started with Yes-No-Maybe: Some Forward Reflections

As you conclude your planning on implementing Yes-No-Maybe, contemplate the following questions:

- What lessons have you already developed that you can adapt to a Yes-No-Maybe lesson?

- What are the social-emotional learning benefits of implementing Yes-No-Maybe for your students as they engage with the curriculum?

- What challenges might you and your particular group of students face with a Yes-No-Maybe lesson on a compelling topic?

- How might you leverage the support of other school personnel in implementing Yes-No-Maybe and enhancing your practice?

Teaching Tip

Finding time for lesson closure can be a challenge as you implement new practices. If this is the case, consider asking students to complete a student reflection exit ticket (find a model at https://www.secdlab.org/stat/book). You can easily adapt the questions to a digital format using Jamboard or Padlet, and you can debrief student responses in the next class.

Respectful Debate: Developing Empathy and Perspective-Taking

Mrs. Biluvay's eyes widened in disbelief. What had started off, in her U.S. history class, as a rather diplomatic debate about the Black Lives Matter movement had taken a sharp and shocking turn into a mudslinging event, complete with name-calling and finger-pointing. "They're standing in their own way!" Trevor yelled at Deja, who had tears streaming down her face. "It's not my problem that they're criminals and crack addicts!"

The class had begun calmly, with Mrs. Biluvay posting the following statement for her students to first research and take a stance on: "The Black Lives Matter movement is a necessary means to combat systemic racism." She didn't assign the students sides; she explained that she wanted them to conduct research, reflect on it, and take an honest position. Her intent was for the students to explore a controversial topic with an open mind.

Mrs. Biluvay had expected that the debate might initially lead to greater polarization, but she felt confident that the debate process would improve the relationships among her students. What she was seeing now was not what she had expected.

The Respectful Debate Strategy

Debate is a cornerstone of democracy as well as a great vehicle for students to learn through experience and make meaning by drawing on prior knowledge. It stimulates critical thinking and helps students strengthen their interpersonal communication skills. Of course, a genuine debate can also provoke strong emotions. In fact, research in social-emotional learning tells us that without the engagement of strong emotions, opinions are not likely to change (Svoboda,

2017). This is why it's so important to maintain a classroom culture where there is trust and where it's clear that emotions are safe to have and to share.

When students are presented with a multilayered and controversial issue, such as systemic racism, and are asked to debate only one side of the issue, they partake in what Budesheim and Lundquist (1999) call "a biased assimilation of the evidence" (p. 106) that reinforces preexisting attitudes as opposed to illuminating both sides of the issue. In essence, when reviewing sources for evidence, students tend to readily seek out and accept any evidence that supports their existing beliefs; evidence that contradicts those beliefs is often distrusted and critiqued.

The STAT strategy of Respectful Debate counters any tendency toward "biased assimilation" by having students do what Lord and colleagues (1984) describe as the "consider-the-opposite strategy." In an attempt to expand their starting perspective, students are asked to defend both the position that aligns with their preexisting beliefs and a side that may be inconsistent with their opinions. Figure 4.1 shows five sequenced steps that will enable you to guide your students in developing the skills of perspective-taking and empathy in the context of a debate.

FIGURE 4.1

The Five Steps of Respectful Debate

---

1. **Introduction and Initial Reflection**
   - The teacher introduces the Respectful Debate strategy and the topic of the debate.
   - Students engage in free writing to reflect on a provocative statement, set of statistics, political cartoon, or quote related to the topic.

2. **Debate Preparation**
   - The teacher divides the students into two groups and assigns them either the pro or con side of the debate, reminding students that they will have the opportunity to argue both sides.
   - If desired, the teacher assigns roles (e.g., note taker, timekeeper, debater, debate researcher) to ensure equity.
   - The teacher presents a controversial statement that will frame the debate.
   - In their groups, students define important vocabulary terms, critically review background sources on the topic, and generate ideas in support of their position.

3. **Debate: Round One**
   - The pro side presents their position and supports it with one or two examples.
   - The con side summarizes the main points of the pro side's argument.
   - The con side presents their position and supports it with one or two examples.
   - The pro side summarizes the main points of the con side's argument.
   - The pro side has the option of providing one additional example to support their position.

- The con side responds by providing one additional example to support their position.

4. Respectful Debate: Round Two
- The teacher announces that to promote perspective-taking, students will "switch sides" and revisit the original debate statement. The pro side will now argue the con side; the con side will now argue the pro side.
- In their groups, students generate ideas in support of their new position.
- Students repeat Step 3.

5. Reflection and Assessment
- Students debrief as a whole class by engaging in a conversation about perspective-taking.

After the introduction and preparation of Steps 1 and 2, in Step 3, students must draw on their social awareness skills to empathically listen to their opponent, putting aside their judgments and devoting their full attention to the opposition's argument. They are asked to pay attention to vocal tone, facial expressions, and body gestures to more fully understand the message the opponent is conveying. Then they restate or rephrase the speaker's main points to confirm their understanding.

In Step 4, students engage in perspective-taking by swapping sides. They repeat the same steps they took in Step 3, only the original *pro* side now argues from the *con* position and vice versa. This step is key to building students' competence in social awareness. The act of perspective-taking challenges them not only to understand an opposing viewpoint but to articulate it, fostering an ability to empathize with the thoughts and feelings of "opponents."

Finally, during Step 5, students respond in writing to several reflection questions that prompt them to think about what they learned about the topic as well as how their opinion may have changed. The lesson concludes with students sharing their insights in a whole-class discussion.

SEL Competency Connection: Social Awareness

Social perspective-taking is the essence of the Respectful Debate strategy. This largely relies on students' metacognitive abilities in that it prompts students to consider the thoughts and emotions of others, as well as the intents and motives underlying their behavior, to analyze a situation and consider how best to respond. Perspective-taking skills are developmental and change as students mature. Therefore, frequent practice is key to building students' competence and confidence.

Planning for a Respectful Debate

It takes only one look at the news or your social media feed to see the lack of civility that people can display when exercising their freedom of speech. This may make planning for a Respectful Debate a daunting task. Many educators avoid topics that may spark controversy. However, as Thomas (2020) points out, our students are counting on us to welcome truth into our classrooms by challenging the distorted "truths" they are likely to encounter elsewhere. Through meaningful dialogue surrounding issues of social justice, we can help students "recognize and analyze the narratives that sustain social inequality" and that pose a threat to "racial, religious, gender, and economic liberty" (p. 86). By addressing these narratives head-on with the strategy of Respectful Debate, we will provide our students with the tools they need to deconstruct the dominant narratives and redefine truth for a more just society.

Although you can implement Respectful Debate across the curriculum (see Chapter 7), we will situate our discussion here around how to use the strategy in the social studies classroom. Specifically, we will draw on a high school lesson related to racial equality in which students will engage in a respectful debate, listen to both sides of the argument to regulate their emotions, and build collective understanding and historical empathy for two civil rights leaders, Malcolm X and James Baldwin. (A detailed lesson plan, "Respectful Debate: The Path to Racial Equality in America," is available both on our companion website, www.secdLab.org/stat/book, and in Appendix B.)

Figure 4.2 shows the steps we suggest you take when planning a Respectful Debate lesson.

FIGURE 4.2

How to Plan a Respectful Debate Lesson

1. **Select a topic for the lesson.**
   - Review the curriculum for controversial social issues that have no clear solution.
   - Consider current events that your students have expressed an interest in discussing.
   - Consult with a colleague or media center specialist for guidance and support.
   - Enlist your students in the process by sharing a copy of the curricular unit with them and having them brainstorm possible topics.

2. Craft a controversial statement.
- Decide whether the statement will be a statement of fact, value, or policy. (See Figure 4.3.)
- Make the statement broad enough to address the relevant objectives and standards.
- Make the statement specific enough to allow each side to engage in a focused argument grounded in specific evidence.
- Present the statement as a single sentence.

3. Select background sources that present all sides of the issue.
- Consider a variety of sources (podcasts, articles, excerpts from speeches, photographs, and so on).
- Tap into the expertise of the media center specialist to fine-tune your selections.

4. Arrange students into groups.
- Consider students' academic and social-emotional strengths and weaknesses; then form heterogeneous groups with positive dynamics.
- Consult with the school social worker, case manager, or special education teachers to find the best group placements for students with 504 plans or individualized education plans (IEPs).
- Decide on one of two formats: *Two groups* (a pro and a con side) to facilitate a single classwide debate or *four groups* (two pro sides and two con sides) to be conducted simultaneously (if support personnel is available in the classroom) or consecutively.

5. Assign roles within the groups to promote equity and individual accountability.
- Consider students' academic and social-emotional strengths, as well as the dynamics within the group when assigning roles.
- Suggested roles include note taker, timekeeper, debate researcher, and debater.
- Alternative roles include facilitator, devil's advocate, harmonizer, elaborator, and ideas connector.

Surveying the Curriculum and Choosing a Topic

Begin by analyzing the curriculum for entry points to discuss controversial topics that students have expressed an eagerness to explore, namely those that relate to the social issues of race, religion, sexuality, gender, disability, and socioeconomic status. For example, in an 8th grade social studies unit focused on the U.S. Civil War, students might analyze the positions of the pro-slavery and anti-slavery parties and consider how the issue of slavery was a major cause of the war. Or, in a high school U.S. history course, as students learn about the "cult of domesticity," they might critically read background sources to evaluate the controversial statement made by prominent physician Charles Meigs in 1847: "A woman has a head almost too small for intellect but just big enough for love." Establishing a safe environment and providing our students with the resources to engage in deeper learning about these topics will enable them to question not only the content but also how issues of the past can influence the dominant narratives of the here and now. The hope is that with enough practice, students will view all information—whether on their social media news feed or in a history textbook—through a critical lens as they make sense of the socio-political information they encounter (Thomas, 2020).

Crafting a Controversial Statement

Once you have selected a curricular topic that lends itself to a Respectful Debate, you're ready to craft a controversial statement. Be sure to frame it with care and draw on the classroom norms of mutual respect and an appreciation for diversity. The statement should be a single sentence that is broad enough to address the relevant objectives and standards, yet specific enough to allow for a focused argument in which each side can cite specific evidence. For example, *"Racial equality is unachievable"* is too broad of a claim, whereas the claim *"Malcolm X believed that the sit-in movement was an unsuccessful means to achieve racial equality because it was too passive"* is too specific. A better choice would be this: *"The path to racial equality in America can be achieved by Black Americans living separately from white Americans."* It may be wise to engage your grade-level or department colleagues in this process, too.

Figure 4.3 shows three different types of statements you can craft and examples of each for the exemplar lesson on racial equality.

Selecting Background Sources

After you have developed a controversial statement to frame the lesson, you can begin the process of selecting background sources. During this step, we encourage you to consult with your media specialist or local librarian to ensure that the sources you select are nuanced and present the issue from multiple angles. These sources can include news or magazine articles, podcasts, statistics, excerpts from books, speeches, and blog posts. We recommend choosing anywhere from two to five sources and homing in on an excerpt for any sources that are particularly lengthy. Sources should be complex and invite interaction on a deep level as students apply the critical reading skills of making connections to prior knowledge and experiences, analyzing, drawing conclusions, identifying evidence to support a claim, and synthesizing information across sources.

In the exemplar lesson on racial equality, we selected two sources: a blog post from the New York City Urban Debate League and an audio recording of a

FIGURE 4.3

Types of Statements for Respectful Debate

Type	Description	Example
Statement of Facts	States that something perceptible exists, has existed in the past, or has the potential to exist	*Proud of being Black and disdainful of passive protests, Malcolm X was responsible for the rise in Black militancy during the 1960s.*
Statement of Value	Presents a qualitative judgment to prove that a person, thing, or event exists at a specific point along a continuum (e.g., good/bad, right/wrong)	*James Baldwin was more effective and honorable in his efforts to achieve racial equality than Malcolm X was.*
Statement of Policy	States that a specific plan of action should be implemented	*To achieve racial equality, Black Americans should live separately from white Americans.*

Source: Marteney, 2020.

1963 televised debate between Malcolm X and James Baldwin. The sources provide context about both civil rights activists, describe their contributions to the movement, present their diverging viewpoints, and offer evidence for both the pro and con sides of the debate. The pro side would agree with the controversial statement that frames the discussion (*"The path to racial equality in America can be achieved by Black Americans living separately from white Americans"*); the con side would disagree with this statement. Further, the sources engage students in multimodal learning, accommodating the diverse learning styles of a wide range of learners.

Arranging Students into Groups and Assigning Roles

Depending on the size of your class and the academic and social-emotional needs of your students, set up two groups (a pro and a con) or four groups (two pro groups and two con groups, which will debate either simultaneously or consecutively).

The next step is to assign roles. This is a simple way to democratize student group work. The roles promote individual accountability and ensures that the workload is fair. When student roles are clearly defined, interactions among group members are more focused and of higher quality. Defining roles also helps prevent students from either feeling left out or dominating the group task (Washington University in St. Louis, 2020).

The roles that we recommend for Respectful Debate include the following:

- *Note taker:* Takes notes to keep a record of group discussions and decisions.
- *Timekeeper:* Keeps group members abreast of time limits so they adhere to the schedule.
- *Debate researcher:* Analyzes background sources to collect information for the debate.
- *Debater:* Serves as the spokesperson, and presents the group's argument and related evidence during the debate.

Depending on the size of the group, you can also assign one or more of the following alternative roles:

- *Facilitator:* Keeps the group on task and arbitrates discussion.
- *Devil's advocate:* Suggests counterarguments that the opposing side may present.
- *Harmonizer:* Supports the group in expressing opinions in a productive way and arriving at a consensus for each round of the debate.
- *Elaborator:* Elaborates on group members' ideas to add more depth and meaning.
- *Ideas connector:* Identifies connections among various group member ideas (Benne & Sheats, 1948).

Eventually you will want to extend your practice of classroom norms to Respectful Debate by having each group establish a set of norms before engaging in the strategy.

Teaching Tip
When planning the lesson, try to anticipate how group dynamics will play out and the social-emotional skills (e.g., active listening, conflict resolution, problem solving, and peer opinion sharing) students will need to work together successfully. You should explicitly teach or reinforce these skills

before the lesson. For example, if you think the group will have a difficult time actively listening to one another, be sure to teach that skill to the whole class *before* you present the lesson. In addition, you may want to refer to Chapter 2 for sample activities to do with the class to facilitate the development of group norms and to engage students in relationship-building exercises to foster a safe and inclusive environment.

Finally, we suggest you consider in advance of the lesson how to adapt it to the digital learning environment. Figure 4.4 offers some suggestions.

FIGURE 4.4

Tips for Respectful Debate in a Digital Environment

- Establish new classroom norms for the remote learning environment. Examples might include "Turn your camera on and mute your microphone unless you are speaking," and "Use the 'raise hand' feature if you have something to say, and use the chat feature to ask a question."
- Digitize and organize any written student materials in the learning management system.
- Use breakout rooms for pro and con groups, and check in on each group frequently to assess their progress, support them if they need help, and hold them accountable for carrying out their assigned roles.
- Provide a five-minute warning to ensure each group has time to generate examples to support their claim. Set a timer to close the breakout rooms after the five minutes are up.
- Plan for a movement break between each round of the debate and encourage students who want to get up and stretch to regain their focus.
- At the end of the debate, engage students in interactive written reflection about the perspective-taking experience by using a program like Jamboard or Padlet.

As you prepare to launch your first Respectful Debate lesson, be sure to keep the purpose of the activity in the forefront of your mind. The goal is not to solve the social or political matter in question; it's to incite a willingness among students to consider others' viewpoints. It's to teach students that it's possible to have strong opinions about an issue while still partaking in meaningful dialogue with those who hold opposing opinions. The focus is on assertiveness rather than verbal aggression, and on developing the ability to listen to ideas that may be disagreeable rather than using underhanded tactics, such as name-calling or finger-pointing, to "win" the debate. Through this experience, students will gain an appreciation for the fundamental values of a pluralistic democratic society and acquire the communication, argument construction, and analysis skills for effective and responsible citizenship (Jagger, 2013; Martinson, 2005).

Implementing a Respectful Debate

Before facilitating a Respectful Debate, assess your students' self-management skills; these involve effectively regulating one's emotions, thoughts, and behaviors by controlling impulses, managing stress, and setting goals (Elias & Schwab, 2006).

Students in Mrs. Biluvay's classroom, which we visited at the opening of this chapter, clearly needed additional work in this area; if they had learned and practiced self-management skills, it would likely have prevented the emotional outbursts that ensued. They might have benefitted from a revisiting (or revision) of class norms and a review of emotional regulation techniques, such as deep breathing, self-talk, and visualization. After practicing these skills in a scaffolded environment, a Respectful Debate activity provides ample opportunities for generalization and transfer (Cartledge & Milburn, 1995).

Just as with the other STAT strategies, we encourage modeling Respectful Debate as part of a fishbowl activity. Select a group of six to eight students and have the remaining students form an outer circle around them to observe and take notes. Choose a topic unrelated to the curriculum that is relevant to students, such as *"Should we lower the voting age?"* or *"Should schools eliminate statewide standardized testing?"* Present a controversial statement related to the topic, such as *"Lowering the voting age will increase civic engagement,"* and walk through the steps of the Respectful Debate strategy. Allow time at the end for students to ask questions. The idea of arguing both sides in a debate will most likely be unfamiliar to many students, so remind them that the goal is not to "win" the debate but, instead, to emerge with a greater appreciation for all points of view on the issue.

Facilitating Controversial Discussions with Your Students

Just as with Yes-No-Maybe, you must be ready to face emotionally charged situations. Continually monitor your students' nonverbal and verbal cues for signs of distress, verbal aggression, or negative group dynamics. If you witness any of these, you need to step back and either revisit your classroom norms to reorient students to the skills of empathy and mutual respect or explicitly teach a specific skill that students appear to be lacking. For example, if you notice that, despite assigned roles, the students within a group are having a difficult time getting others to hear them or engaging in turn taking, set aside some time after the lesson to explicitly teach and reinforce the skill of speaker power (use a talking object to pass around to indicate whose turn it is to speak at a given time). Or, if some students are so passionate about their views on a given topic that they are reluctant to argue the alternate point of view, you'll want to involve them in perspective-taking exercises, such as role-playing scenarios and considering what those involved think or feel. After the lesson, students can also discuss the experiences of a character and how that character's knowledge, likes and dislikes, and background might influence their thoughts and feelings.

Addressing controversial issues like racial equality takes both skill and courage. It may push you beyond your comfort zone, knowing that the polarizing topic of race may invite intense dissension, given the diverse experiences and views of your students. However, the discomfort is worth it. If you assume a "colorblind" approach to discussion surrounding race or avoid the issue altogether, you run the risk of cultivating in your students what Freire refers to as a "magical" consciousness of racism, leading children to believe that racism is not a major concern in society (Husband, 2012). If students don't perceive racism as an issue, they won't be compelled to examine it or address it through social action (Husband, 2012). By consulting resources like Learning for Justice (www.learningforjustice.org) and Facing History and Ourselves (www.facinghistory.org), you can educate yourself in how to talk about race with your students. In the guidebook *Let's Talk!* (2019), Learning for Justice (formerly Teaching Tolerance) offers points to keep in mind when planning a classroom debate about race:

- Give students opportunities to reflect on their comfort level in discussing race.
- Review classroom norms to ensure they reflect clear guidelines for mutual respect and productive dialogue.
- Acknowledge that race is a social construct and has no biological basis.
- Recognize that racial disparities exist but do not have to endure.
- Destigmatize privilege by presenting it as a concept that determines how much power one has in a given situation, depending on the person's identity.

- Offer your own experience with racism (or privilege).
- Have students share their experiences with racism (or privilege).

Although every educator will face a unique set of issues, several common potential hurdles may arise during implementation of the Respectful Debate strategy. Figure 4.5 offers guidance on troubleshooting three possible scenarios.

FIGURE 4.5

Troubleshooting Obstacles During a Respectful Debate Lesson

If ...	Then ...
A student disagrees with the debate's controversial statement (e.g., "There's no such thing as systemic racism")	Invite the student to come to you and discuss their concern. In the spirit of mutual respect, approach students' uneasiness with curiosity and empathy. Remind the student that open-mindedness is a part of learning—necessary to acquire new information and challenge existing beliefs. Also, announcing the topic in advance will enable you to gauge student discomfort early on.
A student refuses to argue the assigned side of an issue	Take the student aside, acknowledge their feelings, and ask why they are so opposed to arguing the assigned viewpoint. If the student entirely disagrees with that viewpoint, remind them of the value of perspective-taking and clarify that the ultimate goal of questioning a dominant narrative is to shed light on marginalized perspectives (Westbrook, 2002). If, after this talk, the student still feels unable to assume the assigned viewpoint, ask that they watch, listen, and learn.
A student becomes emotionally distraught during the debate	Acknowledge and validate the student's feelings, invite them to take a break if they need it, and praise them for remaining open-minded and brave. If you sense the lesson topic is going to stir up strong emotions, meet in advance with your school's guidance counselor or your supervisor to walk through your concerns and to get advice. You may need to revisit or revise classroom norms before the lesson begins to maximize safety and inclusivity.

Teaching Tip

If a student attacks another student's *character,* as opposed to the argument itself, this is called an *ad hominem* argument. These arguments can take many forms, including basic name-calling, dismissing an opponent's argument as absurd without addressing it (*appeal to stone*), and refuting an argument on the premise that the person making it does not have adequate credentials (*credentials fallacy*). It's imperative that you point out that the student is making an *ad hominem* argument, that you clarify the difference between attacking the source of the argument and the argument itself, and that you redirect the focus of the debate.

Participation in such debates engages students in analyzing public issues and figuring out ways to address them, whereas deliberation develops students' civic dispositions of mutual respect, collaboration with others, and tolerance of divergent perspectives. Taken together, participation and deliberation provide students with the skills they need to partake in meaningful and constructive dialogue about essential issues both in and out of the classroom (State of New Jersey Department of Education, 2020).

Extending the Reach of Respectful Debate

Social media has changed the way both students and adults receive information. A platform that once bore cautions and warnings as to the validity of its content has now become, for many students, the primary source of information about current events. Moreover, because technology has found ways to tailor news items and other content to students' personal interests and views, their reality may easily become skewed. Now more than ever, teachers need to find creative ways to discuss current events and incorporate them into lesson plans, all while holding student interest and combating the numerous sources of misinformation.

Teachers can introduce Respectful Debate activities to address news and current events during their regular class times or during their advisory periods. Advisory periods are ideal because teachers can speak with smaller groups of students about important topics that may be sensitive and because they allow for more extensive conversations. Of course, before offering this activity in an advisory period, teachers should first build community by helping students find ways to relate to one another, thus creating a safe space for students to share and demonstrate respect.

Teaching Tip

Given the transdisciplinary application of Respectful Debate, students will likely benefit from having a graphic organizer that lists themes that can focus and guide the debate. For instance, most debates on historical and current events touch on *ethical, legal, scientific,* and *economic* considerations of the topic and proposals. For a sample organizer, check out our "Debate Theme Considerations Graphic Organizer," which you'll find on our companion website, www.secdlab.org/stat/book, under the "Handouts" tab.

Formative Assessment Tools

In Figure 4.5, we looked at ways to handle some of the obstacles you may encounter during implementation. You will also benefit from understanding your students' relative areas of weakness, as well as the social-emotional competencies it will be helpful to address before forging ahead with subsequent debates. We can offer three checklists to help.

Both teachers and students can use the checklist shown in Figure 4.6 to assess the student's perspective-taking skills. After a Respectful Debate, participants fill out this checklist; the teacher does so, too, evaluating each student's performance. Afterward, during a conference, the teacher and student compare and contrast their evaluations, identifying both successes and potential areas of improvement.

The next two tools are student facing. Students can use the checklist shown in Figure 4.7 to assess the social-emotional skills they used (or didn't use) in the Respectful Debate lesson. The checklist in Figure 4.8 can help students evaluate their argumentative reasoning skill through the lens of Webb's four Depth of Knowledge levels. It considers, for example, how well the student was able to synthesize information across multiple sources or spot gaps in reasoning or evidence in the other side's argument.

Collect the completed checklists from the students to gain insight into their self-awareness regarding their skills. If you implement the STAT strategies in the order suggested, you'll be able to use these checklists as pre-assessment data when implementing the Audience-Focused Communication strategy with your students.

FIGURE 4.6

Respectful Debate Formative Assessment Checklist: Perspective-Taking

☐ Student is able to look beyond their own point of view.

☐ Student understands the issue of debate, given the expressed arguments.

☐ Student expresses that a peer's shared point of view broadened or influenced their thinking.

☐ Student communicates that exploring both sides in the argument challenged their thinking.

☐ Student conveys that the evidence presented by the opposing side enhanced their thinking, using phrases like "Before _____ said _____, I hadn't thought of it that way before," "When assuming the opposing side, I found myself surprised by _____," and "I never thought about the issue this way before."

FIGURE 4.7

Respectful Debate Student Self-Assessment: Perspective-Taking

☐ I was able to assume the point of view of the argument I didn't agree with.

☐ I actively listened to the opposing side's argument and communicated my attention in nonverbal ways (e.g., making eye contact, nodding my head).

☐ I acknowledged the feelings of others during the argument and reflection activity.

☐ I asked clarifying questions of the opposing side.

☐ I was able to summarize the opposing side's point of view.

☐ I learned something new or saw the issue from a new perspective.

FIGURE 4.8

Respectful Debate Student Self-Assessment Checklist: Argumentative Reasoning

☐ **Webb's Depth of Knowledge Level 4 (extended thinking):**

    ☐ I noticed the relationships between arguments across sources to strengthen my argument while recognizing the strengths and weaknesses of my opponent's argument.

    ☐ I raised compelling questions for both sides of the argument to consider for deeper understanding.

☐ **Webb's Depth of Knowledge Level 3 (strategic thinking):**

    ☐ I used arguments and supporting evidence from the source(s) to challenge my opponent's argument.

    ☐ I identified some gaps in the reasoning or evidence presented by my opponent.

continued

FIGURE 4.8 *(continued)*

Respectful Debate Student Self-Assessment Checklist: Argumentative Reasoning

---

☐ **Webb's Depth of Knowledge Level 2 (basic skills and concepts):**

☐ I identified major points from the source(s) and can offer reasons for the author's thinking, as well as evidence to support their position when responding to the opposing side's argument.

☐ **Webb's Depth of Knowledge Level 1 (recall and reproduction):**

☐ I recalled some evidence or facts from the source(s) to support my argument.

Source: Aungst, 2014.

SEL Competency Connection: Self-Awareness
Having students reflect on their progress in developing social-emotional skills is key to building self-awareness. Understanding their strengths and limitations, as well as the ways their identity influences their views, gives them a better grasp on their identity and improves their self-knowledge. Further, involving students in the assessment process and highlighting the fact that progress, instead of perfection, is the goal will support them in developing a growth mindset (CASEL, 2021).

Getting Started with Respectful Debate: Some Forward Reflections

As you conclude your planning on implementing Respectful Debate, consider the following questions:

- Which prerequisite SEL skills do you need to teach your students before involving them in a Respectful Debate?
- What are the benefits, in terms of both SEL skills and academics, of implementing Respectful Debate with your students as they engage with the curriculum?
- Think about your current group of students. What specific challenges might you expect to face when presenting a Respectful Debate on a controversial topic?

- What initial steps might you take to extend your practice of Respectful Debate beyond the classroom and commence a dialogue about racial equality within your school?

Audience-Focused Communication: Creating Effective Presentations

Vishal had enjoyed learning about the rise of empires in Africa, Eurasia, North America, and South America during the time period 700–1300 CE. A shy kid, Vishal preferred to sit in the back of the classroom. Although he rarely participated in discussion, he was actively engaged in learning.

Each unit in Ms. Melnik's history classroom concluded with students presenting on a related topic of their choice. Vishal had initially dreaded standing up and speaking in front of his peers, but he found the culminating presentations got easier and easier as the year went on and he learned the art of planning, rehearsing, and delivering a presentation. The strategies he'd learned to help keep himself calm while speaking in front of a group had helped too. Vishal came to appreciate the opportunity to collaborate with his classmates while developing a vision for his presentation and then preparing the materials and outline.

Now, as Vishal prepared to share the poster he had created on the cultural contributions of the Byzantine Empire, he closed his eyes and visualized the presentation playing out successfully from start to finish. He then inhaled to the count of five, held his breath for two seconds, and then exhaled to the count of five, practicing the 5-2-5 breathing technique that Ms. Melnik had taught them. Although his heart pounded and his palms were a little sweaty, Vishal felt excited to share his hard work with his peers.

The Audience-Focused Communication Strategy

Whether students are in math class, describing the approach they took to solve a problem, or in science class, sharing the results of a lab they conducted with their peers, they're frequently asked by their teachers to speak publicly in front of others (Palmer, 2014b). However, although we teach students how to solve math problems and how to carry out science labs, very rarely do we deliberately teach them how to speak in front of others by tailoring their presentations to a specific audience and modulating their voice, tone, eye contact, and gestures accordingly (Palmer, 2014a). This is most likely due to two factors: teachers having limited pedagogical knowledge of how to teach speaking skills and the fact that speaking skills are generally not assessed on high-stakes standardized tests (Webster, 2019).

It's past time to address this deficit. Equipping students with the tools to effectively communicate with others empowers them to be active participants in our democratic society and in the changing nature of work life. More than a decade and a half ago, researchers recognized that public speaking is an essential part of practicing and maintaining a democracy because it enables citizens to share information, develop new ideas, and contribute to the workforce (Evans et al., 2004). For adults, public speaking opportunities are omnipresent—when we make a presentation at work, tell a story to a group at a party, or raise a concern at a local board meeting. In each situation, the person presenting will influence others most effectively if they consider their audience when choosing their words, decide on the best format for their presentation, use strategies to regulate their emotions, and appear confident throughout.

As we saw in the scenario with Vishal that began this chapter, Audience-Focused Communication (AFC) builds students' efficacy by teaching them the skills necessary to present in front of an audience. The audience might be attendees at a community meeting, classmates in a classroom or at an assembly, or a teacher to whom the student is submitting a written product.

The skills of Audience-Focused Communication are tied to both academic and social-emotional learning outcomes. Academically, AFC develops students' college and career readiness skills by teaching them how to present information for a specific purpose and audience, as well as how to use visuals and digital media to elevate their presentations; this has also become a focus on the Common Core State Standards, which promote the development of both digital and presentation skills.

Socially and emotionally, students build on what they learn from Norms, Yes-No-Maybe, and Respectful Debate. They continue to hone their perspective-taking skills, as well as their awareness of the diverse cultural backgrounds of their audience, while, at the same time, developing their self-management skills through emotional regulation techniques. According to Chris Anderson (2016), the curator of TED, "Presentation literacy isn't an optional extra for the few. It's a core skill for the 21st century. It's the most impactful way to share who you are and what you care about" (p. 10).

Figure 5.1 shows the seven sequenced steps of Audience-Focused Communication; these will help you guide your students toward greater presentation literacy and improved social awareness and self-management.

FIGURE 5.1

The Seven Steps of Audience-Focused Communication (AFC)

---

1. Introduction

The teacher introduces the AFC strategy.

2. Outcome Visualization

Students develop a vision for their AFC presentation, which means

- Deciding on or acknowledging the audience.
- Identifying logistical considerations.
- Determining ways to get and maintain their audience's attention.
- Deciding on or acknowledging the format of the presentation.
- Establishing expectations for how the audience will use the information after the presentation.

3. Plan Development

Using the AFT Project Plan Graphic Organizer (available at http://www.secdlab.org/stat/book), students work in small groups or individually to map out

- The objective of the presentation.
- The identified audience and any relevant information.
- The content of the presentation (in bullet points).
- The method of delivery (poster, slideshow, interactive discussion, game, etc.)
- A step-by-step breakdown of the flow of the presentation.
- Assigned parts of the presentation to each group member to ensure equity.

4. Presentation Preparation

Students carry out the plans they developed, consistently taking the perspective of their audience to consider the grammar and language needed to tailor their presentations for maximum effectiveness.

---

5. SEL Skill Practice and Presentation Rehearsal

Students practice SEL skills while rehearsing their presentations to help them regulate their emotions during the presentation. This work includes

- Role-plays to anticipate and plan for obstacles.
- Visualization imagery to help them "cope ahead."
- Preperformance rituals to help them get in the flow (similar to what professional athletes do); this includes keeping calm and deep belly/diaphragmatic breathing, mindfulness techniques, and positive self-talk.
- BEST skills (**B**ody posture, **E**ye contact, **S**aying appropriate words, modulating **T**one of voice; see Figure 5.2).

6. Presentation Delivery

Students present to their intended audience by

- Setting up materials and technology as needed.
- Going through their pre-performance ritual.
- Mentally reviewing the BEST skills.
- Greeting their audience (using the appropriate titles and names), and introducing the group.
- Presenting to the audience, making sure that all group members are equally involved.
- Concluding the presentation, and inviting the audience to ask any questions they might have.
- Thanking the audience for their time.

7. Reflection and Assessment

Students meet in small groups to reflect on their efforts, notice successes, and identify areas of improvement. They then debrief with the whole class.

In Step 1, the teacher introduces the strategy and identifies several real-life examples that illustrate how a presenter takes into consideration the needs of an audience—for example, an interpreter who translates a message into sign language for those who are hearing impaired or the braille labels on elevator panels for those who are blind.

In Step 2, the teacher informs students that they will be planning, practicing, and delivering a presentation to a specific audience on a topic they learned a lot about over the last few weeks. Students will grasp the material better by presenting it to others; they will practice presentation literacy skills, learn how to take the perspective of their audience, and gain recognition for their work. Through a whole-class discussion, students determine the vision of their AFC by deciding on their audience, considering timing or space constraints, selecting the format of their presentation, and, finally, clarifying how their audience might use the information once the presentation concludes.

For example, during Step 2 in Vishal's class, the students might collectively decide to present to 6th graders at the middle school who are studying world history. Each student might decide on a different format for their presentation. Vishal decided to use his creative talents to make a poster, whereas his classmates might compile a photo essay or create a video. Likewise, although Vishal may plan to have the 6th graders write down three takeaways during his presentation and share them during a think-pair-share, his classmates might ask the students to select one topic they have learned about in world history and describe in writing how it relates to the content they presented.

During Step 3, students elaborate on their vision to come up with a concrete plan for their presentations, either in their assigned groups or individually. Teachers can liken this step to that of outlining a paper in an English language arts class or doing background research and brainstorming solutions when applying the steps of the engineering design process. During this step, students will research the demographics and prior knowledge of their audience, determine the content to include in their presentation, and develop a step-by-step breakdown of the flow of the presentation.

For example, Vishal may have reached out to the teacher of the 6th graders to determine their background knowledge on the Byzantine Empire so he would know the level of content to include in his poster. Also, to avoid reading information verbatim from his poster, he may have planned to note the main points on index cards, present the parts of his poster in a step-by-step fashion, and engage his audience with questions.

Teaching Tip

You can abbreviate Steps 1–3 once your students are familiar with the purpose of the Audience-Focused Communication strategy and with how to develop a vision and plan for the presentation. As with all STAT strategies, with repeated practice, students will begin to internalize the steps and skills; in time, they will become second nature.

Oral communication has two distinct stages: building the talk and performing the talk (Palmer, 2014b). In Step 4, students do the former; in Step 5, they rehearse their presentation and focus on the four components of the social awareness skill BEST: **b**ody posture, **e**ye contact, **s**ay appropriate words, and **t**one of voice (see Figure 5.2).

FIGURE 5.2

BEST: The Elements of Presentation Literacy

Communicating in your BEST way involves paying attention to the following aspects of your behavior:

B: *Body posture*
- Standing up straight
- Appearing calm and confident (but not arrogant)
- Matching your gestures to your words
- Considering both body gestures and facial expressions

E: *Eye contact*
- Making appropriate eye contact–soft, not glaring
- Shifting your eye contact to engage with all audience members

S: *Say appropriate words*
- Tailoring your language to the needs of your audience
- Ensuring that your audience hears every word you say
- Enunciating and speaking clearly

T: *Tone of voice*
- Adding feeling to your words
- Practicing different inflections
- Adjusting your pace for greatest effectiveness
- Varying your pace, depending on the content and message

Sources: Elias & Butler, 2005; Palmer, 2014b.

Just as athletes practice numerous times before a game and actors rehearse before a performance, running through the presentation in front of others is an essential part of the AFC process. It enables the speaker to gain familiarity with the content and flow of the presentation and anticipate and plan for how to address potential obstacles that may arise.

In Step 5, students also tap into their self-management skills by practicing techniques to increase their comfort and confidence. They can draw on all their senses to visualize their ideal presentation scenario; they can "cope ahead" by imagining any obstacles that might occur and by seeing themselves successfully address those obstacles. Similarly, students can engage in guided imagery to promote positive thoughts and calm their nerves. They may also use pre-performance rituals, such as deep breathing, mindfulness, or positive self-talk. Note that different techniques will work for different students. For example, Vishal found 5-2-5 breathing effective in calming his nerves and getting in the right mindset for his presentation. However, a classmate might prefer a positive self-talk mantra, such as "I'm confident, I'm prepared, and my presentation will be a success."

> **SEL Competency Connection: Self-Management**
> Having strong self-management skills will support a student in regulating difficult emotions, such as nervousness or anxiety, before, during, and after their presentation. Armed with these skills, students will feel more confident standing before an audience and will take greater pride in the message they're delivering. Self-management skills for a presentation can involve breathing exercises, grounding techniques, and positive self-talk.

In Step 6, when students deliver their presentations, they use the self-management skills they have learned to stay calm and maintain their composure. During this step, students should remember to greet their audience and introduce themselves and any group members, ensuring they use the appropriate names and titles. While presenting, they need to get their audience's attention and keep them engaged by posing questions, relating to the audience, and revealing passion through speech and body language. Students should also have a definitive closure to their presentation in which they thank the audience for their time and invite them to ask any questions they may have.

Finally, during Step 7, students consider several reflection questions to discuss in small groups that prompt them to notice successes, look at how the audience responded to their message, and consider how they might improve next time. The lesson culminates in a whole-class debriefing of how the experience reinforced students' understanding of the material, developed their presentation skills, and offered them skills to regulate their emotions when speaking in front of others.

Planning an AFC Lesson

In Figure 5.3, you'll find the various steps we suggest you take when planning an Audience-Focused Communication lesson.

FIGURE 5.3

How to Plan an Audience-Focused Communication (AFC) Lesson

---

1. **Determine the curricular unit you would like to use for the lesson.**
    - Review the curriculum for content that lends itself to being shared with an audience and taught (by students) to others.
    - Consult with a colleague or media center specialist to determine appropriate resources students might draw on when crafting their presentations.

2. **Determine the assignment topic or range of topics.**
    - Decide whether students will all present on the same topic or a range of topics.
    - Decide whether you will assign students topics or let them choose topics on their own.

3. **Determine whether students will work in groups or individually.**
    - If you decide on groups, consider whether each group will develop its own norms and whether you will assign roles to each group member.

4. **Determine the resources students will use to develop both their presentation and their presentation literacy skills.**
    - Decide what materials students might use, consulting as needed with art and music teachers, the media specialist, and technology support personnel.
    - Consider providing copies of the BEST Guidelines, AFC Project Presentation Plan Graphic Organizer, and AFC Ways to Express Myself—three tools available at http://www.secdlab.org/stat/book.

5. **Develop an essential question that provokes inquiry and focuses on presentation literacy skills.**

6. **Come up with several analogies you can use to introduce the purpose and significance of the AFC strategy.**
    - Focus on what will resonate with your particular students.

7. **Identify the logistical issues and restrictions that students should be mindful of when brainstorming their vision.**
    - Decide who will be in the students' audience: classmates only, other individuals within the school, individuals from outside the school?
    - Decide where students will present and how many people that space will hold.
    - Decide how much time you will allot for presentations.

Reviewing the Curriculum

Start by reviewing the curriculum for units that have topics that will lend themselves to sharing with an audience. For example, a 7th grade social studies teacher may decide that a unit about the foundations of geography, in which students locate geographic locations and analyze features of physical and political maps, would be less engaging for them to present on compared to a unit on globalization, in which they would gain an understanding of the underlying causes and effects of globalization. Or consider multilayered units that students have struggled with. For instance, a high school physics teacher may realize that students tend to struggle with the unit on centripetal forces and therefore identifies this as a unit for students to present on using AFC. Once you select a topic, collaborate with grade-level colleagues across disciplines, as well as with specialists in the media center and technology department, to ensure that adequate resources on the topic are available to students.

Selecting the Topic or Topic Options

When first introducing Audience-Focused Communication, it's best to have everyone present on a single topic. Therefore, a social studies teacher integrating AFC into a unit on the American Revolutionary War might ask all the students to present on the Declaration of Independence. However, once your students have gained comfort and confidence with the strategy of AFC and their presentation literacy skills, you can give them greater choice, either providing them with a list of potential topics from which to choose or suggesting that they conduct preliminary research to propose a topic of their own.

Deciding Between Individual or Group Presentations

Now decide whether your students will work independently on preparing, rehearsing, and delivering their presentation or in small groups of three to four students. Certain situations call for independent presentations, such as a candidate's speech before members of the student council, whereas others lend themselves better to group presentations. See Figure 5.4 for more examples.

If you decide to have students work in groups, refer to Chapter 4 for additional information on how to develop group norms and assign roles to promote equity and individual accountability.

Deciding on the Resources Needed

This part of planning requires you to consider students' previous experiences and comfort levels presenting in front of an audience in order to determine the resources you will use with them, the various logistical considerations, and how you will go about introducing the new strategy. As with any lesson, it is essential to consider the needs of all students, as well as to anticipate all of the directions in which a lesson can unfold.

FIGURE 5.4

Examples of Individual and Group AFC Project Presentations

Individual Project Presentations	Group Project Presentations
High school visual arts. The student explains the steps that went into creating a layered self-portrait. **High school language arts or drama.** The student acts out a scene from a short story to demonstrate their skills in accessing the thoughts and feelings of a character. **Middle school advisory.** The student describes their core values after completing a self-awareness activity and reflecting on what is most important to them.	**High school biology.** Students share the results of a DNA extraction lab, in which they extracted and compared the DNA of strawberries and bananas. **Middle school language arts.** Students describe examples of an author's narrative techniques across several texts during an author study unit. **High school statistics.** Students share a binomial distribution that depicts the outcome of a recent clinical trial of a new drug in treating a disease.

Teaching Tip

When first introducing Audience-Focused Communication, be sure to offer your students sufficient scaffolding and support—and be patient with the process. For example, if you have a handful of students who benefit from structure when planning projects, make the AFC Project Presentation Plan Graphic Organizer available to them. Similarly, if your students tend to struggle with brainstorming ideas, then you may want to inspire their creativity by sharing the AFC: Ways to Express Myself handout.

Developing an Essential Question and Clarifying Analogies

You want to come up with an essential question that will provoke inquiry and highlight presentation literacy skills. An example might be *"How can students consider the perspective of their audience to ensure that their message is well received?"* Or you can make the question more specific to the particular content or to a given presentation skill. For example, *"When describing the steps entailed in creating a layered self-portrait, how might you tailor your presentation to an audience of skilled artists?"* Analogies can help your students understand the purpose and significance of AFC. You might bring up the example of a sign-language interpreter, who translates a speaker's words into a message that can be understood by audience members with hearing impairments, or the way that elevator manufacturers include Braille next to each floor button to communicate with those who can't see the numbers. Seek out analogies that are meaningful for your students, considering their personal and cultural assets and experiences. Also, consider drawing on real-life examples from their shared experiences. For example, if your students have had interactions with individuals with autism spectrum disorder (ASD), they will be aware of how figurative language can be challenging for these individuals to interpret. You can remind them of a specific instance in which this happened and, as a group, discuss considerations to take when tailoring their presentations to an audience that includes people with ASD (e.g., being straightforward, eliminating idioms, excluding sarcasm).

Determining the Logistics

Finally decide the who, what, where, and when of the presentations, identifying any potential restrictions related to physical space, timing, materials, and audience and setting clear parameters. For example, if your school discourages visitors from outside the school, then perhaps establish a parameter that audience members need to be members of the school; you could also present the option of virtually connecting with individuals outside the school. Likewise, if you have students presenting individually, enforce a time limit so presentations don't go beyond the 45-minute class periods we suggest.

As Erik Palmer (2014b) puts it, "Listening and speaking are the water that surrounds everything in our classes and upon which instruction depends" (p. 23). To be effective speakers and listeners, our students need direct instruction of the requisite skills and multiple opportunities for practice and reinforcement, which is exactly what the AFC strategy provides.

Implementing AFC

Going through the steps of an AFC lesson will develop students' ability to give and receive constructive feedback. Using BEST skills will help them be mindful of their body posture, eye contact, language, and tone of voice when presenting. And they will conclude the activity by celebrating successful outcomes and identifying areas in which they can improve. This is of utmost importance, given that our students' communication and presentation literacy skills have declined due to the widespread use of technology. The majority of our students' communication takes place across screens as opposed to face-to-face, which minimizes the need to use proper language, focus on body posture, and interpret social cues.

Although we encourage you to consider topics that pose challenges to students to reinforce their understanding, for your first AFC lesson, we suggest you select a topic that the majority of students understand. Set aside time for students to watch several noteworthy speeches performed by young people, such as activist Adora Svitak and inventor Richard Turere (Chibana, 2015). Using these speeches as examples, have students identify how the speaker tailored their presentation to their audience and engaged them throughout. Next, spend time walking students through Steps 1, 2, and 3—the introduction, visualizing a desired outcome, and developing a presentation plan (see Figure 5.1)—to involve them in the process of determining the audience and format of the presentation. For this first AFC lesson, all students should use the same audience and format (e.g., slideshow, poster, or song); you can gradually release responsibility and allow students greater freedom with each subsequent lesson. For example, an 8th grade science teacher may decide for all students to present on the Coriolis effect to rising 8th grade science students by creating a Prezi presentation. Depending on the needs of your students, you may want to model how to complete the AFC Project Plan Graphic Organizer.

Assigning students roles in their small groups will ensure equity and individual accountability as they prepare their presentations during Step 4. You can support students by reminding them to adhere to group norms, engage in perspective-taking as they consider the grammar and language needed to effectively tailor their presentations, and use strategies for hooking their audience's attention and maintaining it throughout the presentation.

During Step 5, facilitate a whole-class discussion on the various pre-performance rituals that athletes, singers, and performers use. Provide students with an example of a pre-performance ritual they could carry out before their presentation. For example, they might

- Visualize all details of their successful speech from start to finish.
- Engage in positive self-talk, and repeat the affirmation "I believe in myself and my abilities."
- Do 5-2-5 breathing, and repeat three times.

As students rehearse their speeches, have their peers serve as an audience. Liken this experience to a dress rehearsal and if any issues arise, such as technological glitches or lack of audience engagement, capitalize on these opportunities as teachable moments and involve the whole class in brainstorming ways to troubleshoot the issue.

Finally, after students have delivered their presentations during Step 6, have them reflect on their successes (e.g., engaging the audience with consistent eye contact) and identify areas of growth in Step 7. They might, for example, identify engaging the audience with consistent eye contact as something they did well and flag enunciating more clearly and speaking loudly enough for all audience members to hear them as something they might improve. Remind the students that with each speech they deliver, they will become more competent in presentation literacy skills and gain confidence in their abilities. Ultimately, developing these abilities will provide them with the key to reach the hearts and minds of their audience and profoundly affect others.

Over time, as the AFC strategy becomes part of your pedagogical practice, point out to students how they can apply elements of the strategy to a broad range of contexts. For example, when students are handing in an assignment, urge them to consider the perspective of the teacher and how that teacher might feel about getting sloppy work that has not been checked for grammar or spelling. Although they won't formally be going through each step of the AFC process in such a situation, they will be applying the tenets of the strategy by taking into account their audience's perspective and tailoring their oral and written communication accordingly.

Individuals can apply the tenets of the AFC process in a wide variety of situations. These might include

- Running for student council
- Performing a solo during a recital
- Asking your boss for time off
- Presenting the findings of a science lab
- Sharing artwork
- Suggesting to teammates or fellow club members an alternative way of doing something
- Requesting a favor from parents (e.g., an extended curfew, an increased allowance, a separate bedroom from a younger sibling)
- Asking a school administrator for a change in procedures (e.g., more parking spots for high school juniors and seniors, additional transition time in between classes, exemption from physical education during a sports season)

As with all of the STAT strategies, the goal is for students to begin to transfer the SEL skills and tenets of each strategy to contexts in their everyday lives and, ultimately, take action.

Extending the Reach of AFC

The goals of the generic form of AFC are to engage students in deeper learning of content and build their confidence in presenting to an audience. But what about taking action? That's where PLAN Integrative comes in, the focus of the next chapter. PLAN empowers students to take action because it focuses on changing the thoughts or behavior of their audience through their presentation. For example, students may take aim at the unhealthy meals served in their school cafeteria, and their goal will be to effect change by convincing the principal to support them in introducing healthier meal options into the cafeteria.

Scaling up your practice of AFC with PLAN Integrative empowers your students to be change agents and to seize their role as active citizens within a democracy. It helps them find their voice and use it to advocate for causes they believe in. Further, it cultivates assertive communication skills, creativity of self-expression, and ownership of learning. With PLAN Integrative, students see themselves as leaders in the change process, as social change agents in their classrooms, schools, communities, and the wider world.

SEL Competency Connection: Responsible Decision Making

PLAN Integrative combines the practices of ethical decision making and social responsibility. In essence, students must think beyond themselves to consider the ethical implications of a specific decision and take responsibility for the decision they make. For example, if a student collaborates with a friend on a take-home quiz that is supposed to be completed independently, they are not acting ethically. In addition, they are not making a socially responsible decision, as they are getting an unfair advantage over others by pooling their knowledge with that of a friend. Ultimately, the decision should be in accordance with social norms and support the well-being of all parties involved.

Formative Assessment and AFC

Students typically receive two types of feedback when presenting to an audience: immediate feedback from the audience and written feedback from their teacher (Palmer, 2011). However, with AFC, we encourage you to involve the audience members in the evaluation process as well. To that end, we offer a set of simple rubrics for audience members to complete (see Figure 5.5), which addresses the components of BEST: assessing the student's body language (whether they stood up straight, appeared confident, and used appropriate gestures and facial expressions); whether the student tailored the language of the speech to match the audience's prior knowledge and personal, cultural, and community assets; and the student's ability to engage their audience with frequent eye contact, vary the tone of their voice and pacing of their speech, and effectively use visuals or props. Distribute this rubric in advance of the presentation, and provide the audience members with time at the end to thoughtfully complete it. Use your knowledge of your students to best adapt the rubric to suit their needs.

FIGURE 5.5

Rubric for AFC Evaluation

Skill	Beginning	Developing	Approaching	Secure
Demonstrates confident body language	Student does not exhibit confident body posture and does not use gestures and facial expressions to add meaning to their words.	At times, student exhibits confident body language and makes minimal attempts to use gestures and facial expressions to underscore key points and keep the audience alert to the message.	Student often exhibits confident body language and makes frequent attempts to use gestures and facial expressions to underscore key points and keep the audience alert to the message.	Student consistently exhibits confident body language and seamlessly uses gestures and facial expressions to underscore key points and keep the audience alert to the message.

Skill	Beginning	Developing	Approaching	Secure
Tailors speech to the audience	There is no evidence that the student took knowledge of the audience into account when choosing their language and delivering their presentation. Student does not enunciate or speak clearly.	Student made a minimal attempt to fit their language to the context of the audience's interests/prior knowledge and may have attempted to convey the purpose of the presentation to the audience. Student somewhat enunciates their words, but their speech is not always clear.	Some of the student's language fits the context of the audience's interests/prior knowledge and makes the purpose of the presentation clear to the audience. Student enunciates and speaks clearly.	The majority of the student's language matches the context of the audience and makes the purpose of the presentation clear to the audience. Student consistently enunciates each word and speaks clearly.
Engages audience	Student does not use eye contact or visuals/props to engage the audience.	Student makes minimal effort to make appropriate eye contact with the audience or use visuals, props, and information to enhance their presentation. Needs to make more effort to prepare visuals to better capture the attention of the audience.	Student makes appropriate eye contact with the audience from time to time and includes some visuals, props, and information to enhance their presentation. Student needs to refine visuals to better capture the attention of the audience.	Student frequently makes appropriate eye contact with all audience members and uses visuals, props, and information in a manner that continually captures the attention of the audience.

Given that the final step of the generic form of AFC involves reflecting on successes and identifying areas for growth, be sure to have each student evaluate their own presentation literacy skills. The checklist in Figure 5.6 covers the process of developing and rehearsing the presentation, as well as the final product and how the audience received it. Feel free to modify this self-assessment checklist to meet your students' needs.

FIGURE 5.6

Student Self-Assessment for AFC

☐ I used emotional regulation techniques skills, such as deep breathing.
☐ I engaged in a preperformance presentation ritual to ensure I was ready.
☐ I felt connected to myself/felt self-aware during the presentation.
☐ I conveyed confidence through body language and/or facial expressions.
☐ I communicated with an open tone of voice (volume, pace, and/or clarity).
☐ I recognized skills that I need to improve.

Write a brief reflection on the skills you identified as areas for improvement:

Getting Started with Audience-Focused Communication: Forward Reflections

As you conclude your planning on implementing Audience-Focused Communication, contemplate the following questions:

- What previous experiences and knowledge do your students have presenting in front of others?
- What are the social-emotional benefits of implementing AFC for your students as they engage with the curriculum?
- Knowing your students, how do you anticipate they will respond to the AFC strategy?
- How might you leverage the support of other school personnel in helping you implement the AFC strategy and enhance your practice?

PLAN: A Problem-Solving Strategy for Historical Understanding and Social Action

Aneesha slams her locker shut and runs off to make her 12:15 social studies class. She's eager to meet up with her social problem project team—Marc, Rajesh, and Kayla—to share her latest findings on the history of women's rights in the United States. The team has been researching for a few class periods now and has begun developing a strategic action plan focused on winning women the right to vote, informed by the historical conditions in the mid-19th century that were the backdrop to the 1848 Women's Rights Convention in Seneca Falls, New York. Aneesha catches her breath and pulls out her notebook and Chromebook, readying herself to reveal the latest find that will enhance the quality of the group's action plan.

Ready, Set, Go—Social Action in PLAN

PLAN's social action problem-solving goal aligns with social studies standards and disciplinary practices and reflects the spirit of restorative practices. As students make their way through the steps of PLAN, they learn how to repair harm by analyzing causes and listing options to solve a societal problem of the past, a current problem in the news, or even a school-based problem. As such, the process enlivens one's sense of justice.

PLAN also reflects children's natural will to contribute to their world and engage the dispositions of citizenship. In her article "Empowering Kids to Be Part of the Solution," Dana McCauley (2015), an elementary school principal, shares this insight:

> When you can help kids see the impact they can have to solve a problem in their own little corner of the world . . . it's an opportunity to learn something. It's an opportunity to make something good happen. That gives them that sense of belonging and a sense of being a part of something bigger. . . . [They realize that] "here's an issue, here's a problem, and I'm going to lend my part to that, that even I, as a 10-year-old, have something to add." (para. 18)

We live in an era that will see schools make strong shifts toward promoting citizenship and focusing on human rights and civil discourse. PLAN is a concise, elegant way to rehearse the process of democratic change while engaging in desired content.

Specifically, students learn to collaboratively examine and evaluate a problem that has no clear solution and consider the options to solve that problem through inquiry and research. Next, they propose an action plan, considering the views of the various stakeholders who are directly or indirectly implicated, and explore alternative solutions. PLAN ends with a reflective discussion during which students notice successes and consider what they could have improved in view of proposing a more inclusive solution next time. When PLAN is properly executed, students realize that organizing for social change requires ongoing refinement of the problem-solving process and that with each attempt, they can put a better plan into play the next time the situation warrants it.

PLAN democratizes the classroom. PLAN addresses the "hidden curriculum" that defines the traditional power structure of the classroom—the one that teaches students, for example, that a teacher is more likely to call on you if you speak up regularly or that challenging a teacher will get you sent to the assistant principal's office. PLAN provides a way around transactional and compliance-based student–teacher relationships and fosters an environment in which students and their teachers are coleaders of learning. The strategy naturally fosters student leadership skills, infuses democratic practices into the learning, and shows students how to organize for social change.

PLAN empowers student leadership. PLAN flips the script of traditional learning in which memorization—or, as Paulo Freire (2005) calls it, the culture of "the banking system"—prevails in the classroom. It gives students the opportunity to lead their learning and discover information to solve a problem that has no clear solution.

PLAN brings democratic practices and action to the classroom. The wave of activism that we've seen over the last five years—from the #MeToo movement to youth activism in the face of school shootings to the Black Lives Matter movement—illustrates the need to teach active civics learning. Skill building for active and engaged citizenship excites both teacher and student leadership. State social studies standards that mandate civics learning, historical thinking, and critical information literacy skills also align with the aims of STAT.

PLAN teaches students how to consider multiple perspectives. With PLAN, students build empathy for people past and present and for their peers. Students are able to consider an issue not solely from their own experience and point of view; they learn how to listen to another's point of view. This approach gives students the opportunity to check their assumptions, share emotions, and develop social-emotional connections to others who hold differing points of view. This is the beating heart of civil discourse.

Organizing for Social Action

The energy students bring to social issues is a powerful lever for student empowerment and agency. STAT taps into this energy by giving students opportunities to research and examine the root causes of a variety of issues, and it raises awareness of their social, economic, and political effects on the rights of individuals, groups, and communities.

SEL Competency Connection: Self-Awareness
As students uncover how systems of oppression affect innocent people, they will often become emotionally outraged, impassioned, and motivated to express their views. With PLAN, they learn how to make good use of that passion as they explore the content. They practice navigating intense emotions in the presence of their peers, and they learn to empathize with those who strived to make change.

To excite youth to take social action, they must know how to plan for it. Advancing matters of human and civil rights requires that we teach our students not just how people throughout history organized for change. We must also give them the opportunity to *experience firsthand* the social action process while they're students in our classrooms.

Moreover, students will learn that not all action plans are initially successful. By taking the time to evaluate an action plan that they've developed and weigh it against the historical action plan that was implemented at the time, students learn the successful elements of effective social action. Discussing in small groups and as a whole class, and taking note of what was and wasn't successful and why, help generate vulnerable, honest discussions about the action-planning process. And this strengthens trust, which is key to working effectively as a group. This process also reveals to students the threads and responsibilities of social change across generations.

The Four Steps of PLAN

Let's now take a look at the four sequenced steps of the PLAN strategy shown in Figure 6.1, which will help you guide your students through a collaborative problem-solving process.

FIGURE 6.1

The Four Steps of PLAN

1. Create a **problem description** that defines the issue under discussion.
2. Brainstorm a **list** of options to solve the problem.
3. Develop and act on an **action plan** to solve the problem.
4. **Notice** successes as part of an ongoing process of evaluation and refinement.

To assist your efforts, we have scaffolded the strategy into three levels, summarized in Figure 6.2: PLAN Basic, PLAN Comprehensive, and Plan Integrative.

PLAN Basic: Learning the Ropes

To get your students ready for this simplest variation of PLAN, launch a pre-teaching lesson the day before. Inform your students that they will learn a new four-step problem-solving strategy (as shown in Figure 6.1) that they can apply to a real-world scenario, a school-based problem, or a problem of the past. Let them know that when they come into class the following morning, they will work in small groups to solve a problem as a member of the community. Consider developing an anchor chart of the four steps for students to reference throughout their schooling.

FIGURE 6.2

The Three Variations of the PLAN Problem-Solving Strategy

Level	Scope	Problem Type	Duration
PLAN Basic	Introduces the strategy	An everyday problem	1 class period
PLAN Comprehensive	Teaches the full scope of the strategy	A problem aligned with a single academic subject	3–4 class periods (mini-unit)
PLAN Integrative	Teaches the strategy and features presentation skills	A problem aligned with multiple academic subjects	2–3 weeks (full unit)

As students settle into class the following day, let them know that, for this particular lesson, they will collaborate in small groups to familiarize themselves with the four steps of the strategy. The small-group format allows you to monitor students, provide support, or teach a given step as needed. Once you've arranged the students in groups, provide them with chart paper and ask them to use their notebooks. Share that they will be developing their thinking as a group to solve a problem as they work their way through the strategy. Also, let them know that at each step along the way, you will be asking them to share their group's thoughts with the whole class. Setting this expectation will help not only you but also the students, who will hear how other groups sought to solve the problem.

Teaching Tip
The one-page PLAN graphic organizer featured on our companion website (https://www.secdlab.org/stat/book) can help students visualize the process and see the sequencing of the strategy. Students don't necessarily need to fill in the organizer, but it can serve as a visual aid to help them develop the step-by-step knowledge they need to build their understanding of the PLAN strategy. They can keep a copy of the organizer in their notebooks, or you can post it in the classroom.

In the Barking Dog lesson, students tackle the problem of their new neighbor's barking dog, who is causing a public noise disturbance. Students brainstorm potential solutions to the problem (e.g., speak to the neighbor, leave an anonymous note, report a noise disturbance to the police) and decide which is likely to be satisfactory to all parties. Although the lesson's step-by-step approach may feel a bit mechanical, it's valuable to follow it carefully and draw out any student questions during each step's debriefing discussion. The last step of PLAN, notice successes, helps students reflect on their group process—what was successful as a group and what was challenging.

One common issue you will inevitably encounter is a student who may disagree with the group's thinking. Have students build off the Norms lesson as they identify the problem, list options, and develop the action plan, and recognize that disagreement will sporadically emerge. Emphasize that consensus doesn't imply unanimous agreement and that many times in the real world and workplace, the group's work has to proceed, despite a member standing aside.

Recall the goal for PLAN is to solve the problem so that all stakeholders feel included and can come to a solution that is reasonable and hopefully lasting. An example of a consensus opinion is to work through the problem by notifying the municipal animal control board or even knocking on the dog owner's door to have a conversation with the owners as the first step. A divergent opinion might be to write an anonymous letter or immediately call the police. When those moments do arise, a student in the group can say, "I see that you and the rest of the group are far apart on this issue. We recognize the perspective you bring, but at this point, we do have to proceed forward. Will you join us in doing so?" Using language like this shows respect for the other person's contributions and for their right to stand aside, but it also encourages that person to continue with the group's efforts.

SEL Competency Connection: Self-Management

Opposing views do not inevitably lead to conflict. By using language that models how to recognize opposing views, students can create enough space in the discussion to acknowledge the intensity of their own and others' emotions. Creating such space and using such language can improve students' self-management skills during moments of contention.

As with any initial implementation, expect the lesson to feel a bit choppy and, at times, messy. Remember, the goal is to introduce the students to the strategy and for you to build your competence with implementing it. Feel free to conduct the lesson again with a problem that the school community might face, such as whether or not school lunches are nutritious.

PLAN Comprehensive: Connecting to Academic Content and Standards

Once students are familiar with the PLAN strategy, you can introduce them to how the strategy can align with academic content and use standards as the foundation for the problem.

We'll illustrate the process by sharing a lesson that asks students to go back in time to reconsider the gender inequality that women confronted during the 19th century women's suffrage movement in the United States and develop an action plan *they* would have created if they had been among the movement's leaders.

Planning for a PLAN Comprehensive lesson differs from planning the PLAN Basic lesson. Students will need to refer to reading material to build background information (in this case, on women's suffrage in the mid-1800s in the United States); the lesson will require between three to four class periods to accommodate the full scope of the strategy. After students develop their action plan, they will compare their plan to one that the leaders of the historical movement actually implemented. Finally, the lesson culminates with formative assessment linked to the curricular content and standards (in our example, to extend student learning on the topic and on the promise of gender equality).

You can integrate this particular PLAN lesson on women's suffrage into the existing curriculum at the beginning or end of a unit related to human rights, civil rights, or social change. If you have experience with project-based learning, PLAN can serve as a stand-alone unit with supplementary research and presentation skills integrated into the process. Because these are student-centered, constructivist lessons where students actively build their knowledge on the topic, we encourage teachers to communicate with students, parents, and the administration that you're attempting a new strategy that places students in the driver's seat of their learning. For this lesson, you will no longer be the font of knowledge.

We recommend that, on your first attempt, you collaborate with a colleague who teaches the same course and implement the PLAN lesson together. This way you can share your concerns and have someone to collaborate with along the way.

Begin by setting up groups of four to five students. Have them set up norms to guide their collaboration, such as how to communicate beyond the school day or how to work out any unexpected challenges with student absences. Communicate to the students that this PLAN lesson will engage academic content—specifically, gender equality—and will require them to investigate informational sources to build their knowledge of this issue. Have students read the background articles in advance. Make copies of the PLAN graphic organizer; this can help students frame their thinking as they work in groups.

Also, in terms of logistics, let students know that PLAN will be a four-day process: On Day 1, they will identify the problem (P); on Day 2, they will list options to solve the problem (L); on Day 3, they will complete their action planning (A); and on Day 4, they will notice successes (N).

Introducing and Identifying the Problem (P)

This step engages students in building the background knowledge necessary to identify and describe the problem. Be sure to steer students toward identifying the problem (e.g., the lack of legal equality for women) as opposed to accumulating evidence of the problem's effects (e.g., women's issues not being represented in government or public debate not reflecting a diversity of opinions).

SEL Competency Connection: Social Awareness
The rich speaking, reading, inquiry, and listening skills embedded at each level of PLAN promote perspective-taking. Students begin to realize that some of their life experiences or challenges can compare to the plight and struggles of other groups that encounter deliberate acts of violence, injustice, and dehumanization. As students delve into the emotional heartache, anger, hopes, and dreams of the oppressed, they begin to empathize with people of the past and with those who are currently struggling for justice.

Use a do-now activity to launch the lesson. Have students write their reactions to this quote by Elizabeth Cady Stanton in their notebooks: "We are the only class in history that has been left to fight its battles alone, unaided by the ruling powers. White labor and the freed Black man had their champions, but where are ours?" Have the students share their thoughts and feelings as they consider the following:

- What questions does this quote raise?
- Why do you think Stanton said this?
- What, if any, emotional reaction do you have to this quote?

Students may be reticent to step up and lead the conversation with their peers, so encourage one student in each group to lead this part of the discussion.

It's important to debrief the do-now activity. Conduct a whole-class share-out across the groups for each question. Respond with curiosity, underscoring interesting points and affirming the strong feelings this topic may engender, not only on its own, but also as related to its intersectionality with race. Expect this portion of the lesson to be emotionally powerful.

Walk through a whole-class introduction of the reading by noting the dates of the sources and providing a little background information on them. In this lesson, we suggest you use the following two readings:

- An excerpt from "The Cult of True Womanhood: 1820 to 1860" by Barbara Welter (1966, p. 152)
- Elizabeth Cady Stanton's keynote speech at the 1849 Seneca Falls Convention in New York

Have students annotate and highlight in the readings key evidence related to the topic, as well as define specific terms. The students can debrief the articles in their groups, or you can facilitate a whole-class review. As you and your students gain more comfort with this process of debriefing a close reading, you can ask students to lead this process.

Transitioning to the problem description will require students to pull together their thinking independently as a group. Don't give away hints about what the problem is; tell students that they are to arrive at their own understanding of the issue without you confirming their thinking. Allowing your students to engage in a productive struggle and discover the problem on their own is a valuable social learning experience that builds trust and confidence within the group.

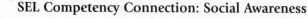

SEL Competency Connection: Social Awareness
The four steps of PLAN—problem identification, list options, action planning, and notice successes—require acute observational skills. Students learn how to read body language; they also learn when to speak up and when to listen. This fosters a situational awareness that makes for meaningful group work as students practice social action planning as democratic citizens.

To support this work, post the guiding questions shown in Figure 6.3 and ask students to walk through them in groups in order to reach a consensus on the problem and craft a description. Monitor the students and listen to their thinking, but resist getting overly involved.

As you monitor the room, notice the tenor and pace of student conversations. Encourage student thinking and offer support as needed. If you note gaps in a student's thinking, ask them to review the issue from a variety of perspectives. After you wrap up the discussion, have students write their problem identification and problem description in their notebooks or on chart paper.

Allow 10–12 minutes for this portion of the activity. Provide an opportunity for student groups to share their problem identification and description.

FIGURE 6.3

Problem Identification and Description: Guiding Questions for Students

- Is there a problem? How do you know?
- What is the problem?
- Where does the event described in the source occur?
- Who is affected by the problem?
- What are the issues of each party involved? How does the issue affect the different individuals and groups involved?
- Who is responsible for the problem? What internal and external factors might have influenced this issue?
- Why are those responsible using these practices?
- Which key people were involved in making important decisions about addressing The problem?

Here's an example of what a student might submit:

> Women were confined to the home in their role as mothers and did
> not have equal rights to men. They wanted to be free and to have
> the right to be represented in the government. Also, they wanted the
> government to revise the many unjust laws that protected men but
> not women. Finally, Black and Brown women felt excluded from the
> efforts of white women to obtain equal rights.

Facilitating a whole-class share-out will provide time for the groups to connect
their efforts. This will be a joyful experience as you see students being confirmed
in their thinking.

Listing Options (L)

Students will now embark on listing options around the problem, whether
it's a historical problem, a current event, or a school-based problem, to come up
with a feasible solution that is inclusive of stakeholders' interests. Students will
need the two original background reading sources on hand. They can add some
original research of their own, or you can work with a media specialist to organize additional sources for students to pull from. It's best to limit the number
of additional resources to keep the content manageable.

To help students consider the varied perspectives of the stakeholders,
have them develop a SMART goal from the perspective of the different groups
involved in the situation, such as the white suffragists, the Black suffragists, veterans of the abolitionist movement, and men in government. The goal must be
Specific and Measurable; it must include an Action plan; and it must be Realistic
and Timely. Here's an example:

> Specific: Draft a constitutional amendment to give Black men
> and women the vote that could be adopted by state legislatures.
> Measurable: The number of states adopting the amendment. Action
> Plan: Rally supporters to lobby state legislatures to adopt the amend-
> ment. Realistic: Women's groups, abolitionists, and freed Black men
> can lobby states legislatures. Timely: Might take 3–5 years.

Allot 10–12 minutes for this activity. You don't need to debrief the groups'
SMART goals as a whole class.

Students will now engage in a quick brainstorm session to plot out potential
solutions in their notebooks. Try to keep this activity at 10 minutes or less; you

will need at least half of your instructional period to weigh the pros and cons of the proposed solutions. Advise the groups to check their thinking against the pragmatic interests of the various stakeholders. Walk around the classroom to encourage, monitor, and listen as students brainstorm their solutions. Students might propose, for example, that the women organize a strike by not carrying out household duties, file complaints and pressure governmental officials to make changes for their equal rights, or protest for equal rights by organizing a rally.

Encourage the groups to select the top two or three options that are the most viable and inclusive. This step of the PLAN directly reflects the social-emotional learning goal of responsible decision making, which is "the ability to make caring and constructive choices about personal behavior and social interactions across diverse situations" (CASEL, n.d., para. 3). *Making a caring and constructive choice* means addressing the needs of the many interests involved, including those opposed to the change. Students are tasked with selecting a solution with the fewest amount of costs across groups.

> **SEL Competency Connection: Responsible Decision Making**
> In the problem identification and option-listing phases, students study the effects of problems on groups and communities and begin to weigh the ethical, economic, political, and social challenges in the decisions they could make. Weighing such factors engenders thoughtful conversations about what is right—and about one's responsibility to *make* things right for those affected for the greater social good.

As the groups debate their two or three options, have them jot down the pros and cons of each, focusing on one option at a time. For example, for the option "women should protest for equal rights by organizing a rally," students might note as a pro that such a protest would show a united force of white women and send a powerful message to men. At the same time, students might note a con, that protesters would face possible arrest and that this option does not involve men in coming up with a solution. This segment of the lesson will take a minimum of 25–30 minutes. By the end, the students as a group should have completed an evidenced-based assessment of each of the options in view of selecting the most caring, constructive, and ethical solution to the problem.

Teaching Tip

To support a thoughtful comparative analysis, offer students use of the pro/con analysis chart on our companion website, www.secdLab.org/stat/book. Students can complete the chart or use it as a guide to develop their own analysis. A side-by-side view of pros and cons can enrich student thinking as they evaluate and determine the most optimal course of action.

Students now examine the solution that the people of the past implemented: organizing the Seneca Falls Convention of 1848, the first U.S. national gathering of women's rights leaders. Investigating what Elizabeth Cady Stanton and her colleagues did will enrich students' evaluation of their proposed solutions as they shift to Step 3 of PLAN, where they develop their own action plan.

Moving to Action Planning (A)

It's not enough to study past injustice. Our youth need to learn how to overcome it by developing an actionable solution to both past and future injustice. At this point in the lesson, direct students to return to their small groups to get ready to develop their action plan. Students can use the guiding questions shown in Figure 6.4, along with their comparative pro and con analyses, to develop their plan.

FIGURE 6.4

Action Plan Design (A): Guiding Questions for Students

> Create a set of action steps that outline how you would solve the problem. To inform your work, consider the following questions:
> - What obstacles might you encounter?
> - Looking at the past, what plan did people decide on to try to solve the problem?
> - How does your plan differ from the historical plan?
> - How was the historical plan carried out?
> - What obstacles did those who carried out the historical plan encounter?

Reinforce for students that they will emulate the same processes that leaders, activists, and citizens engage in when they seek to develop a plan of action. Students discover the value of studying leaders' past attempts to overcome injustice for their action plan development.

Here's a sample, four-step action plan that students might draft as part of the Women's Suffrage PLAN Comprehensive lesson, after they have listed options, conducted a pro-and-con analysis, and participated in a comparative whole-class discussion.

1. Formally gather women to identify inequities in current laws (especially for women of color).
2. Develop the details of the rally—the place, time, and message to convey.
3. Anticipate and prepare for any pushback from law enforcement personnel and from men in general.
4. Convene with men to discuss revisions to voting laws and governmental documents.

Posting a model like this can help students visualize what an action plan should look like and what action-oriented steps it might include. Allow 25–30 minutes for groups to develop their action plans.

Noticing Success (N)—and Reflecting on the Learning

Approach this step of PLAN with a shared sense of accomplishment. As you end the lesson, it's crucial to take stock, recognize what went well, and reflect on the process. Debrief the learning in small groups or as a classroom, and facilitate a discussion around the set of questions shown in Figure 6.5.

FIGURE 6.5

Noticing Success (N) and Reflecting on the Learning: Guiding Questions for Students

---

1. How did the plan work in history?
2. What went well?
3. What did not go well?
4. How would your plan have worked differently?
5. What can we learn from the historical experience that is relevant to the present?

Here's an example of how students engaged in the Women's Suffrage lesson might respond to these guiding questions.

1. **How did the plan work in history?**

Answer: Many women, including Elizabeth Cady Stanton and Lucretia Mott, called for the first women's rights convention in 1848 in Seneca Falls.

2. What went well?
Answer: About 300 attendees drafted and debated the Declaration of Sentiments, which was modeled after the U.S. Declaration of Independence.

3. What did not go well?
Answer: Only 100 of the 300 attendees signed the document, and the convention did not secure suffrage for women.

4. How would your plan have worked differently?
Answer: The PLAN would have been more inclusive as it included advancing the causes of citizenship and voting rights for Black Americans. It also included convening at the end with male politicians to review and advocate for equal human rights and yield very different outcomes.

5. What can we learn from the historical experience that is relevant to the present?
Answer: Although the organizers didn't see the full results of their work at the time, this event did mark the beginning of the women's rights movement.

If students noticed that their action plan wasn't successful, encourage them to contemplate what revisions they could make to improve its success. Using the SMART goal as a criteria barometer, students can evaluate whether the goal was not specific enough, if the timing clashed with other forces, or if the plan failed to address the immediate needs of the stakeholders. In this instance, the sample action plan may not have taken into consideration the broader national political climate of 1848, particularly the states' rights tensions over the expansion of slavery that would influence the success of women's causes.

SEL Competency Connection: Relationship Skills

As students listen, discuss, and organize their group to solve a social problem, they experience the emotional vulnerability and trust to take the courageous step of taking action. Building healthy relationships during this collaborative problem-solving practice will translate into building healthy relationships in other areas of students' lives.

As with all lessons, you will want to know if students are meeting the learning aim, so it's worthwhile to invest the time to have them reflect in writing (perhaps in their journal) on their learning. We recommend offering prompts that invite reflection on the PLAN process and on the content itself. So appropriate questions for the Women's Suffrage lesson might include the following:

- How does brainstorming as many solutions as possible influence your action plan, and what does this say about thinking outside the box?

- How does anticipating obstacles influence your action plan and likely outcomes?

- With the 19th century women's rights movement, how were the rights of one group tied to the rights of other groups?

- What issues of the women's rights movement of the 19th century are still relevant today?

- How did looking at the issue from many sides enrich the development of your action plan?

- Considering Elizabeth Cady Stanton's leadership, what skills are crucial for social action?

Students could select one or two questions to address and share their response with the class. Or they might respond to several questions in their notebooks or journals, with their responses serving as evidence of learning.

If you'd like to take a more formal snapshot of student progress on the targeted learning outcome, you can create assessment rubrics keyed to the lesson's skill targets. We provide three illustrative assessment rubrics, keyed to the Women's Suffrage lesson. One focuses on an academic standard (Figure 6.6), one on a 21st century skill (Figure 6.7; see p. 108), and one on a social-emotional learning competency (Figure 6.8; see p. 109). Used in combination, these kinds of rubrics provide comprehensive assessment of the student's progress and will help you make adjustments for the next time students practice the skills.

These rubrics are intended to provide formative feedback, so it's best not to enter the indicator in a gradebook. Further, given the novelty and controversy around assessing social-emotional learning, we chose not to include an exemplary level in that rubric. Because the academic and 21st century standards are more straightforward and familiar to the repertoire of teacher practice, we did decide to include an exemplary level for those standards.

Set aside time after the lesson to have students read through the rubrics. You may host a question-and-answer session, asking students to name the distinctions between the categories and the terms that stand out. Then encourage your students to gather evidence that demonstrates how they met a given progress indicator, and have them circle where they fall on the indicator spectrum. Let them know that you will assess them independently, as well as consider their self-assessment. You may also use the rubrics to confer with students on their progress. Remember, like the other components of the lesson, your tone, optimism, and sense of commitment to a shared open process will frame the formative assessment experience.

FIGURE 6.6

Sample PLAN Formative Assessment Rubric: Academic Standard Proficiency

Progress Indicator: Academic Standard

Student uses primary and secondary sources to assess whether or not the ideals found in the Declaration of Independence were fulfilled for women, African Americans, and Native Americans during this time period.

Possible evidence:
- Annotates texts addressing rights
- References sources in verbal contributions
- Engages with text while collaborating with the group
- Asks questions about the text to investigate women's voting rights and examine the ideals
- Uses words associated with democratic ideals in relation to women's voting rights
- Creates an action plan that draws on sources and attends to democratic ideals and women's voting rights
- Reflects in writing on relevant formative assessment questions

Beginning	Approaching	Secure	Exemplary
References the sources in a superficial manner. Most sources are left out of the thinking to develop an evaluation of women's voting rights and democratic ideals.	Integrates some lesson sources into emerging thinking about the lack of fulfillment of democratic ideals for women. Some sources are left out, and ideas are not fully developed for a balanced evaluation.	Integrates all lesson sources into a balanced evaluation, weighing the democratic ideals with the rights not granted to women. Doesn't include reasons for the lack of fulfillment of voting rights for women.	Integrates all lesson sources into a thoughtful and critical evaluation of democratic ideals and points out reasons for the lack of fulfillment of voting rights for women.

FIGURE 6.7

Sample PLAN Formative Assessment Rubric: 21st Century Skill Proficiency

Progress Indicator: 21st Century Skill

Student assesses how point of view or purpose shapes the content and style of a source.

Possible evidence:
- Discusses words that reveal tone to show the source's attitude on the issue(s)
- Identifies words and parts of sentences in the text that indicate the source's intended purpose
- Explains how the source's point of view influences the style and content of a text

Beginning	Approaching	Secure	Exemplary
Considers the source's message in a superficial manner. Doesn't make a connection between the message and the content and style of the source.	Engages the source's attitude on the issue and the language expressed. Begins to make a connection between the message and the content and style of the source.	Weighs the source's attitude toward the issue and the language expressed. Makes connections between the message and the content and style of the source.	Weighs the source's attitude toward the issue and the language expressed. Makes critical connections between the source's stance on the issue and the content and style of the source.

PLAN Integrative: Adding AFC Presentation Skills

If you or your students have built up muscle in implementing PLAN, then PLAN Integrative is for you. You can take your practice to the next level by having students present their action plan to a mock or an authentic audience. In addition, PLAN Integrative connects the lesson concepts and skills to related disciplines—to science, English language arts, and math—through research. And it includes the option to add Audience-Focused Communication after students develop an action plan.

FIGURE 6.8

Sample PLAN Formative Assessment Rubric: Social-Emotional Learning
Competency

Progress Indicator: Social-Emotional Learning Competency			
Responsible decision making: Develop, implement, and model effective problem solving and critical thinking skills.			
Possible evidence: • Creates an options cost-benefit sheet • Creates an action plan document • Solicits peer feedback and comments on the action plan • Responds in writing to a reflection question			
Beginning	**Approaching**	**Secure**	**Exemplary**
Offers a solution to the problem. However, fails to engage multiple sources, as well as action planning tools, in designing an effective and a responsible solution.	Develops a solution and weighs evidence to design that solution but may leave out some crucial information needed to solve the problem.	Designs a solution that considers all stakeholders. Integrates the use of action planning tools to develop a thoughtful and an inclusive solution to the problem.	Not available for SEL competency.

Let's take a quick look at how PLAN Comprehensive differs from PLAN Integrative. The chart in Figure 6.9 (see p. 110) lists the sequence of activities, those that are the same in both approaches and those that differ, and where you'd need to adjust for those differences.

Preparing to Rehearse the Presentation

If you conducted a PLAN lesson with small groups, the groups can use their action plans to present. If you conducted a whole-class PLAN lesson, you'll need to group students, assign roles, and determine who will present. Or you can require all students to present using the same presentation materials.

You will likely need between three and four class periods for students to rehearse the skills for presentation. If you allow class time for developing the presentation, you will also need to take that into consideration in your planning. If the class is delving into this skill for the first time, build this preparation time into your class time or homework efforts.

FIGURE 6.9

PLAN Comprehensive and PLAN Integrative: A Comparison

Factor	PLAN Comprehensive	PLAN Integrative
Problem-solving approach	Yes	Yes
Lesson resources	Yes	Yes, with interdisciplinary connections
Collaborative small-group work configuration	Yes	Yes
Problem Description (P) step	Yes	Yes, and it will draw from a wider array of research and resources, and will demand more time.
List Options (L) step	Yes	Yes
Action Plan Development (A) step	Yes	Yes. Additional interdisciplinary research adds complexity to this step.
AFC presentation skills	No	Yes, with language added to account for audience interests and rehearse BEST communication and presentation skills.
Action plan presentation	No	Yes. It is presented to either a mock or an authentic audience, followed by a question-and-answer session.
Notice Successes (N) step	Yes	Yes. Incorporates feedback on action planning, the integration of comparative analysis, and the presentation of the action plan to the target audience.

To prepare students for this work, you should likely include a lesson on each of the following:

- Visualizing the intended outcomes for the audience
- Developing a presentation plan using the planning guide at www .secdLab.org/STAT/Book
- Practicing the presentation

You can use your creative discretion and planning skills to design the lessons, referencing the implementation guidance in Chapter 5 as needed.

Teacher as Coach

Be sure to make a deliberate mindset shift to play the role of coach to monitor the students as they engage in these activities. It's time to put on that coaching hat! While students are planning and rehearsing, encourage them to give one another constructive feedback after modeling what that kind of feedback might look like. Be sure to coach students to give feedback on the core steps of BEST (body posture, eye contact, say appropriate words, and tone of voice). To ensure that all students have the chance to rehearse presenting, have students present in small groups and then switch roles. Your students may begin to do this naturally as they build confidence with the skills.

John Dewey (1938) once wrote, "We do not learn from experience, we learn from reflecting on experience." With that in mind, at the end of each lesson, do take time to reflect on the goal. Also, debriefing with brief questions pertaining to a given skill offers students a safe space for feedback.

PLAN Integrative as Project-Based Learning (PBL)

PLAN Integrative presents a rich and an exciting opportunity for project-based learning. You can design it as a longer-term project for your students that might take two to four weeks to complete. If your school or district has a project-based or problem-based component to the curriculum, you can attach PLAN Integrative to that sequence of learning. You can also make the presentation of the action plan a summative assessment, because it comes at the end of the PLAN lesson template.

John Larmer and colleagues (2015) at the Buck Institute offer the gold standard of project-based learning—seven research-based design elements that are reflected in the PLAN Integrative lesson (see Figure 6.10).

FIGURE 6.10

Gold Standard Project-Based Learning

Source: From *Setting the Standard for Project Based Learning* (p. 34), by J. Larmer, J. Mergendoller, & S. Boss, 2015, ASCD and Buck Institute for Education. Copyright 2015 by ASCD.

If you're unfamiliar with project-based learning, Figure 6.11 shows how the two approaches align.

FIGURE 6.11

PLAN Integrative and Project-Based Learning: A Comparison

PLAN Integrative	Project-Based Learning
Compelling social problem/issue	Challenging problem/question
Deep research and probing analysis to understand and solve problem	Sustained inquiry
Real-world/relevant problems and relevant skills-based activities	Authentic work
Collaboration; students share in decision making, speaking, and presentation skills	Student voice and choice
Debrief on efforts, with a reflect-and-grow after the presentation	Reflection
Reflective whole-class discussion and individual reflection on a problem of presentation; reattempt presentation if unsuccessful	Critique and revision
Presentation of action plan to audience publication/distribution of action plan	Public product

Source: Adapted from *Setting the Standard for Project Based Learning*, by J. Larmer, J. Mergendoller, and S. Boss, 2015, Alexandria, VA: ASCD. Copyright 2015 by ASCD.

The natural connections between PLAN Integrative and PBL offer up a rich and rewarding opportunity for you and your students. Because of the class time that project-based learning requires, and because it is complex and seems all-encompassing, in Figure 6.12 we offer some tips for designing a PLAN Integrative lesson as a project-based unit.

Don't hesitate to make changes to the student project sheet if you need more or less time for a step or two in the lesson plan. Having a digital document on hand is a nice way to seamlessly make those adjustments as students engage in the steps of the lesson. Share the exciting news of the project with your students' families because they are critical partners in their child's education. Lean on a colleague or your supervisor for guidance after a challenging lesson. And remember to maintain perspective: yes, project-based learning can be messy, but authentic learning is anything but linear. We have found that project-based learning is rewarding and empowering work—not just for students, but also for ourselves as professional learners.

FIGURE 6.12

Tips for Preparing a PLAN Integrative Unit with a PBL Approach

- Identify the summative assessment plan specifying the skills you intend to assess (presenting the action plan).
- Use the AFC skill rubrics to show students what you intend to assess.
- Use a calendar and the PLAN Integrative lesson plan to sketch out the core lesson activities backward from the summative assessment plan and date. Review the calendar with students to make any necessary adjustments.
- Develop a student project sheet that they can refer to along the way as a reference point.
- Build in buffer time to be responsive to student needs and to provide direction.
- Include time in class to teach the presentation skills.
- Use a digital learning platform to organize the learning activities.
- Encourage feedback and reflection through check-ins as needed to tweak the steps of the PLAN Integrative lesson.
- Let students know that you will be taking on more of a role of coach, guide, and facilitator and that they will experience uncertainty as you and they colead the learning together.

Implementing PLAN: Some Forward Reflections

As you contemplate integrating PLAN into your classroom, consider the following questions:

- What natural problems lingering in your curriculum or in the current events you are discussing might you use as anchors to develop a PLAN lesson or even unit?
- How can PLAN help you deliver on the promise to meet the needs of all learners in your classroom?
- In what ways could the PLAN strategy empower your students to become engaged citizens and give them hope for the future?

STAT Integration Across the Curriculum

It was May, and Miss Jackson's junior students were beginning to turn their thinking toward their summer activities and away from American Studies II. This year, the school district had abolished final exams, and the department chair encouraged end-of-year project work. Jacob, a student who always enjoyed bantering about politics and current events with Miss Jackson (and with his parents at home), brought in a New York Times *article titled "Right-Wing Views for Generation Z, Five Minutes at a Time." He was jazzed about the article and suggested they take a look at it in class.*

Miss Jackson devoured the article along with her lunch and began to consider how it might inspire a meaningful end-of-year project. A few weeks later, armed with their research, students debated which of the five issues was the most pressing in a series of Socratic circle discussions. The debates fueled passionate discussions about their future. The post-discussion reflections brought tears to Miss Jackson's eyes, seeing how passionate her learners were about the issue they had selected. It was a beautiful and liberating experience for both her and her students.

Schools must be places where we encourage students' best selves—and give them opportunities to direct their best selves toward humane outcomes. As bell hooks (1994) writes,

> The classroom, with all its limitations, remains a location of possibility. In that field of possibility, we have the opportunity to labor for freedom, to demand of ourselves and our comrades an openness of mind and heart that allows us to face reality even as we collectively imagine ways to move beyond boundaries, to transgress. This is education as the practice of freedom. (p. 207)

The way in which Jacob's article fueled a whole new avenue for learning in Miss Jackson's class is just one illustration of what can happen when we nurture students' interests and inclinations. Much of this book has focused on how STAT teaching techniques can enrich students' learning in social studies classes. Let's now look at how they can do the same in English language arts; science, technology, engineering, and math (STEM); and visual and performing arts (VPA) curricula.

Integrating STAT Across the Curriculum

In *The Metacognitive Student*, Cohen and colleagues (2021) illustrate the power of teaching students a mindset and problem-solving strategy that they can use in many domains. In the authors' view, this leads to a metacognitive "frame" that students then apply as they encounter new content in familiar subject areas, as well as novel issues and problems they face, whether in college, careers, or civic engagement. Fostering student voice, literacy skills, research skills, peer-to-peer discussion, and collaborative problem solving applies to any academic course. Moreover, developing speaking, listening, debating, and collective problem-solving skills helps students become innovative contributors to the world around them. Paulo Freire (2005) captures this spirit poignantly when he writes, "Looking at the past must only be a means to more clearly understand what and who you are—so you can more wisely build a better future" (p. 84). When teachers build these and related STAT skills, they combine content competencies with the shared mission of giving students the tools to take action in a democratic society.

Key to any curricular change is teacher ownership and collaboration. The interdisciplinary team model found in some middle schools is a natural place to implement a STAT strategy. At the high school level, department curriculum supervisors can coordinate the integration of STAT as they work with their teachers. Working collaboratively is essential to support the professional learning, ongoing problem solving, and tweaking that go on during the implementation period. Further, teachers are much more likely to engage in curricular innovations when working with colleagues who they can rely on for advice and feedback and with whom they can share frustrations.

Some districts have made STAT a year-long or multiyear curricular goal. Whether you're teaching in a middle school or high school, STAT's focus on fostering civil discourse, social-emotional learning, and social justice applies to a variety of curricular contexts where dilemmas, debates, unsettled matters, or problems exist. The crosswalk table shown in Figure 7.1 provides examples of the transdisciplinary applications of each of the five STAT strategies in the areas of social studies, math, science, English language arts, and the visual and performing arts.

STAT Strategies in the STEM Classroom

Taking a social justice or global approach in STEM disciplines helps students acquire an in-depth understanding of current social issues and serves as a constant reminder that they live in a "social world" (Garner et al., 2018). Further, the skills of self-reflection and emotional regulation that STAT strategies reinforce support students in engaging in scientific inquiry and extending their conceptual understandings to broader contexts (Garner et al., 2018). In inquiry-based classrooms—a rising trend in contemporary science education—students must engage in peer opinion sharing and provide evidence to support their thinking, which are the very tenets of Yes-No-Maybe and Respectful Debate. Finally, many STEM tasks, such as planning and carrying out investigations and solving problems, require strong collaboration skills that are intrinsic to STAT (Bahnson et al., 2020).

STAT teaching techniques also complement the iterative nature of the engineering design process, which involves solving problems by performing background research, brainstorming solutions, testing the solution, reflecting on improvements, and communicating the results (Science Buddies, n.d.). The process is iterative because the steps are repeated as many times as needed, but they're not always carried out in a linear fashion. Figure 7.2 highlights how the five STAT strategies complement the process.

Teachers can also use the STAT strategies to teach the Next Generation Science Standards, which involve students in complex tasks that require effective collaboration and participation in constructive discussion with their peers (Bahnson et al., 2020; Sneider, 2018). A Yes-No-Maybe lesson in which students reflect on an anchor phenomenon and share their initial reactions enables students to practice active listening and peer opinion sharing, whereas facilitating a Respectful Debate about the risks and benefits of harnessing nuclear power for civilian purposes engages them in perspective-taking and gives them practice providing strong reasons to support their thinking. Finally, a PLAN lesson inviting students to tackle the global environmental issue of widespread plastic

FIGURE 7.1

A Crosswalk of STAT's Transdisciplinary Applications

STAT Strategy	Social Studies	Math	Science	ELA	VPA
Norms	Classroom discussions	Collaborative teams	Laboratory procedures	Book club discussions	Giving and receiving peer feedback
Yes-No-Maybe	Discussing positions on controversial issues and questions	Determining whether the recommended method is the most effective multiplication method	Reflecting on and sharing initial reactions to an anchor phenomenon	Considering the article/text's conclusion about the most fitting theme of a fictional text	Discussing and sharing opinions about whether art is a valuable way to express one's political views
Respectful Debate	Analyzing critical turning points/decisions in history—such as the Treaty of Paris, the signing of the Americans with Disabilities Act (ADA), Supreme Court decisions like *Brown v. Board of Education,* and legislation such as the Voting Rights Act of 1965 and the War on Drugs—as to whether, on balance, these led to benefit or harm	Considering the most efficient method (graphing, substitution, or elimination) to solve a system of equations in Algebra II	Considering the risks and benefits of harnessing nuclear power for civilian purposes	Analyzing a poem's meaning by considering the use of literary devices to convey certain thoughts and emotions	Debating whether artistic talent is inherent or can be acquired over time or how to evaluate a particular artistic product

STAT Strategy	Social Studies	Math	Science	ELA	VPA
Audience-Focused Communication	Presenting your verdict to a Supreme Court justice in 1974 about whether Nixon was guilty or innocent in the Watergate scandal	Presenting a method for determining the volume of a historic building, such as the World Trade Center, by applying principles of algebra and geometry	Determining the best format for a science project or a presentation on the effect of population on the environment after learning about human carrying capacity	Presenting an analysis of the theme, narrative techniques, and goals that an author uses across multiple books	Preparing a creative presentation to convince a local art gallery to display your work or a local band or orchestra to play your composition
PLAN	Identifying ways communities can resolve the challenges of racial injustice in the United States as identified in Martin Luther King Jr.'s "I Have a Dream" speech or in current articles and books assigned to students	Exploring ways to increase confidence in vaccines by using probability and analyzing the effects of variables on confidence	Determining ways to reduce the use of plastic bags or designing environmentally friendly substitutes	Considering a character's response to a challenge, as well as alternative solutions and their possible outcomes	Offering solutions to the dilemma of public museums charging admission or considering the context and purpose of a given artistic work and how that work might have evolved if circumstances and decisions were different

FIGURE 7.2

How STAT Strategies Support the Engineering Design Process (EDP)

EDP Steps	Supporting STAT Strategies
Define the problem	With **PLAN,** students craft a written problem description.
Conduct background research	With **Yes-No-Maybe, Respectful Debate,** and **PLAN,** students consult background sources to conduct research on the issue.
Brainstorm solutions	With **Norms,** when conflict arises in the classroom, students brainstorm solutions to revise the class contract. With **PLAN,** students list options for solving the problem.
Evaluate and choose the best solution	With **PLAN,** students evaluate the pros and cons of each possible solution to choose the best one.
Test the solution	With **PLAN,** students notice the successes of their action plan.
Communicate results	With **Audience-Focused Communication,** students factor prior knowledge and their audience's needs into message design and delivery.

bag use hones their problem-solving skills. All lessons support the underlying goals of fostering effective collaboration skills and productive dialogue, enabling students to successfully meet the science standards.

In the mathematics classroom, integrating STAT strategies engages students in deeper learning. Unfortunately, in an effort to cover the curriculum, many math classrooms focus on procedural fluency and applying "plug and chug" procedures at the expense of students developing conceptual understanding and mathematical reasoning (Dean & Brookhart, 2013–14). Students become so intent on following a series of steps to arrive at the correct answer that they bypass opportunities for engaging in critical thinking and fostering a deep understanding of the concepts. Further, a focus on right and wrong answers and on the precise application of memorized procedures cultivates a classroom environment that is stratified by ability, where students are fearful of taking risks and discussion is dominated by the strongest math students.

However, that's where the STAT strategies come into play. With classroom norms, you can establish a sense of equity in your classroom, challenging the notion that math ability is fixed and that some people are naturally good at math whereas others are not. With the Respectful Debate strategy, students will develop their ability to construct viable arguments and respectfully critique their peers' reasoning, which is one of the eight Standards for Mathematical Practice (Common Core State Standards, n.d.). You could do this in an Algebra II class by presenting students with a system of linear equations and having them consider the most efficient method—graphing, substitution, or elimination—by which to solve the problem. This type of lesson would encourage students to focus on the *process* and build their conceptual understanding as opposed to focusing on the *product* by applying a prescriptive series of steps. This complements yet another Standard for Mathematical Practice, which involves persevering when working through difficult problems.

STAT in Action in the STEM Classroom

Let's look at two examples to give you an idea of how you might integrate Yes-No-Maybe and PLAN in the science or mathematics classroom. The first shows you how you might use the Yes-No-Maybe strategy in a geometry classroom to have students analyze proofs, and the second describes a PLAN lesson, in which students address climate change.

Yes-No-Maybe in the geometry classroom. An ongoing goal for students in the mathematics classroom and one of the eight Standards for Mathematical Practice is constructing viable arguments and critiquing the reasoning of others. In essence, students must be able to make a conjecture and then consider how definitions, theorems, postulates, and results from similar problems can support their thinking. To craft a viable argument, they must develop statements that follow in a logical progression to justify their reasoning. The final step involves communicating their argument to their peers and engaging in mathematical discourse. During this step, students actively listen to their peers to consider the plausibility of their peers' arguments and distinguish correct reasoning from flawed logic.

SEL Competency Connection: Relationship Skills
Constructing a viable argument and effectively communicating it to others require strong relationship skills. Students must actively listen to their peers, consider the arguments and perspectives of others, and tailor their message in such a way that their audience will understand it. Further, when

engaging in mathematical discourse, students must successfully navigate any disagreement and conflict that arise.

Geometry focuses heavily on argumentative reasoning. Yes-No-Maybe can bring to life the often-dreaded process of working through two-column proofs by presenting students with a statement such as this: *"If Angle A and Angle C are complementary and Angle B and Angle C are complementary, then Angle A is congruent to Angle B."* Students can work independently to first consider theorems, postulates, and previous problems that may shed light on the statement. Next, they develop an example to either support or disprove the statement. A supportive example for the former statement would be if Angle A was 35°, then its complement (Angle C) would be 55°. Therefore, if Angle C was 55° and complementary to Angle B, then Angle B would be 35°, making Angle A and Angle B both 35° and, hence, equal.

At this point, students engage in the first round of Yes-No-Maybe, taking a stance on whether they agree with (Yes), disagree with (No), or are not sure about (Maybe) the statement provided. In triads, they provide reasons to support their thinking. After the first round, students critique the reasoning presented by their peers and work through a two-column proof to map out the flow of their logic. Finally, they engage in a second round, determining whether the process of peer opinion sharing influenced their initial stance, and they move to a location in the room (that is, one labeled "Yes," "No," or "Maybe") that best aligns with their reasoning.

A PLAN lesson and environmental science. PLAN enables us to take any issue—such as climate change, access to clean drinking water, the risks of genetically modified food, or the debate surrounding CRISPR gene editing—and plan a lesson that engages students in not only analyzing the issue, but also developing a plan to take social action. Instead of just reading articles to respond to questions, memorizing content to recall on a quiz, or following a series of steps to complete a lab, students lead their own learning and feel empowered to implement their solutions to bring about change.

We have developed a lesson titled "PLAN: Students and Climate Change in Schools" that you can refer to on our companion website (https://www.secdlab.org/stat/book). Students learn about the global challenge of climate change and develop solutions to address the environmental injustices that society faces when students don't learn about this issue in schools. Students begin by reading two articles—one that sheds light on climate change education in the United States and one about a youth-led campaign in the United Kingdom advocating for legislation to mandate climate change education. They then analyze data on climate change. All three background sources, the articles plus the data, help them develop a problem description related to the negative ramifications of a lack of climate change education. Students then collaborate to develop a SMART goal to address the problem. This may involve crafting a petition for a local high school to teach a course on climate change and presenting it to stakeholders, including the superintendent and Board of Education. Finally, students reflect on the PLAN process and compare the hypothetical success of their action plan with that of actual social action initiatives that students have carried out in recent years.

Teaching Tip

You can easily adapt this lesson to other school-based problems, such as whether students can choose the texts they read in English class, how the school handles discipline, how to curb cheating on exams, and how to deal with cyberbullying.

STAT Strategies in the ELA Classroom

Over two decades ago, researchers noted that "adolescents entering the adult world in the 21st century will read and write more than at any other time in human history. They will need advanced levels of literacy to perform their jobs, run their households, act as citizens, and conduct their personal lives" (Moore et al., 1999, p. 3). The STAT strategies lessons integrate rich English language arts standards to help students foster the skills needed for informed citizenry and engaged civic life.

Unfortunately, as students move into middle and high school, teachers devote little time to explicit instruction of reading and writing skills (Vacca, 1998). The late Steven J. Mayer, who served as a school superintendent in central New Jersey, emphasized the need for a commitment to such skills: "We teach students to learn to read," he said, "so they can read to learn." STAT emphasizes that literacy skills are a shared commitment across a student's curricular experience and that they're needed to prepare future citizens for informed social action.

Reading to Build New Knowledge

STAT lessons support comprehension and understanding by taking the time to explore the academic vocabulary of an article or a topic. (In a lesson focused on neuro-abilities, for example, students might encounter unfamiliar terms like *autism, neurodiversity,* and *disability.*) This exploration will broaden student thinking, not just about the vocabulary in the article, but also about how to best interact in this world because students will encounter other-abled individuals and neuro-diverse individuals across the course of their civic and career life.

The STAT lessons expose students to a wide range of primary and secondary sources, everything from newspapers and magazines to government agency publications, novels, white papers from think tanks, political cartoons, and speeches and quotes from leaders of all ages. Tapping into the practice of critical literacy, students learn that sources are never neutral and that words convey power. Knowing how to apply this critical lens when examining sources that address injustice, inequality, and inequities is fundamental to igniting social justice learning in the classroom.

In addition, engaging a variety of sources sets up readers for synthesis. Synthesis skills support students in building their writing and communication skills so they're able to effectively exchange new knowledge with others. This is especially important in a society that requires us to continually make sense of a barrage of new information (Ludstrom et al., 2015). By embedding effective reading strategies, STAT lessons underscore the idea that readers are active and critical consumers of information. This is the first step in nurturing civil discourse—committing to teaching citizens to become informed on issues affecting their community.

Teaching Tip
Whenever you're assigning sources for your students to read, it's a prime opportunity to reinforce the tenets of STAT strategies without actually doing full STAT lessons. For example, if you're a history teacher assigning primary source documents on the Cold War, be sure to include sources from both the United States and the Soviet Union. If you're an English teacher introducing students to *Hamlet*, capitalize on what students can learn by analyzing it from multiple points of view. For example, what is real within the world of the play, what are figments of Hamlet's imagination, and how do we determine that? Encourage

students to analyze multiple characters' perspectives on the events of the play, share their opinions with peers, and discuss key plot points in small groups.

Speaking and Listening Integration

The Common Core State Standards in English language arts call for 12th graders to be able to engage in collaborative discussions and build on the ideas of others. To do so, they must know how to actively listen to others (Tyson et al., 2014). Although Norms lay the foundation for active listening skills, the Yes-No-Maybe and Respectful Debate strategies provide opportunities for reinforcement. When establishing your classroom norms, be sure to define active listening as *listening for understanding* (Tyson et al., 2014). Engaging your students in creating a chart like the one shown in Figure 7.3 is a way to help define the elements of this rather abstract skill.

FIGURE 7.3

Characteristics of Active Listening: Clarification Exercise for Students

---

What Is Active Listening?

— Maintaining eye contact with the speaker

— Sitting up straight when listening

— Concentrating on what the speaker is saying

— Tuning out distractions

— Using body language (like smiling, nodding, or gesturing) to show understanding

— Listening without interrupting the speaker

— Paraphrasing what the speaker said or asking a clarifying question to confirm understanding Examples:" So, what I heard you say was ____." "It seems as though you're saying _____. Is that correct?"

In Yes-No-Maybe lessons, students must actively listen to their peers when meeting in small groups as each student shares their reasons for taking a stance on an issue. Students must also have listened well to fulfill the role of spokesperson for their or other groups because they'll need to summarize main points. Similarly, in Respectful Debate lessons, active listening skills are necessary when students engage in collaborative discussion in their assigned pro or con group and, of course, when evaluating an opponent's point of view, explaining their reasoning, and giving evidence during each round of the debate.

Just as telling students to listen often doesn't translate into good listening skills, providing your students with the occasional opportunity to present in front of their peers will not make them good speakers. Just as with active listening, students will only improve their speaking skills through explicit instruction and deliberate reinforcement (Palmer, 2014b). Implementing these strategies in your classroom multiple times throughout the year will enable your students to explore ways of presenting information that will have the greatest effect on a given audience.

Writing to Elevate Student Voice

Each STAT lesson features an opportunity for students to express themselves by writing on the topic at the end of the lesson. Following the speaking and listening activity with a writing activity will strengthen a student's sense of competence and confidence. Because students will have listened to discussions of the topic and debated the issue, they will have thought about it fairly deeply. These experiences enable students to sew the ideas together to clarify their point of view to reach new states of understanding. Expect them to have a lot to say.

With all STAT strategies, students will also exercise the skill of drawing out evidence from their learning, their background resources, and the poignant points that surfaced during discussions to use in their writing. Students will begin to dig into the content, analyzing and comparing, to formulate their own point of view. They will discover how empowering it is to realize the power and purpose of one's words.

STAT in Action in the ELA Classroom

Let's look at transdisciplinary applications of STAT strategies in the English language arts classroom. The first example focuses on developing norms in student-led book clubs. The second highlights a Respectful Debate lesson in which students consider the ways that ableism, stereotypes, and the failure to embrace disabilities and disability culture exclude individuals with disabilities from mainstream American society. You can find this lesson plan at https://www.secdlab.org/stat/book.

Norms and student-led book clubs. It's a good idea for students to establish four or five norms for their book club before reading or discussing a book. Students can write down the norms in their notebooks or create a collaborative document available online. They each will need to sign off on one another's notebooks or type their signatures on the collaborative document, indicating their agreement with the group contract. Figure 7.4 shows a sample set of norms established by a book club in a 5th grade classroom during a period of remote learning.

FIGURE 7.4

Sample Set of Student-Generated Norms

> **The Pretty Potatoes Book Club: Our Norms**
> 1. Be respectful to other members of the club.
> 2. Only read our selected book during designated school hours.
> 3. Only one person speaks at a time.
> 4. Keep webcams on for the entire reading period.
> 5. Stay focused and pay attention to what other members say.

Norms also play an important role when students work with a partner to offer each other feedback on their writing. Before students begin the peer review process, you might support them as follows:

- Cocreate a rubric with your students that will encourage them to give specific suggestions for improvement instead of vague feedback.
- Develop a protocol for providing feedback to ensure consistency.
- Use structures such as
  - One "glow" (positive comment) and one "grow" (suggestion for improvement).
  - "Warm feedback" (positive comments) and "cool feedback" (suggestions for improvement).
- Model how to give feedback.
- Hold students accountable for reacting to the feedback they receive.

Respectful Debate and individuals with disabilities. Works of literature naturally open many doors for possible debates in the ELA classroom. With fiction texts, step back and look at the universal themes. Then consider possible controversial statements that you could generate to frame the debate, as well as background sources to provide students with a broader context and an under-standing of the issue.

We took the aforementioned approach when developing the exemplar les-son "Respectful Debate: Are Those with Disabilities Still Invisible in America?" (You can find this lesson plan at https://www.secdlab.org/stat/book.) Fifth grade students had just finished reading the following fiction texts in book clubs: R. J. Palacio's *Wonder*, Sharon M. Draper's *Out of My Mind*, and Lynda Mullaley Hunt's *Fish in a Tree*. The teacher identified ableism as a universal theme that cut across all texts. The students then crafted the following statement to frame the debate: *Walls of exclusion still persist in how we treat those with disabilities in America.* They also found a *New York Times* article titled "We're 20 Percent of America, and We're Still Invisible" written by well-known disability rights activ-ist Judith Heumann and civil rights lawyer John Wodatch (2020). The teacher facilitated smaller debates by dividing up each book club into pro and con groups and assigning roles. The lesson encouraged synthesis across multiple texts, a deeper analysis of the texts, and perspective-taking.

STAT Strategies in the Visual and Performing Arts Classroom

Visual and performing arts are a prime vehicle through which to engage stu-dents in social action. In fact, social practice art is a burgeoning movement in education in which individuals and communities collaborate to use art to effect social or political change (Sholette et al., 2018). Moreover, social-emotional learning competencies are naturally embedded in the arts. Therefore, it's no surprise that the STAT strategies align with these disciplines.

As we've noted, the five STAT strategies have two goals: to infuse civil dis-course and civic engagement into the curriculum and build students' social-emotional learning skills. According to the National Art Education Association, the arts do the former by providing an opportunity to "raise critical conscious-ness, foster empathy and respect for others, build community, and motivate people to promote positive change" (NAEA, 2018, p. 1). Consider *The Laramie Project*, a 2001 play by Moisés Kaufman and Stephen Belber about the murder of gay college student Matthew Shepard, or the song "Imagine" by John Lennon and Yoko Ono, a call for world peace released during the Vietnam War. Or con-sider 12 Black Artists/24 Protest Posters, part of the Fine Acts Collective through

TED Fellows, in which Black artists created posters to hang in communities to combat systemic racism. We want to empower our students to follow suit and see art as what Fine Acts calls a "playground for social change" (Fine Acts, n.d.).

In terms of the second goal—building students' social-emotional skills—the VPA standards and SEL competencies are inextricably linked. Figure 7.5 illustrates that relationship, as well as their connection to STAT strategies.

FIGURE 7.5

Connections Among SEL Competencies, VPA Standards, and STAT Strategies

SEL Competency	VPA Connections	Complementary STAT Strategies
Self-Awareness	Performing arts promote students' awareness of their place within a performing ensemble.	**AFC** encourages students to reflect on their audience and anticipate how their message may be perceived.
	Visual arts offer opportunities for self-reflection.	**All STAT strategies** embed opportunities for self-reflection.
Social Awareness	Visual arts engage students in perspective-taking to interpret meaning in art and consider the social/historical context of artistic works to deepen understanding and appreciate diversity.	**Yes-No-Maybe and Respectful Debate** engage students in perspective-taking by having them consider and appreciate the opinions and arguments of others.
Self-Management	Both visual and performing arts teach students how to set goals and remain disciplined and focused, which is essential in arts education.	**PLAN** walks students through the process of goal setting and action planning to ensure they reach their goals.
	Performing arts provide students with opportunities to use mindfulness and breathing techniques to deal with performance anxiety.	**AFC** permits students to rehearse for competency building before presenting by practicing visualization and breathing techniques.

continued

FIGURE 7.5 *(continued)*

Connections Among SEL Competencies, VPA Standards, and STAT Strategies

SEL Competency	VPA Connections	Complementary STAT Strategies
Relationship Skills	Both visual and performing arts support students in balancing their own ideas with the input of others during the creative process. Both visual and performing arts teach students how to work collaboratively–especially when performing with others–to carry out an artistic vision.	**All STAT strategies** prompt students to reflect on their own opinions and views, listen to others' opinions with an open mind, and determine how others' views may have influenced their own. **Norms** for collaboration can be foregrounded in classroom discussions and projects. With **PLAN, Respectful Debate,** and **AFC,** students must work with others and effectively communicate, navigate conflict, and carry out their responsibilities to achieve the vision of the group.
Responsible Decision Making	Both visual and performing arts teach students perseverance in problem solving, even in the face of obstacles and constructive criticism and feedback.	**PLAN** provides the support of a collaborative group in which all members must work through potential challenges and disagreements as they develop a solution and an action plan to solve the problem at hand.

STAT in Action in the Visual and Performing Arts Classroom

Here are two examples of what integrating STAT strategies into the VPA classroom might look like. The first focuses on a Yes-No-Maybe lesson, in which students take a stance on whether or not they feel that public art is a form of activism. (You can find this lesson, "Yes-No-Maybe: LGBTQIA+ Murals and Activism," via a link on our companion website, https://www.secdlab.org/stat/book.) The second example demonstrates how the AFC strategy can help students tailor a presentation of a song, dramatic performance, or shared piece of art to a specific audience.

Yes-No-Maybe and public art. Given the use of art as a platform to raise political consciousness and ignite social activism, it often stirs up strong opinions about social and political issues. You might use this strategy to address any number of topics in the VPA classroom, including the following:

- Public museums should be able to charge admission.
- Art is a natural-born talent.
- Music censorship violates First Amendment rights.
- Plays that include content related to sex, alcohol, drugs, and homosexuality should not be banned from high school theaters.

The exemplar lesson, "Yes-No-Maybe: LGBTQIA+ Murals and Activism," prompts students to reflect on their opinions about the artistic display of such murals in city spaces and their effect on public consciousness. After engaging in peer opinion sharing during the first round of Yes-No-Maybe, students watch a video on Chicago artists aiming to paint LGBTQ murals across the city; they also read an article about muralist Sam Kirk's exploration of identity and culture through public art to broaden their understanding of the issue. The students consider how their peers' opinions and their analysis of background sources influenced their initial stance on the issue. Students then engage in the second round of Yes-No-Maybe, indicating whether or not their beliefs changed. Finally, the students respond to several questions to reflect on what they learned about the topic and themselves and how—if at all—their opinions changed from the first to the second round.

 Teaching Tip
Given the sensitive nature of the topic (LGBTQIA+ murals and activism), you may want to preview the lesson a few days before. Discuss with students the importance of being mindful of how they present their opinions to others and how their peers may receive those opinions. Also, remind your students of the need to practice speaker power so that one voice speaks and is heard at a time.

Audience-Focused Communication and artistic performance. Artists often create a work with the intent of sharing it with an audience; therefore, the audience plays a crucial role. The generic version of AFC is a natural fit in any VPA classroom as students consider the point of view of their targeted audience, rehearse the presentation for competency building and self-management techniques, and anticipate the audience's reactions so they're prepared to address those reactions appropriately.

For example, let's say that high school students are studying the style and techniques that artist Keith Haring used to address controversial issues like racial inequality and AIDS. The students might select a cause of their own and apply at least two techniques that Haring uses in their own artistic work to communicate a message about that cause to a group of middle school students. The high school students could do this collaboratively in small groups or individually. Before presenting to the middle schoolers, they would need to consider their audience's prior knowledge about the topic and the audience's possible perspectives to tailor their language, gestures, intonation, and pacing appropriately.

Students would then rehearse their presentation multiple times in front of a mock audience, reflecting after each rehearsal to determine if they need to make changes. They would also practice visualization and breathing techniques, such as imagining the details of a successful presentation and 5-2-5 breathing. Finally, the high schoolers would present to their actual audience, celebrate their effort and accomplishments at the conclusion of the presentation, and identify areas of improvement moving forward.

STAT and Student Autonomy

As you become more comfortable with implementing the STAT strategies, coach your students to apply them to novel circumstances. Try modeling them as situations arise in the classroom to promote student autonomy to make class decisions. For example, if the class is nervous about an assessment, they could use a Yes-No-Maybe to decide if the assessment should be an open book test or to discuss whether the assessment really has life-affecting consequences that should warrant their nervousness. Or they might apply a quick round of Respectful Debate to decide if a project should be an individual or a group effort. Or they might use the Norms strategy to ensure equitable participation in group efforts. The point here is to widen opportunities for students to practice and apply the STAT strategies to everyday problems to increase the chances the students will generalize the skills to social situations in settings beyond the classroom and school.

STAT's pliability to a variety of curricular and cocurricular experiences can help schools meet their mission of fostering student leadership and civic readiness to participate in a democratic society. Economic, social, and political problems are naturally interdisciplinary in their scope and effects. Therefore, strategies that support civil discourse should reach into all academic courses of study to promote more participatory and problem-based learning. With their extended reach, STAT strategies can pave the way for transformational learning experiences. They can nurture citizens who understand more deeply how we have gotten to the present moment and who possess the skills and dispositions needed to lead social change from a position of civic and civil collaboration.

Integrating STAT Across the Curriculum: Some Forward Reflections

As we end this chapter, consider the following questions that explore how educators might integrate STAT strategies across the curriculum:

- What curricular initiatives in your school or district align particularly well with the intended outcomes of STAT?
- What curricular revisions are in the pipeline in your school or district that would allow for the integration of STAT?
- What are some barriers your school or district would need to overcome to integrate the STAT strategies in particular content areas?

8

STAT in the Inclusion Classroom

Reviewing her class roster of 22 5th graders, Ms. Bell saw that four of her students had individualized education plans (IEPs). She let out a sigh. Would she get the support she needed to give these four students the best education possible? Would the lesson plans she had access to contain accommodations, or would she have to create them herself (as usual)? As she dug into each of the four students' files, she did a quick search for their IDEA classification: Freddy—autism spectrum disorder, Jeremiah—Down syndrome, Lily—ADHD, and Aniyah—dyslexia.

"Four IEPs!" Ms. Bell sighed aloud. When she glanced up, she realized that Sarah, the school social worker, was within earshot and had heard her comment. Sarah turned to her and said, "Jackie, you know there's much more to these students than their labels. And the best way to avoid behavioral issues and give a great class for everyone is to get to know them and to recognize and communicate their strengths."

This scenario happens all too often in education. Educators may perceive students' challenged abilities as liabilities as opposed to assets (Armstrong, 2012). We prefer the term *challenged abilities* to *disabilities* because it reflects the many circumstances that can impair students' learning and behavior in school and the accommodations required in light of these. Many teachers don't have experience with students carrying particular labels, nor do they feel they get adequate support in those situations. At least Ms. Bell had a school mental health professional to turn to. Of course, as we understand more about the effects of trauma, we're coming to realize that many students who are not diagnosed bring learning or behavioral difficulties into the classroom. We hope you adopt a wider frame as you read about the inclusive classroom. It undoubtedly includes more children with challenged abilities than meet the eye—certainly more than just Ms. Bell's identified quartet.

A common feature of students with challenged abilities is that they struggle with social relationships and with perceiving and interpreting the social behavior of their peers, as well as other social cues. For example, students with challenged abilities may need extra guidance controlling physical impulses, recognizing personal space, and effectively reading others' body language and facial expressions. These difficulties can become labeled as "problem behaviors," such as hyperactivity, withdrawal, and aggressiveness (McConaughy, 1986).

Students with challenged abilities benefit from explicit SEL skills instruction to successfully navigate the school environment and understand the hidden curriculum. According to Alsubaie (2015), the hidden curriculum involves the norms, values, and expectations of social behavior that are implicitly communicated to students and that are crucial to their social skills development. Although including students with challenged abilities in the mainstream provides them with access to positive peer models, it does not guarantee their social skills development and their understanding of the hidden curriculum. It's wiser to assume that these students—and there are many in most classes—will appreciate instruction in the social skills related to communicating with others, problem solving, decision making, peer and group interaction, and self-management, rather than expecting them to pick those skills up from the milieu (Elias, 2004).

Enter STAT

Programs like STAT are a proactive means to address the social competence of individuals with challenged abilities because they focus on skill building for success rather than on eliminating problem behaviors. Empathy, discernment, and interpreting social cues are often considered higher cognitive and affective skills and too abstract for such students to acquire. However, STAT addresses them in a spiraling approach, providing students with multiple opportunities for reinforcement and mastery. Finally, given that individuals with challenged abilities make up well over one-fourth of the U.S. adult population (Centers for Disease Control and Prevention, 2018), STAT intends to prepare *all* students with the social-emotional and character development competencies required to take meaningful democratic action.

STAT creates opportunities for students to engage in social and emotional skill development through nontraditional activities and tasks, such as Norms, Yes-No-Maybe, Respectful Debate, and PLAN. Through the STAT model, students engage in needs-based learning in an approach that highlights their strengths. This builds confidence and self-efficacy and increases the likelihood that students will be willing to participate.

Although students may engage in activities related to a teacher-selected topic, they can often choose a topic of intense interest on their own to explore. This also promotes a more strengths-based approach (Kluth & Schwarz, 2008), as well as ensuring the topic's relevance for the student. In addition, STAT gives students the freedom to express their views or share their opinions uninterrupted (for example, as the speaker for a Yes-No-Maybe triad or the reporter for either the pro or con side in a Respectful Debate). At the same time, the students' peers have the opportunity to exercise yet another SEL skill—self-management (that is, restraint and respect). And of course, through Norms, students collaboratively establish ground rules tailored to the needs of the individuals in the group.

Teaching Tip

Students can contribute to developing norms through a variety of methods. For example, a teacher might execute a lesson on Norms unconventionally, allowing students who benefit from movement and who have difficulty focusing for long periods of time to stand, move around, or fidget. Students with handwriting difficulties can dictate their choice of norms to the teacher or to another student who writes the suggestions down (Armstrong, 2012).

Teachers find that STAT fosters skill acquisition through repetition, practice, and modeling. In fact, studies have shown that repetition and practice are most effective for students with challenged abilities (Niemiec et al., 2017). Finally, to strengthen students' confidence and competence, teachers might also look at their IEPs and 504 plans for specific skills the students are working on in view of explicitly reinforcing those skills.

STAT in Action in the Inclusion Classroom

Before implementing a STAT lesson in the inclusion classroom, teachers may need to modify lesson resources, take steps to ensure students with challenged abilities will be socially included, and differentiate assessments to best reflect student understanding. Figure 8.1 lists a variety of accessibility factors to consider.

FIGURE 8.1

How to Implement STAT Strategies in the Inclusion Classroom

1. **Consider ways to make the learning environment inclusive and accessible:**
   - Use tiered lessons to enable students to learn at levels that provide challenge but do not overwhelm them.
   - Ensure that the classroom decor (e.g., posters or banners) don't create distraction or sensory overload. Make sure visual displays reflect the diversity of the classroom and the community beyond the classroom.
   - Arrange the instructional space to promote both inclusion and comfort.
   - Include literature that portrays individuals with challenged abilities as productive members of society.
   - Use language that is straightforward, and check for understanding.
   - Make expectations and directions (norms) accessible in multiple ways (visually
   - and verbally), and refer to them often.
   - Give all students opportunities to display and share their best work.

2. **Consider ways to promote a more inclusive classroom community:**
   - Engage students in ongoing community-building exercises.
   - Convey the belief to students that they can all learn and succeed.
   - Be mindful that all students should feel as though they are accepted and belong.
   - Model the values of empathy, compassion, acceptance, respect, and fairness for others.
   - Recognize each individual student's successes, and show that you value them.
   - Focus not on students' labels but on their strengths and positive qualities.
   - Dissuade the use of stereotypical language in the classroom.

3. **Consider ways to modify lesson resources:**
   - Provide access to materials that enable the text-to-speech feature, or obtain recorded audio excerpts for students.
   - Offer students reading materials that are at their level.
   - Remove jargon or unnecessary text from reading materials for students with comprehension or processing difficulties.
   - Provide students with graphic organizers, and demonstrate how to use them effectively to categorize and organize information.
   - Use color-coding strategies to help students distinguish key words or categorize information.

4. **Consider ways to promote social inclusion:**
   - When developing norms at the beginning of the year, intentionally focus on showing respect for others, regardless of their differences. Frequently revisit the norms throughout the year.
   - Explicitly teach and reinforce skills that support success in cooperative learning groups, such as active listening, perspective-taking, and empathy.
   - Ask students to establish norms for their small-group work.
   - Be mindful of diversity when grouping students.
   - Assign roles to students in cooperative learning groups to promote equity. When assigning roles, keep in mind the students' strengths.

continued

FIGURE 8.1 (*continued*)

How to Implement STAT Strategies in the Inclusion Classroom

> - Assign peer advocates, mentors, or buddies to students with challenged abilities to provide them with ongoing support and encouragement.
> - Enlist the help of other school personnel (e.g., a special education teacher or paraprofessional) to "coach" students who need it during small-group work.
>
> **5. Consider ways to differentiate assessment:**
> - Ensure that each assessment generates valid evidence of students' content understanding and progress toward IEP goals.
> - Let students choose their preferred modalities to express their understanding.
> - Support students to reflect on their progress and set goals for their learning.
> - Reword questions and read them aloud to students.
> - Grant students additional time to complete assessments.
> - Let students record their reflections or responses in the form of a video or voice recording or enable the speech-to-text feature to facilitate typing.
> - Provide frequent, meaningful feedback.
> - Balance teamwork and individual work.

Sources: Land (2017); Ontario Ministry of Education (2006).

Planning for an Inclusive STAT Lesson

Although STAT lessons are designed to meet the needs of a diverse group of learners, every group of students is unique; you will, of course, need to adapt the lesson plan to your particular situation. For example, if your class includes a student with dyslexia, make reading materials during a Respectful Debate lesson accessible in an audio format and allow the student to use speech-to-text software to take notes in preparation for the debate portion of the activity. Although students generally have five minutes to write down their ideas in support of their position, you may want to eliminate or extend the time limits or replace the role of *timekeeper* with that of *group motivator*.

Applying the tenets of universal design for learning (UDL) when planning helps you factor in the needs and abilities of all learners and eliminate potential barriers in the learning process. When planning STAT lessons, focus on

- Representing content in multiple ways (e.g., visually, aurally).
- Employing a flexible means of engagement as students learn (e.g., role playing, videos, and podcasts).
- Allowing students multiple ways of expressing their understanding of content (e.g., writing, drawing, and speaking) (Land, 2017).

Teaching Tip

In advance of a lesson, take your students with challenged abilities aside and give them relevant reading materials, vocabulary, or handouts to review with a paraprofessional or for homework. Also, offer them several ways of engaging during the lesson and demonstrating their learning. You can either list these or provide a choice board. Have the student select their preference, and clarify what their performance should look like.

Likewise, offering students tiered lessons means they can learn at a level that challenges them but doesn't overwhelm them. Tiered assignments are parallel tasks that vary in depth, abstractness, and complexity and that offer students varying levels of support and scaffolding (Williams, 2002). All students work toward achieving the same goals and standards, but with accommodations that address differences in student readiness and performance levels.

Remember the PLAN lesson on women's suffrage that we looked at in Chapter 6? Figure 8.2 illustrates how this lesson might be conducted with tiered assignments.

Supporting Students During Implementation

When carrying out a STAT lesson in the inclusion classroom, flexibility is key. The STAT lesson plans in this book aren't recipes that you must perfectly execute to yield a successful result. Focus on the process as opposed to the product, and be mindful of how you may need to adjust the ingredients. Let's look at some of those ingredients.

Timing. Even if the STAT Yes-No-Maybe lesson plan suggests that it should take two 45-minute periods to complete, it may take longer. For example, if your students struggle with active listening skills and speaker power, you might designate a full period for each round of Yes-No-Maybe to coach students in developing these skills during their small-group discussions. Or you may have several students in your class with challenged reading abilities. In that case, you may wish to allocate more time for the reading portion of the lesson and ensure that the appropriate supports are in place. With STAT, less is always more; the focus should be on presenting fewer skills or lessons to promote mastery and generalization.

FIGURE 8.2

A PLAN Lesson on Women's Suffrage with Tiered Assignments

Lesson Component	Tier 1 PLAN Basic	Tier 2 PLAN Comprehensive	Tier 3 PLAN Integrative
Content	Elizabeth Cady Stanton's keynote speech at the Seneca Falls Convention	"The Cult of True Womanhood" and Elizabeth Cady Stanton's keynote speech	"The Cult of True Womanhood," Elizabeth Cady Stanton's keynote speech, and primary source documents related to current issues of gender inequality
Process	Students will analyze the problem-solving process that Elizabeth Cady Stanton and women's rights activists went through in 1848 with the Seneca Falls Convention.	Students will analyze the problem-solving process of the women's rights activists at that time and develop SMART goals to reflect a short- and a long-term solution. Students will develop a detailed action plan to achieve the solution.	Students will analyze "The Cult of True Womanhood" and Elizabeth Cady Stanton's keynote speech to determine how the women's rights activists addressed issues of gender inequality at that time. They will then identify and closely read several primary source documents related to current issues of gender inequality.
Product	Students will complete the PLAN graphic organizer to evaluate the effectiveness of the activists' plan.	Students will present the action plans they developed to hypothetical audiences of women's rights activists, men in government, or other groups whose rights were previously violated (for example, freed Black men).	Students will develop a policy to address an issue of gender inequality and present it to relevant local stakeholders.

Grouping. Cooperative learning groups—the essence of all STAT strategies—can foster a sense of belonging for students with challenged abilities. According to Stevens and Slavin (1995), students with challenged abilities benefit greatly from such groupings and from hearing their peers' explanations of the work at hand. In addition, cooperative learning groups provide multiple opportunities for students with challenged abilities to practice social skills in authentic contexts. Here are some guidelines to keep in mind when grouping students:

- Keep groups small—no more than four students.
- Assign roles based on the students' strengths.
- Within groups, partner students with challenged abilities with another student's strengths to buttress their weaknesses.
- Have students engage in reciprocal teaching to ensure their comprehension of the text.
- Group students with challenged abilities with their assigned peer mentors, advocates, or buddies.
- Keep groups intact for several lessons to promote relationship building. However, create diverse groupings after several lessons to expose all students to those with different backgrounds and abilities.

Technical support resources. When executing the "recipe" or lesson plan, make sure your "kitchen" or classroom is fully stocked with the resources to ensure your students' success. You should have reading materials on hand at a variety of levels and text-to-speech programs for those students who need them. Have devices available for students who need support with the physical task of writing, and offer Flipgrid videos or the option of creating an illustration as alternative assessment opportunities.

Human support resources. Have school personnel, such as paraprofessionals, special education teachers, and mental health professionals, on call to support students' emotional needs. Expect that students may experience anxiety or have strong emotional responses to a lesson's content, which may require extra processing and reflection time. Although paraprofessionals can help students reinforce emotional regulation strategies or encourage them to retreat to a calming center in the classroom to collect themselves, school mental health professionals can directly intervene in lessons to address students' behavior intervention plans. Special education teachers can help deliver instruction through coteaching models and strategies, as well as monitor the progress of the students with challenged abilities, tailor instructions, and provide supplemental learning materials.

Assessment. Design your assessments so they're also inclusive. Assessments should provide evidence of the student's understanding of the lesson objectives and standards, as well as progress toward any IEP goals. Give students the choice in how they want to express their understanding, and grant additional time to complete assessments. In addition, provide students with prompt, constructive, and ongoing feedback, as well as support in using this feedback to improve their learning. The goal is for students to reflect on their learning and to set goals based on their reflections to drive that learning.

Teaching Tip
Depending on your students' needs, feel free to modify any of the formative assessment tools presented at the end of Chapters 2–6. When modifying the tools, sit down with a special education teacher or school social worker and refer to goals established in the student's IEP or 504 plan. Work together to come up with a means of giving feedback to the student that highlights their strengths, and set reasonable goals in areas in which they can improve.

Making STAT Inclusive: Some Forward Reflections

As you conclude this chapter on making STAT lessons inclusive to all learners in your classroom, contemplate the following questions:

- To what degree is your learning environment inclusive and accessible to students with challenged abilities?
- In what ways do you engage in inclusive planning practices by offering activities that appeal to various ways of learning and provide students with choice and alternative assessments (Tomlinson, 2017)?
- How do your instructional practices focus on students' strengths and positive qualities, instead of on their labels?
- How could you leverage the support of other school personnel to assist you in planning and delivering STAT lessons to meet the needs of students with challenged abilities?

Scaling Up STAT

We're excited that you have continued on this journey with us to read about the prospect of scaling up STAT in your school or district. This chapter focuses on ways to increase social-emotional learning, civil discourse, and social justice in your community. Recognizing that innovation and creativity in education are never a one-size-fits-all process, we return to the crux of this book—that anyone in a school community, from the superintendent to the students themselves, can lead the transformation of student learning.

First, a Look at Outcomes

Before going any farther, let's pause to take stock of what STAT can help you achieve in your school.

In addition to supporting STAT implementation in 13 schools, we have a mailing list of more than 1,000 educators who are receiving STAT materials and teaching tips. We instituted a practice of soliciting ongoing feedback about STAT (Hatchimonji et al., 2017), and our findings, summarized in Nayman (2019), Tavarez (2021), and Cedano (2021), testify to its overall benefits.

Linsky and colleagues (2018) provide an extensive analysis of the connection of STAT procedures with best-practices pedagogy along with a detailed case study of how one urban school effectively implemented STAT despite numerous logistical challenges. Notably, students in this school enjoyed the movement aspect of the Yes-No-Maybe instructional strategy and the opportunity it gave them to share their opinions and hear the opinions of others. This exchange of perspectives, they reported, helped them to think differently about topics under discussion.

Generally, these students recognized the value of having norms to facilitate respectful engagement in discussions and underscored the importance of listening to and recognizing others' perspectives. Teachers observed improvements in students' empathy and civility during discussions, and reported an increase in student enthusiasm for coursework. In addition to highlighting STAT's benefits, feedback provided practical suggestions for improvement that have been integrated into STAT procedures.

Cedano (2021) and Tavarez (2021) focus particularly on how STAT participation affects BIPOC students. In Figure 9.1, you can see a collection of phrases surveyed teachers used to describe STAT.

FIGURE 9.1

Teacher Feedback on STAT Program Design, Practicality, and Content

"Easily implemented."

"Flexible."

"Strategies don't require extensive training."

"Designed to include students."

"Well-aligned with state standards."

"Adds structure."

"Easy to use in a distance learning environment."

"Practical. A commonsense approach."

"Fosters communication and collaboration skills in students."

"Encourages students to think more critically."

"Infuses SEL into other content."

"Elevates student voice."

"Supports student learning."

Source: Cedano, 2021.

Avenues to Scaling Up STAT

Due to the pluralistic ecosystem of schools, multiple pathways exist to scale up STAT in your school. Let's look at some of them.

Teacher Leadership

Teacher leaders naturally question the status quo, delving into the hidden curriculum in their efforts to improve student learning. Such teachers, often the early adopters, can integrate STAT strategies into their practice and serve as advocates of the approach. As productive disruptors, they can spark discussion and healthy disequilibrium. If you're a teacher leader and are interested in implementing this approach, find a critical colleague or school leader to coach you through any resistance, help steer you through the politics, and, mostly, to share in your joy.

Maybe you don't regard yourself as a teacher leader. To you, we say that if you want to improve student learning outcomes, you're ready to lead. A teacher's courage is the first step toward commitment. Get comfortable with STAT and with generating student products to share with colleagues. Start innovating your lesson planning for student-driven learning.

You can advance your professional practice and hone your burgeoning teacher leadership skills through any of the following channels:

- Annual professional development goal setting
- Professional development workshops
- Professional learning communities
- Departmental and grade-level initiatives
- Teacher-led professional development opportunities
- School climate and culture committees
- Curriculum writing opportunities
- Mentoring pre-service teachers
- Coteaching partnerships and interdisciplinary teaming

Getting started as an instructional leader may seem at first as though you're "faking it to make it" because that initial foray into implementation can unleash self-doubt. Following the STAT lessons closely at the beginning will build your competence and confidence. Over time, as you develop more awareness and more ease with the strategy, you can begin to blend in your own original content. Start with an essential inquiry and an objective aligned to formative assessment, and you will be well on your way to transforming your planning to align with STAT strategies.

SEL Competency Connection: Self-Awareness

As you experience the risk taking and vulnerability of stepping into leadership, you will begin to experience a heightening of your emotions. This can be destabilizing at first, but as you become more aware of this effect, you can intentionally slow down an excitement that may overwhelm clear thinking. You will become more fully present to meet your students' needs and find joy in the learning.

Making your formative assessment plan clear in the lesson will help you engage in backward lesson design. Start from the learning outcomes you're aiming for and set up the scaffolded activities and steps of the lesson you'll conduct over consecutive days and class periods necessary to bring students to those outcomes. You want students to dig into deeper learning, practice crucial social-emotional skills, and engage in the demands of the cognitive academic process.

Professional Communities of Practice

Communities of practice can serve as petri dishes of curricular innovation to integrate STAT. They can be formal structures created by building-led professional learning communities or informal ones that grow out of mutual partnerships. Small professional communities of change will encourage and renew your professional commitment. Collegial connection and community can fuel resilience when a lesson doesn't go as hoped. You may be tempted to go it alone, but it's easier, more fun, and more rewarding to engage in curricular innovation with a group.

Partnering with School Leadership

Partnering with your supervisor or taking part in a departmental or grade-level STAT initiative is another pathway to bring STAT to your community. Leading a STAT integration as you strengthen your relationship with your building leadership can be a joyful experience. Be sure to keep your supervisor informed of such shifts in your practice so they can support your efforts and guide you through the change process. Sharing the lesson resources, reviewing lesson plans, and providing samples of student learning can help educate your building leadership on the approach. You will need to serve as an advocate for the learning, displaying the positive outcomes that your students have demonstrated. Such outcomes will be observable in students' generalizing the strategies in their interactions with peers. You may even hear from colleagues that your students are explicitly using a STAT strategy in their class or suggesting that everyone in the class use a particular strategy to help regulate their emotions, show empathy for a point of view they don't agree with, strive for a balanced view on controversial issues, or reduce disciplinary issues. As the leader that you have become and continue to evolve into, you can show how to implement curricular change in the context of the school community.

Partnering with your supervisor can excite meaningful dialogue around student learning outcomes. With their awareness of the community's political climate, supervisors can help steer your implementation with care and act as a sounding board to discuss student resistance or parent concerns. Be sure to keep parents in the loop, too; let them know what their children are learning and why. Don't get discouraged by resistance; it's a sign that you're challenging traditional perspectives on education.

SEL Competency Connection: Relationship Skills
Partnering with colleagues or your supervisor will offer you a rich opportunity to stretch your communication and social skills. These interactions can enhance your ability to interact with others in healthy, highly effective ways and enrich your professional relationships. Innovating the curriculum can be a thrilling prospect for both your students and your professional community.

Student Voice and Leadership

Because STAT elevates student voice, it can put students in a position to lead its integration. For example, students might author an article for the school newspaper or the district website that explains how STAT is affecting their learning outcomes. Be sure to coordinate any such plans with your supervisor or principal; they are critical partners who can help steer you in the right direction.

Showcasing student successes in the classroom and sharing evidence of student learning with colleagues, your supervisor, your principal, and even parents are other ways to advocate for the integration of STAT strategies. Such evidence might include samples of student learning and growth demonstrated in the self-reflections, a writing sample expressing social awareness and empathy for the people affected by an issue, growth over time on the STAT skills rubrics, and ultimately students organizing to make change in the community. Summative assessment products stemming from PLAN and Audience-Focused Communication can excite the potential for integrating STAT on a wider scale beyond the school and into the community.

School Mental Health Professional Leadership

School mental health professionals can lead change in their spheres of influence. As they collaborate to address student behavioral or transition challenges, support families in need, work to educate teachers on students' psycho-social development, and support intervention and referral services committee processes, they can infuse STAT strategies into their practices to ensure inclusive and equitable practices.

For example, they might integrate Norms and the Yes-No-Maybe strategies into the various group sessions they lead, or they might help develop norms in the classroom. Or they might use STAT strategies to help develop critical thinking, self-management, and social awareness skills during Respectful Debates. Or they could integrate STAT strategies in meetings and student-to-student restorative practice sessions. In this vein, they might adapt a Yes-No-Maybe lesson to surface student misconceptions about how to interpret, respond to, and act on their peers' behaviors. The counselor could share SEL strategies for how to best respond in a given situation.

Working closely with building administration and families, counselors often sit on multiple school-based committees, such as the school climate and culture committee, child study teams, Section 504 committees, and the intervention and referral services committee. Establishing norms early on and employing Yes-No-Maybe can help honor multiple perspectives as committee members look at shared evidence of student progress. Further, school counselors are uniquely positioned to serve as advocates for student-centered practices that elevate student choice, voice, and leadership across the school community.

Teacher-Driven Professional Development

Another avenue to expand the integration of STAT is to present your learnings during in-district and out-of-district professional development events. In-service professional development affords opportunities to share STAT strategies, lesson plans, effects on student learning, and implementation challenges, which can help prepare your colleagues to attempt the strategies on their own. Advocating and advancing professional learning on STAT are worthy ways for teachers to elevate their voice, enrich their professional learning communities, and foster the psychological safety needed for professional risk taking.

If you want to expand the reach of your STAT experience and share this knowledge with a wider community, you can take it a step further. Submit a proposal to present at professional conferences; EdCamps; or local professional association workshops such as those offered by ASCD, the Association for Middle Level Education (AMLE), the National Education Association (NEA), and the American Federation of Teachers (AFT). Or partner with local university pre-service teacher programs to infuse STAT into their professional learning experiences. Expanding the reach of the STAT strategies will take additional time, but remember that the goal is to empower students to develop the skills and practice of leading change in a democratic society. To lighten the load, find a willing partner who shares your commitment and passion to collaborate with on these experiences.

Formal and Informal Instructional Observations

Although they may seem like unlikely avenues, both formal and informal observations can serve as pathways to extend the reach of STAT. Not only will you receive feedback from the observation itself, courtesy of your building leader or department supervisor, but you'll also have an opportunity to highlight the STAT learning that's occurring in your classroom. Announced observations allow you to choose which kind of lesson to highlight.

Your observer will see how your implementation of STAT increases opportunities for student voice and choice and enhances the classroom culture. Be sure to share the lesson and the link to the STAT website in advance to help your supervisor understand the strategy. Also, specify what feedback you're looking for, and set up a follow-up meeting to gather the supervisor's input and feedback.

You might also host peer visitations so your colleagues can see a STAT lesson in action. That can generate fruitful discussion around facilitating challenging conversations with students, elevating student voice, and ensuring inclusive class environments. Soliciting positive feedback from observers in the form of an exit slip can also enrich the teacher's practice of a given strategy.

Parents as STAT Advocates

Never forget that some of your best advocates are your students' parents and guardians. You can share and celebrate student progress resulting from STAT lessons formally at parent conferences, informally during meetings, or even while touching base over the phone or by email. You can show the power of STAT learning at the high school level by sending an email to a parent expressing your delight in their child, who finally overcame their reluctance and volunteered to speak in a Yes-No-Maybe.

Be proactive with parents and guardians, explaining what the STAT strategies are and how they relate to the content standards. Doing this before implementation or as part of your beginning-of-the-year orientation with parents can support the idea that parents are partners in their child's education. Explaining the why of an assignment or a classroom activity can be a wonderful way to let parents know about the learning experiences you include in your lessons. In addition, check out Appendix E for elevator pitches you can use to advocate for STAT with parents and other critical stakeholders in the school community.

SEL Competency Connection: Relationship Skills
Whether you send parents a single email about their child or broadcast a monthly newsletter, communicating to families about what their child is learning, and why and how they're learning it, is a positive and proactive way to build relationships. Ongoing communication with families about classroom successes with STAT can help maintain healthy parent–school relationships and even open avenues for parents to serve as advocates for STAT out in the community.

School Leadership-Driven Implementation of STAT

Leading collaborative instructional change is a dynamic process of decision making, gauging feedback, and ongoing improvement. It's crucial to clearly envision the outcomes that you and your leadership colleagues desire early on. STAT integrates effortlessly with social studies and the visual performing arts curricula. Also consider how to integrate STAT into academic courses that are subjected to state-mandated testing as there may be some cause for concern about how STAT strategies align with the standards.

As you work with your team, connect the instructional change to the district's vision and core values. Rallying hearts and minds may seem "fluffy," but identifying the organization's beliefs and vision for student learning can lift attitudes and foster aspirations for change. As guidance, we recommend John Kotter's three-phase, eight-step process:

Create a Climate for Change

1. Increase urgency.
2. Build the guiding team.
3. Get the right vision.

Engage and Enable the Whole Organization

4. Communicate for buy-in.
5. Empower action.
6. Create short-term wins.

Implement and Sustain Change

7. Don't let up.
8. Make it stick. (Kotter & Cohen, 2012, p. 6)

Readying a Faculty for Implementation

Surfacing a shared need among your professional community can be the spark to fueling teacher practice. Identifying recent student mental health concerns, lagging academic achievement, student disciplinary issues, or even disengagement in the classroom highlights for teachers the relevance of the change. Examine and present district data demonstrating disparities between student subgroups or demographic changes that would necessitate a change in teaching practices. Personalizing the data with student stories can really bring the cause for change into a concrete and an emotional focus for faculty. Examples like this can excite doubt, ignite professional discussion, and cause rethinking.

As you begin this work, gauge the readiness of your staff: who is eager and willing, who is reluctant but may need time and training, and who might be resistant and demand intensive support? Tailor professional learning experiences to meet your faculty's needs. Be sure to listen to and treat those who are reluctant and resistant with compassion and dignity.

You might share that recent leadership discussions around student needs have indicated that we need to shift our practices to engage our students in new ways. This signals to teachers that the curricular change is connected to their practices. Bringing a curricular initiative to your teachers is going to stretch your leadership, so think about partnering with an administrative intern or a teacher leader early on to help you adjust your processes.

Taking Steps Toward Integration

To prepare teachers to integrate the STAT strategies, offer a professional learning experience that includes some light resource exposure. Consider having your faculty read the *SmartBrief* article "Civility and Society: How to Boost Civil Discourse in K–12 Classrooms" (*SmartFocus,* 2019); the *Phi Delta Kappan* article "Empowering Students for Social Action in Social Studies" (Bond et al., 2021); or the *Greater Good* article "Three Strategies for Helping Students Discuss Controversial Issues" (Fullmer & Bond, 2021). Further, to give teachers a glimpse of the strategies in action, have them explore some of the STAT project resources, such as the videos on the website of the Rutgers Social-Emotional and Character Development Lab (www.secdlab.org/STAT).

Reviewing the articles in greater depth with teachers or hosting a Socratic circle activity or readthrough with a reading protocol can help them envision using the strategies in their own practice and can surface early on any barriers to and breakthroughs for integration. You can then connect these discussions to any revised state curriculum standards that need to be integrated into the curriculum. Be sure to openly gather feedback, take questions, and hear concerns because this will help you pace your next steps to launch a pilot of STAT.

An inclusive scaling up begins with organizing a community of voluntary practitioners. You can fashion this as a pilot program of STAT, as a professional learning community, or even as a book club with a given grade level, a given department, or even with the whole school using the one book/one school approach, using this book as your selection. Working with a small group of willing teachers can serve as an engine of exploration and experimentation. Partnering with teacher leaders can be a powerful way to foster distributive leadership and signal the trust you have in your faculty to colead their learning.

For wider engagement with a department or a whole school, you can connect STAT to an academic standard in one or more content areas or to any social-emotional learning or character development goals or initiatives your school has established. With the prevalence of Zoom conferencing, you can host book clubs or professional learning sessions online. You might even consider options for parent participation if you're willing to hold sessions in the evening. Truly, the only thing that may stand in your way is your imagination. So get creative, and see where it takes your school or department.

Expanding Implementation

If your leadership responsibilities extend across multiple buildings, we recommend implementing STAT one building at a time. Be mindful to differentiate for any building-based needs and district strategic aims. For example, the high school might want to implement STAT in social studies to foster healthy student discussion, an upper elementary school may want to implement STAT in English language arts to support speaking and listening skills, and the middle school may want to implement it in the visual and performing arts to enhance a focus on how SEL resides and thrives in the arts. If resources are available, it may even be worthwhile to focus on a single strategy for each department.

Setting annual professional development goals linked to implementing STAT can make that implementation an ongoing focus across the school year. Because this is a shift in instruction, you might decide to make participation voluntary the first year and then requisite for all faculty the following year. Figure 9.2 provides an overview of how a multiyear implementation process might be staged.

FIGURE 9.2

Sample Multiyear STAT Implementation Process

Year 1	Year 2	Year 3	Year 4
Explore and build knowledge capacity.	Pilot integration and widen knowledge networks.	Expand implementation further by tying it to annual professional development goals.	Tie the full-scale implementation to annual professional development goals.

Outcomes and Obstacles

As you scale up STAT in your school, stay focused on the outcomes. The ready-to-use assessment tools and reflection questions that are embedded in these chapters will assist teachers in tracking those outcomes.

Any time you collaborate with adult learners in the change process, you're bound to encounter resistance. It's a natural human response when the status quo is challenged. In his 2016 *Educational Leadership* article "The Tug of War Between Change and Resistance," Michael Murphy provides perspective on how to address resistance when implementing a new instructional practice:

> When thinking about managing resistance, it's useful to keep two big ideas in mind: (1) reluctance or open resistance to changes a leader proposes is often predictable and understandable, and (2) you can move beyond resistance by observing how those affected by the

change react and then altering *your* behavior, rather than decrying the resisters' behavior. (p. 66)

True to the social-emotional character of STAT, as you adjust your behavior, you will retain the trust you have built with your teachers and safeguard relationships.

SEL Competency Connection: Responsible Decision Making

With each decision you make, you have the opportunity to evaluate the personal, safety, ethical, and civic effects of that decision. Adjusting your own behavior can seem to run counter to your instincts. Yet when you weigh the personal benefits of maintaining relationships, keeping an eye on long-term goals, and fueling aspirations for both your teachers and students, it makes sense to accept some discomfort and delay gratification for healthy and sustained change.

Bear in mind that adult learners need plenty of time to make sense of the why and how of adapting their practice. Virginia Satir's model of change is a powerful visual that reminds us just how much time it takes for a single individual to move from clinging to the old status quo to moving into a new one (Newton & Wolf, 2017). We recommend taking a few moments to learn more about Satir's model via the material at http://www.satirworkshops.com. It's a worthy read for any leader committed to respecting the dignity of faculty and families as they adjust to a new status quo. Like Satir, we believe that growth and change are possible for everyone. So returning to this model after a challenging day of working with adult learners on implementing STAT can help you empathize with how trying it is for someone to adapt to change.

Don't forget to take a breather every now and then. Remember that you're helping to lead work around social justice, social-emotional learning, and civil discourse. It's complicated. It will take time. And yes, remind yourself that there will be breakthrough moments for your teachers and their students that will fill you with joy.

With our focus on student outcomes, we encourage active use of each STAT strategy's assessment rubrics and formative assessment tools to gauge student progress. Solicit teacher feedback on what they're noticing in their implementation; what you learn can help you design your next leadership steps in teacher support and professional development. Bring samples of student work or assessment results to discuss in greater detail with the faculty to surface any patterns and exceptions in the outcomes.

You will, of course, run into obstacles that impede the implementation, but they don't have to determine how you *perceive* the obstacles. Recognizing that resistance is natural can change the way you respond to that resistance. John Schermerhorn and colleagues (2005) argue that people resist change for eight reasons:

1. Fear of the unknown
2. Lack of good information
3. Fear of loss of security
4. No clear reasons to change
5. Fear of loss of power
6. Lack of resources
7. Bad timing
8. Habit

You can overcome all the factors in this list with skill and leadership moves that foster a positive climate for change. Your role as leader is to collaborate with your leadership team and everyone on the faculty to remove systemic, structural, and cultural barriers that impede implementation. Addressing those barriers will require nuanced problem solving, strategy work, and seizing opportunities for bold conversations. If you'd like to dive into a deeper read on how to address obstacles, consider John P. Kotter and Leonard A. Schlesinger's 2008 article "Choosing Strategies for Change," published in the *Harvard Business Review*.

Students Taking Action Together: Case Studies

The purpose of Students Taking Action Together is just that—teaching adolescents to discover the power of their voice and empowering them to take action in their communities. Wherever you implement STAT, finding platforms for students to advance their advocacy work and engage in social change can be a meaningful and thrilling experience.

We now turn our attention to the voices of our youth who yearn to take action, no matter how small or local, to make a difference in this world. Empowered by STAT program participation and the strategies it has taught them, they are realizing these ambitions in their own communities. We share these stories with the hope of inspiring you to bring STAT to your school community. The timeless words of Martin Luther King Jr. seem relevant here. Yes, the arc of the moral universe is long and bends toward justice, but school leaders need to commit to helping each generation of citizens, each new class of tomorrow's leaders, learn how to take action toward bending it.

Students as Changemakers

One suburban New Jersey school district is infusing STAT strategies in 4th and 5th grade classrooms across the district as an extension of their language arts curriculum and to complement a program they have adopted that focuses on teaching students to be changemakers.

This integration of STAT begins with introducing BEST and Respectful Listening to provide students and teachers with a way to infuse social-emotional learning and practice into the existing language arts curriculum. By using Yes-No-Maybe and PLAN strategies, students practice the skills to empower them to effectively listen to and feel empathy for others with opposing views, approach social problem solving, and speak effectively to effect change in their community and beyond.

In these language arts lessons, students interact with a variety of sources (books and other media resources) that feature SEL themes. A guide includes talking points and activities to underscore the social-emotional components of the selected resources. In one lesson, students read and discuss Jacqueline Woodson's book *The Other Side*, guided by the following prompts:

- Think about struggles we face in our own lives.
- Identify some of the same social issues in this book.
- Think about the issues and ask yourself, "Why is this important?"

Finally, students work in groups to pick a social issue and create a poster or video on how they can address their social issue and empower others.

Further, students engage in introductory lessons focused on STAT principles and strategies, as well as five units that coincide with their existing language arts units. The five units focus on what we consider to be keys to success to develop the skills to lead positive change in their lives:

- Acceptance (of self and others)
- Inquiry (having flexible thinking)

- Empowerment (how to bring about positive change)
- Transformation (understanding historical content to transform ideas to the present day)
- Transcendence (how to move on to middle school as mature and responsible students)

In the Empowerment unit, for example, students read articles and watch videos that display a variety of individuals their age who found ways to fix and work through problems in everyday life to help others. One lesson for 5th graders centers on reading the 2015 book *One Plastic Bag: Isatou Ceesay and the Recycling Women of the Gambia* by Miranda Paul, which tells the story of how an African woman began a movement to recycle the plastic bags that were polluting her community. The lesson includes prompts and reflection questions to encourage students to analyze character growth and change and to discuss the term *changemaker*. As one student noted, "I like [the program] because it teaches us some good things that we can use in life, like acceptance, not just standing by but being changemakers to help other people. Even if you think that one thing won't matter, it will make a difference or change." In that vein, the school gives students ample opportunities throughout the year to become *changemakers* in their school and community. An extension of this lesson asks students to pick one of the individuals from their gallery walk of articles and videos about young changemakers. They are given the opportunity to write a letter to their chosen individual introducing themselves and reflecting on something in the world they would like to change, why they believe it should be changed, and various ways in which they might help bring this change about through action, invention, or advocacy.

Seeing the World Through Others' Eyes

One small independent school in rural Idaho serves at-risk teens—including students who have failed at their local high school, have a child to care for, have been the target of bullies, and have struggled with mental health issues. Many lack self-confidence when it comes to academic success.

The only 10th and 11th grade U.S. history classes in the school experienced a resounding success with teaching respectful disagreeing. In one unit, students focused on the factors that shape our identities and then related those factors to the topics under study—the Indian Removal Act of 1830 and the Trail of Tears. After researching the indigenous tribes, students created identity charts to better understand those nations affected by this government policy, including the Cherokee and Seminole. The identity charts helped students understand indigenous people through the struggles they encountered. They recognized how some traits that were imposed on them were not how the indigenous peoples authentically saw themselves. This activity enabled students to take the perspective of Cherokee and Seminole people during the Jackson administration and see the Indian Removal Act through their eyes. Taking on the persona of a member of either the Cherokee or Seminole Nation, students were tasked with writing a letter to President Jackson critiquing his 1830 speech to Congress. The social-emotional skillset helped the students show compassion and empathy, and they were able to make more meaningful connections between this event in history and the current living conditions of indigenous peoples on tribal land.

Promoting Awareness of Social Justice Issues

At Heron Bridge College in Johannesburg, South Africa, 11th and 12th grade students taking geography class were studying developing and developed countries. Their teacher asked them to design either a takeaway coffee cup or a sleeve for a coffee cup that would bring awareness to a social justice issue. The items had to meet two other criteria: they had to be environmentally friendly, and they had to be affordable yet profitable.

Students made cups and sleeves out of a variety of biodegradable materials, but what was truly noteworthy were the campaigns they highlighted with their designs (see Figure 9.3 for examples of the students' work). Many of the students designed cups or sleeves that highlighted social justice issues, such as racial injustice, women's rights, climate change, gender-based violence, and forced labor camps. Armed with solid social-emotional learning, these students showed off the skills that would prepare them to take on the world's biggest problems.

Empowering All

The beauty of STAT is that through professional growth, you will empower your educators to empower their students to become change agents. This is the underlying moral imperative entrusted to school leaders around the world—to help educators help their students to become the best versions of themselves as they strive to contribute to society. Such experiences can liberate the individual and renew the soul of education. Truly, there is no limit to what students can accomplish when students take action together.

FIGURE 9.3

Student-Designed Coffee Cup Sleeves

Source: Photographs courtesy of Samantha Wilke.

Acknowledgments

This book began more than three decades ago, when Rutgers University's Social Decision Making/Social Problem-Solving Program created lesson plans around "taming tough topics," using a problem-solving approach to discuss current events. Karen Haboush (of blessed memory) did the first study of the effectiveness of this approach in middle school social studies classes and found it made a positive difference, including for students with special education classifications. Since then, many teachers have used these lessons and made suggestions that have led to their evolution into Students Taking Action Together (STAT). The most enduring champions of the current, mature iteration of STAT have been school counselors Andrea Sadow and Grace Rivetti, along with Yenny Tavarez, who is entering doctoral study and will be a catalyst for social action.

We owe a great debt of gratitude to all the teachers who have tried STAT and have given us feedback directly and in the many surveys we have distributed. STAT methods have benefited from all this practical input as well as from the work of the Rutgers Social-Emotional and Character Development Lab—specifically from Danielle Hatchimonji and Arielle Linsky, Kellie McClain and Nina Murphy, Sarah DeMarchena, and our cherished Jersey City colleagues, Karen Colello, Paula Christen, Franklin Walker, Robert Brower, Margaret Critelli, Roslyn Barnes, and Francine Luce. We also thank the New Jersey Education Association (NJEA), particularly Janet Royal, Steve Beatty, and Patrick Rumaker, who gave us many opportunities to share STAT with NJEA membership.

Finally, and with tremendous gratitude, we acknowledge the guidance of Allison Scott, our editor, and her team. Their grasp of this book, their belief in its importance, and their help with communicating our ideas more effectively than we ever could have managed on our own have inspired and impressed us. Indeed, it takes a village to make a resilient and sustainable effort to help students take action together. Onward!

A personal note from Lauren: I am grateful for the best partner I could ask for on this project, Laura, who always helped me see the bigger picture and brought such creativity and energy to the project. I am filled with gratitude for my wonderful family's ongoing support and encouragement. They have been as understanding of the early mornings and late nights I spent working on the book, as they are supportive of my passion to equip teachers and students with the tools necessary to take social action and make the world a better place. I am especially thankful to my amazing husband, Dave, and our sons, Cade and Rhys, for instilling me with confidence, believing in me, and for the giggles and hugs that kept me going along the way.

A personal note from Laura: I am beyond thankful for my talented collaborative partner Lauren and for the zeal and commitment she brought to our collective collaboration during this project. Maurice, thank you for taking a chance on me; this has been an amazing journey of restoration for all the students whom I didn't teach with a whole child lens in mind. Boundless appreciation goes to my life partner, Chris, whose love and support have inspired me to new destinations I never imagined in my journey; to my Jack and Katie, for always reminding me that we must see the world and justice through the eyes of an adolescent; and to my Crosswicks Meeting Friends, who amplify my light. I wish to thank my mother, Marlene, who nurtured my curiosity and wonder to explore the world, and Maya Angelou, who instilled in me a love of words and a recognition of their power to expand the potential of our humanity. Words do empower and can propel change!

A personal note from Crystal: Thank you to my parents, Thomas and Marian Molyneaux, who supported me by encouraging me and praying for me. Dad, thank you for the wisdom and knowledge you poured into me; you have always had full confidence in my abilities. You are the epitome of strength and compassion, and I thank you for instilling the same in me. Mom, you have always seen my potential. You have cheered me on, affirmed me, and provided me with a safe space full of joy and love. You have been my example. Thank you for all the conversations and advice. To my son, Brandon, thank you for being understanding and patient with me as I set out to achieve this goal and for the hugs and kisses while I worked. I love you all very much.

A personal note from Sam: A primary goal of Students Taking Action Together (STAT) is to create positive change in our world through open-minded, creative, and collaborative problem solving. I am grateful for my coauthors who brought this goal to life, both through the writing of this book and by how they lead their lives.

A personal note from Maurice: I have been blessed with a supportive family that cheers me on as I embark on too many projects, and I want to thank all of them for taking such good care of me: my wife, Ellen; daughters, Sara Elizabeth and Samara Alexandra; sons-in-law, Josh and Paul; and grandchildren, Harry, Isaac, and FP.

Appendix A: Matrices for Available STAT Lessons

The matrices that follow provide an overview of the STAT lessons available on this book's companion website (https://www.secdlab.org/stat/book). They also suggest how to use essential questions to organize and inspire the lessons. The grades 5–8 band features nine lessons in world and U.S. history, as well as in current events in the categories of race, class (socioeconomic status), and gender. The grades 9–12 band features 10 lessons in world and U.S. history as well as current events.

We have highlighted only three of the STAT strategies on these matrices: **Yes-No-Maybe, Respectful Debate,** and **PLAN.** Refer to Chapters 2 and 5, respectively, for lesson ideas and exercises for the Norms and Audience-Focused Communication strategies. All lessons with an asterisk (*) are featured in Appendix B: Four Sample STAT Lessons and appear as exemplar lessons throughout the instructional strategies chapters (Chapters 2–6).

Additional lessons that are referenced throughout the book are available at this book's companion website: **https://www.secdlab.org/stat/book.**

Grades 5–8 Band: Lesson and Strategy Mapping for World and U.S. History

STAT Strategy	Race: Historical Content	Class: Historical Content	Gender: Historical Content
Yes/No/Maybe	**Do actions or words heal the injustices of the past?** *Source:* Bill Clinton apologizes for the Tuskegee Experiment www.c-span.org/video/?c4584112/user-clip-bill-clinton-apologizes-tuskegee-experiment	**Are police strike-breaking activities ever justified?** *Source:* The Strike for Three Loaves: The plight of mill workers in Lowell, MA www.alyve.org/english/docs/apat/05-ThreeLoaves.pdf	**Did women's involvement in WWII contribute to a shift in the attitude regarding the role of women in society?** *Source:* Women's involvement in WWII and empowerment thereafter https://dp.la/primary-source-sets/world-war-ii-women-on-the-home-front/
Respectful Debate	**Can social equality be attained while honoring states' rights?** *Source:* Jim Crow Laws and excerpts from the Green Book www.smithsonianmag.com/smart-news/read-these-chilling-charming-guides-black-travelers-during-jim-crow-era-180957131	**Can a real democracy exist in the presence of social stratification?** *Source:* "Does America Have a Caste System?" https://theconversation.com/does-america-have-a-caste-system-89118	**Did a lack of access to quality education affect women's rights in ancient civilizations?** *Source:* The role of women in ancient civilizations (including Mexican and African women); "Women's Footprints in History" https://interactive.unwomen.org/multimedia/timeline/womensfootprintinhistory/en/index.html#section01

STAT Strategy	Race: Historical Content	Class: Historical Content	Gender: Historical Content
PLAN	**Would African Americans have migrated north had they been treated with dignity in the South?** *Source:* "The Long-Lasting Legacy of the Great Migration" www.smithsonianmag.com/history/long-lasting-legacy-great-migration-180960118	**Empire Redo: What were possible alternatives to the exploitation of groups for labor?** *Source:* Historical look at the exploitation of groups of individuals in the ancient world; "America Cannot Bear to Bring Back Indentured Servitude" www.theatlantic.com/politics/archive/2018/03/american-immigration-service-slavery/555824/	**When a government is organized in a way that excludes groups of people, do we run the risk of social disorganization?*** *Source:* Seneca Falls Convention in 1848 and the consequences it had for women thereafter https://susanbanthonyhouse.org/blog/wp-content/uploads/2017/07/Elizabeth-Cady-Stanton-Seneca-Falls-1848.pdf *This lesson is available in two separate versions (PLAN Comprehensive and PLAN Integrative) on the companion website.

Grades 9–12 Band: Lesson and Strategy Mapping for World and U.S. History

STAT Strategy	Race: Historical Content	Class: Historical Content	Gender: Historical Content
Yes-No-Maybe	**Do leaders have to be charismatic to bring about social change?** *Source:* Nelson Mandela's June 1990 speech to the U.N. Special Commission on Apartheid https://www.un.org/en/events/mandeladay/legacy.shtml) **Does racism backfire on the people it intends to privilege?** *Source:* TED Talk: Racism has a cost for everyone https://www.ted.com/talks/heather_c_mcghee_racism_has_a_cost_for_everyone/transcript?language=en#t-207388	**Is it justifiable for strikers to compel a national emergency to have their demands met?** *Sources:* (1) BBC: "On This Day 1972: Miners Strike Against Government"; (2) Lib.com Chapter 5: The 1972 Miners Strike http://news.bbc.co.uk/onthisday/hi/dates/stories/january/9/newsid_2515000/2515917.stm http://libcom.org/library/chapter-05-1972-miners-strike	**Although it was outlawed in 1912, was foot binding in China an expression of beauty?** *Source:* Leveled reading passage: Foot Binding in China https://www.rif.org/literacy-central/reading-experience/leveled-reading-passage-chinese-foot-binding-easy

STAT Strategy	Race: Historical Content	Class: Historical Content	Gender: Historical Content
Respectful Debate	**The path to racial equality in America can be achieved by Black people separating from white people.** *Source:* Democracy Now: summary and video https://www.democracynow.org/2001/2/1/james_baldwin_and_malcolm_x_debate	**Was the Chinese government crackdown on the 1989 student protests justified?** *Source:* "PBS Timeline: What Led to the Tiananmen Square Massacre" https://www.pbs.org/wgbh/frontline/article/timeline-tiananmen-square/	**Was the Stonewall incident a riot or rebellion?** *Source:* "Was Stonewall a Riot, an Uprising, or a Rebellion?" https://time.com/5604865/stonewall-riot-uprising-rebellion/
PLAN	**How can communities resolve the challenges of racial injustice in America identified in MLK's "I Have a Dream" speech?** *Source:* Black Past: "I Have a Dream" speech https://www.blackpast.org/african-american-history/speeches-african-american-history/1963-martin-luther-king-jr-i-have-dream/	**How can those who are marginalized organize to overcome injustice?** *Source:* "A Lesson About Cesar Chavez and Civil Rights" https://www.edutopia.org/blog/lesson-about-cesar-chavez-civil-rights-maurice-elias	**What are alternatives to state-imposed population control programs like the one in India?** *Source:* "1 in 3 Indian Women Has Been Sterilized" https://www.pop.org/project/stop-forced-sterilizations-in-india/

Grades 5–8 Band: Lesson and Strategy Mapping for Current Events

STAT Strategy	Race: Current Events	Class: Current Events	Gender: Current Events
Yes-No-Maybe	**Discrimination related to the novel coronavirus has affected relationships.** *Source:* "As Coronavirus Spreads, So Does Xenophobia and Anti-Asian Racism" https://time.com/5797836/coronavirus-racism-stereotypes-attacks/	**Are gangs trying to do good for society?*** *Source:* "Gangs Are Good for Society" https://docs.google.com/document/d/1y9_ufIKSkdy_h8wbipYS-fcmguHyv_UtkngHipDH8EoU/edit	**Can you change the mindsets of influential groups that see women's rights as limited?** *Source:* Malala Yousafzai's Nobel Speech https://www.indiatoday.in/world/story/nobel-peace-prize-malala-yousafzais-nobel-speech-kailash-saty-arthi-230641-2014-12-10
Respectful Debate	**Can a lack of representation serve as fuel for social change?** *Source:* Windows and Mirrors: A Collection of Diverse Literature https://www.ronniesawesomelist.com/blog/windows-mirrors	**Can a real democracy be achieved in a socially stratified society?** *Source:* "Does America Have a Caste System?" https://theconversation.com/does-america-have-a-caste-system-89118	**Is it possible for sports to be inclusive of the LGBTQIA+ community?** *Sources:* (1) "Sports Remain Hostile Territory for LGBTQ Americans"; (2) "Inclusiveness Growing for LGBTQ Athletes" https://theconversation.com/sports-remain-hostile-territory-for-lgbtq-americans-157948 https://www.diverseeducation.com/home/article/15093066/inclusiveness-growing-for-lgbtq-athletes

STAT Strategy	Race: Current Events	Class: Current Events	Gender: Current Events
	How has the Black Lives Matter movement influenced systemic racism?	How have U.S. immigration laws influenced society's perceptions of immigrants over time?	Do women have to sacrifice their role as "homemakers" to close the gender wage gap?
	Source: "Black Lives Matter 13 Guiding Principles"	*Source:* "How U.S. Immigration Laws and Rules Have Changed Through History"	*Source:* "Take Five: At the Current Rate of Progress, No Equal Pay until 2069"
	https://www.dcareaeducators4so-cialjustice.org/black-lives-mat-ter/13-guiding-principles	https://www.pewresearch.org/fact-tank/2015/09/30/how-u-s-immigration-laws-and-rules-have-changed-through-history/	https://www.unwomen.org/en/news/stories/2017/2/take-five-chidi-king-equal-pay
PLAN			

Grades 9–12 Band: Lesson and Strategy Mapping for Current Events

STAT Strategy	Race: Current Events	Class: Current Events	Gender: Current Events
Yes-No-Maybe	**Should police wear body cameras to help address implicit bias?** *Source:* Bill de Blasio: "We can't let what happened to Eric Gardner happen again" https://twitter.com/billdeblasio/status/1166085488027021313?lang=en	**Is the $15-an-hour minimum wage a living wage?** *Source:* "Why the U.S. Needs a $15 Minimum Wage" https://www.epi.org/publication/why-america-needs-a-15-minimum-wage/	**Should all women heed the advice to "lean in"?** *Source:* "Should All Women Heed Author's Advice to 'Lean in'?" https://www.npr.org/sections/13.7/2013/03/31/175862363/should-all-women-heed-authors-advice-to-lean-in **Is public art always a form of activism?** *Source:* "Muralist Sam Kirk explores identity, culture through public art" https://chicago.suntimes.com/murals-mosaics/2019/10/4/20887122/chicago-murals-sam-kirk-pilsen-identity-culture-housing-lgbtq-pride-public-art

STAT Strategy	Race: Current Events	Class: Current Events	Gender: Current Events
Respectful Debate	Would a policy of open dialogue help us overcome systemic racism? Source: "We Must Talk About Race to Fix Economic Inequality" https://www.youtube.com/watch?v=caarVAS40jQ	Does the high school grade point average (GPA) contribute to social inequality? Source: "Another Advantage for Wealthy Students" https://www.usnews.com/news/education-news/articles/2018-09-19/the-gpa-gap-rich-students-have-grades-inflated-more-often-than-poor-students	Should the workplace adopt gender-neutral signage? Source: "He, She, They: Workplaces Adjust as Gender Identity Norms Change" https://www.npr.org/2019/10/16/770298129/he-she-they-workplaces-adjust-as-gender-identity-norms-change
PLAN	How can schools address racial bias in school discipline? Source: "Implicit Racial Bias in School Discipline" https://www.youtube.com/watch?v=1kCE-ejP5fY	How can we address the lack of access to quality healthcare in rural America? Source: "The Health Care Worker/Hospital Shortage in Rural America" https://www.ncsl.org/blog/2019/12/18/the-health-care-worker-hospital-shortage-in-rural-america.aspx	What are the alternatives to the current design in public space that can address sexism? Source: "The Credibility Gap: How Sexism Shapes Public Space" https://www.youtube.com/watch?v=HJjqtUUDhaxA

Additional Lessons Available on Our Companion Website

STAT Strategy	Lesson Topic	Source(s)
Yes-No-Maybe (current event)	Was the January 6 insurrection an attack on U.S. democracy?	"Pro-Trump mob storms U.S. Capitol, tries to overturn election" https://newsela.com/read/trump-mob-storms-capitol/id/2001017795/https://newsela.com/read/trump-mob-storms-capitol/id/2001017795/
Respectful Debate (current event)	Are those with disabilities still invisible in the United States?	"We're 20 Percent of America, and We're Still Invisible" https://www.nytimes.com/2020/07/26/opinion/Americans-with-disabilities-act.html?auth=login-email&login=email&referringSource=articleShare
Generic Audience-Focused Communication	How can students consider the perspective of their audience to ensure that their message is well received?	Academic content/book on which student will present
PLAN Basic	How would you respond responsibly to a neighborhood problem?	N/A

PLAN (current event)	How can students lead schools to adequately foster learning on climate change?	"Teachers and students push for climate change science in California" https://edsource.org/2019/teachers-and-students-push-for-climate-change-education-in-california/618239 Climate Science Data from National Oceanic and Atmospheric Association (NOAA) https://www.climate.gov/maps-data

Appendix B:
Four Sample STAT Lessons

YES-NO-MAYBE: GANGS DOING GOOD FOR SOCIETY

Are gangs trying to do good for society?

Rationale: In this lesson, students will learn how to take a stance by answering "yes," "no," or "maybe" to a statement about gangs, and they will explain their stance. This will enable students to develop the fundamental habits for respectful listening, engaged dialogue, and peer opinion sharing, which are the foundations of democratic action.

Objective: Students will reflect on their opinions related to gangs, on the people involved in gangs, and on the effect gangs have on society. Also, they will discuss the perceptions that surround gangs and gang-related activity.

Target Grade Levels: 5–8

Social Studies and ELA Standards:

- **NJSLS-SS.6.1.8.CivicsPI.4.** Investigate the roles of political, civil, and economic organizations in shaping people's lives, and share this information with individuals who might benefit from this information.

- **NJSLSA.R1.** Read closely to determine what the text says explicitly and to make logical inferences and relevant connections from it; cite specific textual evidence when writing or speaking to support conclusions drawn from the text.

Focal SEL Skill: Social awareness

Recognize and identify the thoughts, feelings, and perspectives of others

Materials and Resources:

- Signs that indicate "Yes," "No," and "Maybe" (to post in the corners of the room)
- Pencil/pen
- Highlighters
- Notebook
- Copies of Yes-No-Maybe Student Resource (https://docs.google.com/document/d/1AIF9FYRyNa8dFTbF7RAapXc8AdNyxl4BgOSWOgoxHyA/edit)
- Pictures of "Early Street Gang" (https://themobmuseum.org/blog/the-chicago-mob-vs-chicago-street-gangs) and "East Coast Crips"
- Copies of the article "Gangs Are Good for Society" by Caspar Walsh (https://www.theguardian.com/society/joepublic/2011/nov/10/gangs-good-society-youth-crime)
- Copies of Yes-No-Maybe Lesson Reflection (https://docs.google.com/document/d/1NnIt9nLZW7RzICAaliMzzl2RKaOgzNHnkHXzg21zt9s/edit)

Timing: Two 45-minute lessons

Lesson Procedure:

Step 1: Introduction and Initial Reflection (15 minutes)

1. Present two pictures to the students ("Early Street Gang" and "East Coast Crips") and explain that they both show gangs at different points in history. Say, *"Today we're going to examine your views on gangs by engaging in activities with your classmates. We will then explore several statements related to gangs and have the opportunity to take a stance on each."*

2. Explain that students will engage in free writing related to the four prompts below. First, they will record the statements on their worksheet. Then, for each statement, they will write a few sentences of initial reflection. Tell students, *"For each statement below, write whatever comes to your mind, and do not focus on the structure or conventions. The intent is to help you sort out your thinking."*

    A. *There is a link between gangs and drugs, violence, and crime.*

    B. *People can be motivated to join gangs to make money and gain power.*

    C. *Gangs can give people a sense of purpose.*

    D. *Young people who live in an area where gangs are prevalent are often pressured to join.*

Step 2: Yes-No-Maybe Round One (25–30 minutes)

1. Tell students, *"Today we're going to start learning some skills that you will need, now and as you get older, to be effective and involved citizens of your classrooms, your school, your community, and the wider world. It involves thinking about our own opinion on issues and considering others' opinions as well."*

2. Designate three separate areas in the room for "Yes," "No," and "Maybe."

3. Tell students, *"I'm going to read a sentence and when I'm done, you will move to the Yes, No, or Maybe spot of the room depending on if you agree or not with the statement. If you agree and move to 'Yes,' you have to share one reason why you agree. If you move to 'No,' you have to say why you do not agree. If you pick 'Maybe,' you have to share both something you agree with and something you disagree with about the statement. Then a spokesperson from each of the areas will summarize the main points of their group's discussion for the whole class."*

    A. *There is a link between gangs and drugs, violence, and crime.*

    B. *People can be motivated to join gangs to make money and gain power.*

    C. *Gangs can give people a sense of purpose.*

    D. *Young people who live in an area where gangs are prevalent are often pressured to join.*

4. Have students return to their seats and reflect in their journals on the following questions: "What surprised you about the activity? Did your opinion change after hearing your classmates' responses? If so, how?"

Step 3: Background Source Analysis (15 minutes)

1. Have students read the article "Gangs Are Good for Society," by Caspar Walsh. As they're reading, encourage them to annotate the parts of the article that relate to the four statements (you can either display the statements on the board or have the students refer to them in their notebooks). Students can annotate by assigning a color for each statement or using the letters (A–D) assigned to each statement when writing notes in the margin.

2. Have students respond in their notebooks to this question: *"What argument is the author trying to make? What evidence does he have to support the argument?"*

Step 4: Yes-No-Maybe Round Two (10–12 minutes)

1. Tell students, *"I will read the same statements from before, and you will move to the Yes, No, or Maybe spot of the room depending on your thoughts about the statement. We will briefly share our thoughts after each Yes-No-Maybe round. Reflect on this experience when you're back in your seat."*

Step 5: Reflection and Assessment (5 minutes)

1. Have students respond in their notebooks to each of the following reflection prompts. (If you prefer that students have a copy of the worksheet with the reflection questions, refer to the Materials and Resources section.)

   • **Reflection 1:** Did your responses to any of the prompts change during this round? If you did experience a change, explain why that occurred as best you can.

   • **Reflection 2:** What did you learn from this activity? Please be specific.

2. Have students discuss as a whole class how their perspectives changed from the beginning to the end of the activity.

Formative Assessment: You can present the reflection questions as an exit slip or in an interactive format, using a tool like Jamboard (https://jamboard .google.com). You can also have students create a Flipgrid video (see info .flipgrid.com), in which they present their answers orally.

Lesson Extension: Identify two examples of the media's negative portrayal of gangs; these can be video clips, articles, or social media posts. Write a letter to the media outlet challenging its biased portrayal of gangs, and ask them to consider all sides of the story.

RESPECTFUL DEBATE:
THE PATH TO RACIAL EQUALITY IN AMERICA

The path to racial equality in America can be achieved by Black people living separately from white people.

Rationale: As students study historical developments, they will encounter debates that ensued over change. In this lesson, students will consider opposing perspectives held by two civil rights leaders in the 1960s about the path to racial equality in the United States. Students will engage in a respectful debate, argue both sides to regulate their emotions, and build collective understanding and historical empathy for the civil rights leaders. Such skills are necessary for students to participate in and lead respectful debates for healthy civil discourse.

Objective: Students will debate the arguments made by two civil rights leaders on how to achieve racial equality in America by listening to, summarizing, and reflecting on the key points of the argument to build their perspective-taking skills.

Target Grade Levels: 9–12

Social Studies and ELA Standards:

- **NJSLS-SS. 6.1.12.History CC.13.a.** Compare and contrast the leadership and ideology of Martin Luther King Jr. and Malcolm X during the U.S. Civil Rights Movement, and evaluate their legacies.

- **NJSLSA.SL.11-12.3.** Evaluate a speaker's point of view, reasoning, and use of evidence and rhetoric, assessing the stance, premises, links among ideas, word choice, points of emphasis, and tone used.

- **NJSLSA.W.11-12.1.** Write arguments to support claims in an analysis of substantive topics or texts using valid reasoning and relevant and sufficient evidence.

Focal SEL Skill: Social awareness
- Recognize and identify the thoughts, feelings, and perspectives of others

Materials and Resources:

- Notebook
- Pencils/pens
- A computer connected to a projector for the teacher
- Chromebooks for students (optional)
- Copies of the background source: A blog post on the June 1963 debate between Malcolm X and James Baldwin
- An audio recording of the debate (https://www.youtube.com/watch?v=tJ-d _JgJfuQ)

Timing: Two 45-minute lessons

Lesson Procedure:

Step 1: Introduction and Initial Reflection (10 minutes):

1. Do-Now/Introductory activity

As students get settled into class, say, *"Today we're going to engage in a respectful debate about the path to racial equality in America by learning the views from both sides of an actual debate that took place between two activists during the civil rights movement in the early 1960s."* To prime students' thinking after they settle in, have them respond in writing to the statement below as a focusing/do-now activity:

"The path to racial equality in America can be achieved by Black people living separately from white people."

Step 2: Debate Preparation (40 minutes)

1. Debate introduction

Divide the class into two groups; one group will assume the "pro" side, and the other will assume the "con" side. Tell the students, *"Today we will engage in an activity called Respectful Debate to practice the skill of perspective-taking. This is a skill that you will need to be an effective and involved citizen in your school and community as well as a global citizen. It involves debating not just the one side of a debate you agree with but also taking the side of a debate that you don't agree with."* Inform the class that *"taking the position of a side you disagree with is the essence of Respectful Debate; this part of the lesson will help you build mutual understanding on the topic."*

2. Prepare for the Respectful Debate

   Distribute materials (now or in advance): Pass out the background information and have students read it to gain a general overview of the debate. Tell the students, *"You're going to meet two civil rights leaders, James Baldwin and Malcolm X. In June 1963, they met on television for a debate on the path to racial equality in the United States."* You may have students underline/highlight the main points that informed James Baldwin's and Malcolm X's views in the debate to get students thinking about their perspectives on racial equality.

   Next, play approximately 12–15 minutes of the audio recording of the Malcolm X and James Baldwin debate. (Listen to this in advance so you can tell the students which voice is Baldwin's and which is Malcolm X's.) Ask students to listen carefully with their full attention as the debaters present their ideas in detail with historical background content. Feel free to assign listening to the debate as homework to help students familiarize themselves with the debate beforehand. They can even take notes on the key points made by each of the debaters for homework.

Generate ideas: Both pro (in support of Malcolm X's position) and con (in support of Baldwin's position) sides have five minutes to write down as many examples supporting their position as they can.

Assign roles: You may wish to have students assign roles in their respective groups, determining who will be the *note taker,* the *timekeeper, debaters,* and *debate researchers* who can go back to the debate between Malcolm X and James Baldwin to gather key points. Note that the number of debaters can range from one student presenting every point to multiple students presenting fewer points each. Explain to the students that your role is to guide the students through the debate steps.

Step 3: Respectful Debate: Round One (15 minutes)

1. **Reconvene** as a whole class.

2. **Pro side starts the debate.** The pro side (in support of Malcolm X's position) gives their position and supports it with one or two examples.

3. **Con side summarizes** ("reflects back") what the pro side said and confirms with the pro side whether they summarized accurately. If not, the pro side can offer clarifying statements. Then the con side (in support of Baldwin's position) gives their own position and supports it with one or two examples.

4. **Pro side responds.** The pro side summarizes what the con side said and confirms with the con side whether they summarized accurately. If they did not, the con side can provide clarifying statements. The pro side then has the option of providing one additional example in support of their own position.

5. **Con side responds.** The con side summarizes what the pro side said and confirms with the pro side whether they summarized accurately. If not, the pro side can provide clarifying statements. The con side then has the option of providing one additional example in support of their own position.

Step 4: Respectful Debate: Round Two (15 minutes)

1. **Debaters swap sides to gain perspective.** Using the same debate statement, have the pro side and con side switch sides; have students repeat the Step 3 actions after having once again completed the "generate ideas" and "assign roles" steps. The switching of sides is a *crucial element of the lesson* to help stretch student thinking to see the topic from a different perspective.

Step 5: Reflection and Assessment (8–10 minutes)

1. Facilitate a conversation about the skill of perspective-taking, which is the ability to see situations from multiple perspectives.

   Sample questions:

   • Has your opinion changed at all about charismatic leadership and social change from when we started? How so?

- Did summarizing what the other side said or switching sides change your opinion? What about the summary activity was helpful?

- What lessons does this activity teach us about our opinions on issues in the news or historical events?

- How might debates like this help you question issues in history, current events, or school and consider other perspectives?

- How does exercising mutual respect for opposing views bring different results from debating opposing views?

- How did it feel to disagree with someone's point of view but also hold an appreciation for their point of view? How might this skill be helpful in society today?

Formative Assessment: After the discussion, have students choose any one of the questions above to respond to (or have them respond to the lesson debate statement) on a paper exit ticket or a digital Padlet posting website. Feel free to modify this step for your learners.

Lesson Extension: For an extended writing activity and to practice argumentative writing skills, have students develop a claim reflecting their stance on the debate statement. Have them integrate into their response evidence from the debate and any additional research they wish to include to support their claim.

AFC GENERIC:
PRESENTING A PROJECT OR BOOK REPORT

*How can students consider the perspective of their audience
to ensure their message is well received?*

Rationale: The generic form of Audience-Focused Communication (AFC) helps students take the perspective of their audience when planning their presentation, as well as consider how their message will be received by their audience. Through perspective-taking, students will learn how to focus their message in a way that is entertaining and memorable and that conforms to constraints with regard to available technology, space, and time.

Objective: Students will reflect on the perspective of their audience to communicate their message and present a book report or final project in a way that is effective, engaging, and memorable.

Target Grade Levels: 5–12

Career Readiness, Life Literacies, Key Skills, and ELA Standards:

- NJSLS-9.4.8.IML.12. Use relevant tools to produce, publish, and deliver information supported with evidence for an authentic audience.

- NJSLS-SL.9-10.6. Adapt speech to a variety of contexts and tasks, demonstrating command of formal English.

- NJSLS-SL.11-12.4. Present information, findings, and supporting evidence clearly, concisely, and logically such that listeners can follow the line of reasoning and the organization, development, substance, and style are appropriate to purpose, audience, and task.

Focal SEL Skills: Social awareness, emotion management

- Recognize and identify the thoughts, feelings, and perspectives of others

- Regulate the tendency to present in a way that *you* would like, as opposed to what might best suit your audience, or in a way that is simply easiest for you

Materials and Resources:

- Notebooks
- Pencils/pens
- Student Chromebooks
- Computer hooked up to projector
- Copies of worksheets (see Appendix C)
  - BEST Guidelines (https://docs.google.com/document/d/1AjktINfiibzZEC9G540vIDq4idVmnArSQ4iCDqAv-nY/edit)
  - AFC Project Presentation Plan Graphic Organizer (https://docs.google.com/document/d/1sKMb-nx-yuHRtl27k1E1uMIjCCUuHdPzlIQoI04E5XQQ/edit)
  - AFC SEL Skills for Rehearsal & Competency Building (https://docs.google.com/document/d/1hfURYr7X-d2co-Jq_gFxkB-yVg5_GESxoW7kopymL5hM/edit)
- Materials for presentation:
  - Books/articles
  - Notes
  - Visuals (charts, posters, pictures, etc.)

Timing: Two to three 45-minute periods

Preparation: You can apply this lesson to any content area; it should take place at the end of a unit. If this lesson is conducted in an English language arts classroom, students can present on a book they just finished reading. If it's conducted in a science classroom, students can present on a topic they learned about during a recent unit. Make sure students hold onto all notes and resources, because they will need them during Step IV.

Arrange students into groups of no more than four to five students. Also, assign students roles within their respective groups. Consider the following: *note taker, timekeeper, facilitator,* and *materials manager.*

Step 1: Introduction (5–8 minutes)

1. As students get settled into class, tell them, *"Today we're going to learn a strategy called Audience-Focused Communication or AFC. It will help us focus our message when communicating with others and keep the perspective of our audience in mind."*

2. Post the following questions on the board for students to reflect on and respond to in writing in their notebooks:
   - Have you ever been in an elevator and noticed the raised bumps next to the floor numbers?
   - Have you ever crossed a street and noticed the flashing signs that indicate when it's safe to cross?
   - Have you ever been at an event where an interpreter uses sign language to translate what the speaker is saying?
   - Have you ever used Google Translate?

3. Facilitate a whole-class conversation, asking students, *"What is the purpose of the bumps, flashing signs, interpreter, and Google Translate?"*

4. Guide them to the understanding that when people are blind, deaf or hard of hearing, or speak a different language than you do, you have to deliver your message in such a way that they can understand it. Tell students, *"Anytime we have an important message to communicate to someone else, we have to ask ourselves how we can most effectively communicate it so that our audience will be able to best understand it. The way we communicate with one audience will differ from the way we communicate with another."*

Step 2: Outcome Visualization (10 minutes)

1. Explain to students that today they are going to plan, practice, and deliver a presentation on a topic that they just learned a lot about over the last few weeks. Doing so will not only give them the opportunity to learn the material better by presenting it to others, but also enable them to practice presentation literacy skills, learn how to take the perspective of their audience, and gain recognition for their work.

2. Facilitate a whole-class conversation about the points below, and create a chart to reflect some of the ideas the class proposes.

3. Tell students that now that they have a clear understanding of the AFC strategy, as a class they will develop a vision for their AFC, keeping the following in mind:
   o Decide on/determine your audience.
      - Describe the audience (their prior knowledge, communication needs, and their anticipated views on the topic)
      - Why is the audience attending? Are they coming to see their children present? Has their attendance been assigned? Do they need to make a decision based on the presentation?
   o Identify any logistical considerations, such as timing, space, etc.
   o Decide on how you will get and maintain your audience's attention.
      - Interactive activities
      - Storytelling
      - Visuals
      - Planning for a break, if needed/allowed/possible
   o Decide on the type of presentation
      - Slideshow
      - Poster and discussion
      - Interactive game
   o Clarify your expectations for the audience's use of the information after the presentation
      - Provide additional resources
      - Offer opportunities for note taking

Step 3: Plan Development (15–20 minutes)

1. Explain to the students that they will meet in their groups and come up with a plan for their presentations. They will record this on the AFC Project Presentation Plan Graphic Organizer (https://docs.google.com/

document/d/1sKMbnx-yuHRtl27k1E1uMIjCCUuHdPzlIQoI04E5XQQ/
edit). The elements that their plan will reflect include the following:

○ Objective of the presentation

○ Identified audience and relevant information

○ Content of the presentation (in bullet points)

○ Method of delivery (for example, posters, slideshow, interactive discussion, game)

○ Step-by-step breakdown of the flow of the presentation

○ Assigned parts of the presentation to each group member (to ensure equity)

Step 4: Presentation Preparation (30 minutes)

1. At this time, students will carry out the plans they developed. This is the most important part of the process because they will consistently take the perspective of their audience and consider the grammar and language needed to effectively tailor their presentations.

2. Also, remind students to imagine the presentation from start to finish. They should

○ Greet the audience and introduce the group.

○ Introduce their topic.

○ State the goal of the presentation.

○ Begin discussing the main points of the topic.

- Provide evidence for the points made.

- Summarize each point before moving on to the next one, linking ideas from point to point.

- Clarify when moving on to the next point.

- Conclude.

— Signify the end of the presentation using a phrase such as "As we conclude/wrap up . . ."

— Restate the topic and goal of the presentation.

— Summarize the main points.

- Thank the audience and invite questions.

Step 5: SEL Skill Practice and Presentation Rehearsal (15 minutes)

1. Explain to students that just as they practice before a sports game or a recital, they will do the same with their presentations to increase their comfort level and confidence and make sure all the details work out as they intended.

2. Part of this rehearsal involves students using social-emotional learning (SEL) skills to regulate their emotions and be their BEST selves when presenting. Use the AFC SEL Skills for Rehearsal & Competency Building checklist (https://docs.google.com/document/d/1hfURYr7X-d2co-Jq_gFxkB-yVg5_GESxoW7kopymL5hM/edit) with your students. These skills include
   - Practice and role plays (to anticipate and plan for obstacles)
   - Visualization (imagery, "cope ahead")
   - Pre-performance rituals (to get in the flow, similar to what professional athletes do)
     - "Keep calm" and deep/belly/diaphragmatic breathing
     - Mindfulness
     - Reminding oneself to stay focused on the goal
     - Positive self-talk
   - Reminding oneself of one's BEST skills (https://docs.google.com/document/d/1AjktINfiibzZEC9G540vID-q4idVmnArSQ4iCDqAv-nY/edit; refer to Appendix C

3. Allow students time to rehearse and practice SEL skills.

Step 6: Presentation Delivery (timing will vary, depending on the length/number of presentations)

1. Allocate enough time for each group to present. If the students are part of the audience, have them take notes on their peers' presentations.

2. When each group presents, remind them to do the following:
   - Set up materials and technology.
   - Go through their pre-performance ritual.

- Mentally review the BEST skills.

- Greet their audience (use the appropriate titles and names), and introduce the group.

- Present to the audience, making sure all group members are equally involved.

- Conclude the presentation, and invite the audience to ask any questions they have.

- Thank the audience for their time.

Step 7: Reflection and Assessment (10 minutes)

1. Have each group meet to reflect on and celebrate their efforts and successes by addressing the following questions.

   - What went well?

   - What did not go well?

   - How would your plan have worked differently?

   - How did your audience respond to your message? Could they have responded better?

   - What SEL skills did you rely on before and during the presentation to regulate your emotions and build your confidence?

   - How could you improve the planning, rehearsing, or the delivery of your presentation if you were to do it again?

2. Debrief reflective responses as a whole class.

Formative Assessment: Have students respond in writing or record a video response (via an app like Flipgrid) to two of the three following questions:

- How did the presentation affect your understanding of the topic?

- How did tailoring your presentation to the needs of your audience affect how they received your message?

- How would the presentation have changed if you were to have delivered it to a different audience? (Give an example to support your reasoning.)

PLAN COMPREHENSIVE:
ELIZABETH CADY STANTON AND
SOCIAL JUSTICE FOR WOMEN

*How can disenfranchised groups organize to
secure their natural rights?*

Rationale: Students will engage in a social problem-solving strategy, PLAN, to learn how women approached the issue of unequal social, civil, and religious rights in the United States in the mid-1900s by partaking in meaningful dialogue. They will think about the perspectives of all parties involved in this historic issue and develop solutions to address the social injustices women faced. Students will consider their audience when presenting their solutions.

The PLAN framework stands for Problem description, List of options, Action plan, and Notice successes. Through this framework, students will analyze a problem, generate their own solutions, create an implementation plan to solve the problem, and reflect on the problem-solving process. They can apply the framework to a variety of issues, such as current events and historical events.

"The best protection any woman can have . . . is courage." (Elizabeth Cady Stanton). PLAN helps students take this lesson to heart and learn from the mistakes of the past by analyzing what worked well and what did not. Students weigh the options and consider potentially better alternatives, rather than passively learning about what took place or what simply didn't work. It nudges students to think about what people could have done differently.

The point of PLAN is to help students learn and use a specific problem-solving strategy. If you or other teachers in your grade already are using such a strategy, perhaps as part of an SEL education, a character education, or a bully/violence prevention program, you may want to use that as a framework instead of PLAN for the sake of consistency for students.

Objective: Students will analyze the keynote speech at the 1848 Seneca Falls Convention in New York to evaluate the effectiveness of the measures that

Elizabeth Cady Stanton took in leading women to advocate for equal rights. Students will develop an action plan reflecting alternative solutions to this issue.

Target Grade Levels: 5–8

Social Studies and ELA Standards:

- **NJSLS-SS.6.1.8.Civics DP.3.a.** Use primary and secondary sources to assess whether or not the ideals found in the Declaration of Independence were fulfilled for women, African Americans, and Native Americans during this time period.

- **NJSLS-SS.6.1.8.Civics PI.4.** Investigate the roles of political, civil, and economic organizations in shaping people's lives, and share this information with individuals who might benefit from this information.

- **NJSLSA.R6.** Assess how point of view or purpose shapes the content and style of a text.

- **NJSLSA.W9.** Draw evidence from literary or informational texts to support analysis, reflection, and research.

SEL Focal Skill: Responsible decision making

- Develop, implement, and model effective problem-solving and critical thinking skills

- Evaluate the personal, ethical, safety, and civic effect of decisions

Materials and Resources:

- Pencils/pens
- Notebooks
- Computer with audio and projectors
- Background source documents
  - Excerpt from "The Cult of True Womanhood" by Barbara Welter (p. 152) (https://english.hku.hk/staff/kjohnson/PDF/WelterBarbaraCULTWOMANHOODinAQ1966.pdf)
  - Elizabeth Cady Stanton's keynote speech from the Seneca Falls Convention (https://susanbanthonyhouse.org/blog/wp-content/uploads/2017/07/Elizabeth-Cady-Stanton-Seneca-Falls-1848.pdf)

- ○ "Five You Should Know: African American Suffragists" from the National Museum of African American History and Culture (https://nmaahc.si.edu/blog-post/five-you-should-know-african-american-suffragists)
- Chromebooks/laptops for students to use
- Copies of graphic organizers
  - ○ Problem Description Graphic Organizer (https://docs.google.com/document/d/1z46gA4PUey-Qo4entmEPJ8dMHQICW3y2uFlkXWPkCD9w/edit)
  - ○ PLAN Graphic Organizer if time doesn't allow for the more detailed problem description (https://docs.google.com/document/d/1DkY3IEEGP4_9A61-DsA-ql_I-mEykHEzEWnE9Z0wBD8/edit)
  - ○ SMART Goal Graphic Organizer (https://docs.google.com/document/d/17VqHPQJDGrft247CTpkicEXqh1X_bCBXwVgRIwU-CA0/edit?ts=5e9a361c)
  - ○ Pro-Con Options Graphic Organizer (https://docs.google.com/document/d/1VpBgztaBG6PlTv-OPrfSEGG_751XIc_MNREbR45GzhU/edit)

Timing: Four 45-minute periods

Preparation: Organize students into small groups of no more than four to five students. Inform them that they will be learning about several suffragists, including Elizabeth Cady Stanton, one of many courageous leaders involved in the women's suffrage movement who initiated the first organized women's rights movement in 1848. Her efforts extended well beyond securing voting rights for women to areas such as employment rights, parental and custody rights, and liberal divorce arrangements. Today students will work in groups to examine primary source documents related to Stanton's efforts in the women's rights movement to determine how leaders plan for collective action and to reflect on the process.

Have the graphic organizers and excerpts ready to hand out (links provided in the Materials and Resources section):

- Problem description
- SMART goal
- Pro/Con options

Lesson Procedure:

Step 1: Introduction and Problem Description (45 minutes)

1. **Do-Now (activity for students as they enter the room):**

   Students will write down their reactions in their notebooks to the follow-ing quote by Elizabeth Cady Stanton: "We are the only class in history that has been left to fight its battles alone, unaided by the ruling powers. white labor and the freed Black man had their champions, but where are ours?" Have students process their reactions to the quote as a whole class by posing the following questions:

   - What questions does this raise?
   - Why do you think Stanton said this?
   - What, if any, emotional reaction do you have to this?

2. **Provide Background Information:**

   - Give students time to read the excerpt from "The Cult of True Womanhood" by Barbara Welter (p. 152). Explain that this provides them with a historical context for the problem. Then have them define the terms *piety, purity, submissiveness,* and *domesticity.*

   - Students will read and annotate Elizabeth Cady Stanton's keynote speech at the Seneca Falls Convention in 1848.

   - Finally, provide students with the resource from the National Museum of African American History and Culture to shed light on the African American suffragists involved in the women's rights movement.

3. **Problem Description:**

   In their groups, students will craft a written **problem description** in their notebooks after answering the questions below about the problem —who it affects, the perspectives of the various individuals/groups involved, and other factors at play—to prompt their thinking. Use the problem description graphic organizer (https://docs.google.com/

document/d/1z46gA4PUeyQo4entmEPJ8dMHQICW3y2uFlkXWPk-CD9w/edit) to support students' collaborative efforts to define the problem.

- Is there a problem? How do you know?

- What is the problem?

- Where does the event described in the source occur?

- Who is affected by the problem?

- What are the issues of each perspective/party involved? What is the impact on the different individuals/groups involved?

- Who is responsible for the problem? What internal and external factors might have influenced this issue?

- What is causing those responsible to use these practices?

- Who were the key people involved in making important decisions?

To conclude, have each group draft a description of the problem. Feel free to select a few students to read aloud their descriptions to check for understanding.

Example problem description students might generate:

Women were confined to the home in their role as mothers and wives and did not have equal rights with men. They wanted to be free and to be represented in the government. Also, they wanted the government to revise the many unjust laws that protected men, but not women. Finally, Black women felt excluded from the efforts of white women to obtain equal rights.

Step 2: Listing Options and Action Planning (70 minutes):

1. Have students **list options** for solutions for how they might have solved the problem.

   - Identify a SMART Goal (Specific, Measurable, Action plan, Realistic, and Timely) from the perspective of different groups involved in the situation (for example, white suffragists, Black suffragists, veterans of the abolitionist movement, men in government).

   - List as many short- and long-term solutions as you can think of.

- Pick two or three solutions, and think about the pros and cons of these options (see graphic organizer).

2. Facilitate a whole-class discussion so students can process and report on what they discovered about how individuals at that time addressed the actual historical event and reflect on their solution development. Another option is to have students conduct this discussion first, then list options for solutions afterward.

- What options did students consider to be acceptable ways to resolve the problem?

- What do you think about their solution?

- What would your solution be?

- What solution did the suffragists ultimately decide to pursue?

Example options students might generate:
File complaints and pressure governmental officials to make changes for equal rights for women, protest for equal rights by organizing a rally, call for a meeting of women to draft a document of the rights they would like, organize a strike by not carrying out household duties.

Options students might pick: Protest for equal rights by organizing a rally

Pros: Shows united force of white women and sends a powerful message to men

Cons: Participants would face possible arrest, and men are not involved in coming up with a solution

3. Have students create their own **action plan** they might have used for addressing this problem, and analyze the plan that was used in history.

- Create action steps to outline how you would solve the problem. (Create action steps for different groups, if relevant.)

- What obstacles might you encounter?

- What plan was created at that time to solve the problem? (Allow students to research here.)

○ How is your plan different from the plan created? (Students will need to conduct research on the Declaration of Sentiments.)

○ How did they carry out the plan in history?

○ What obstacles did they encounter?

Sample Action Plan:

• Formally gather women to identify inequities in current laws (for women, especially women of color).

• Develop the details of the rally, with the place, time, and message to convey.

• Anticipate and prepare for any pushback from law enforcement personnel and from men in general.

• Convene with men to discuss revisions to laws and governmental documents.

4. Present action plans (additional 45 minutes/full class period): Student groups can present their action plans to a hypothetical audience of women's rights activists, men in government, or other groups whose rights were previously violated (such as freed Black men). Different subgroups in the class can target different audiences. Consider also having students present their action plan to a real audience. This can include having members of the school community—such as a female student council representative, a school counselor, a female school administrator, or a social studies teacher—serve on a panel, or it could involve presenting to an out-of-school audience, such as parents, community groups, historical societies, or local government/civil rights officials. This would enable students to rehearse their public communication skills with the STAT strategy of Audience-Focused Communication.

Students can accompany their speeches with slides and visuals, crafting their presentation for the specific audience and taking into account both the time and context of the presentation. Reference the Audience-Focused Communication guidelines in Chapter 5 to help students prepare their presentations. Consider following up the lesson with an Audience-Focused Communication lesson.

Step 3: Notice Successes and Reflect on the PLAN Process (20 minutes)

1. **Notice successes!** Debrief in small groups or as a whole class by addressing the following questions.

   - How did the plan work in history?

   - What went well?

   - What did not go well?

   - How would your plan have worked differently?

   - What can we learn from their experience that is relevant to the present?

   Example: Many women, including Elizabeth Cady Stanton and Lucretia Mott, called for the first U.S. women's rights convention in 1848 in Seneca Falls, New York. About 300 attendees drafted and debated the Declaration of Sentiments, which was modeled after the U.S. Declaration of Independence. Although only 100 of the 300 attendees signed the document and the convention did not secure suffrage for women, it did mark the beginning of the women's rights movement in the United States.

   Example: Many women of all different backgrounds convened to discuss ways to raise awareness about the inequities women were facing. This was beneficial, as it was the first time that some women of color were involved in these efforts. While they effectively organized a rally outside the White House and nearly 500 women attended, the protest broke out in violence. Approximately 15 of the protesters were assaulted by men who opposed their efforts. Despite the women's nonviolent approach, 30 of them were arrested by law enforcement personnel. Although the rally inspired more violence than the women intended, it ultimately generated wider support for the women's efforts to combat inequities in the current laws.

If students noticed that their plan wasn't effective or didn't speak to the specific stakeholders, have them revise their plan.

Formative Assessment: Have students write a reflection in their journals in response to at least two of the following questions:

- How does brainstorming as many solutions as possible influence your action plan, and what does this say about thinking outside the box?

- How does anticipating obstacles influence your action plan and likely outcomes?

- With the women's rights movement, how were the rights of one group tied to the rights of others?

- What issues of the women's rights movement of the 19th century are still relevant today?

- How did looking at the issue from many sides enrich the development of your action plan?

- Considering Elizabeth Cady Stanton's leadership, what skills are crucial for social action?

Lesson Extension: Identify an issue of gender inequality that still persists today. Draft an amendment to the U.S. Constitution to ensure that "all men *and* women are created equal."

Appendix C: Teaching Tips

Teaching Tips for YES-NO-MAYBE

1. **Collaborate with a mental health professional in your school.** Activities such as Yes-No-Maybe or any similar open-ended exchange of opinions could elicit strong feelings from some students. This is good and correlates with deep learning, but it can also bring about some discomfort. If you have any hesitation, speak to a school mental health professional either in advance or as a debrief or ask that person to attend, colead, or even model an activity to help you feel more comfortable.

2. **Take an interdisciplinary approach.** Consider introducing and modeling activities like Yes-No-Maybe during advisory time or team activities. Given that students are arranged in teams in many middle schools, seek opportunities to implement Yes-No-Maybe in all content areas, taking a team-based approach. The more exposure students have to the strategies, the more adept they will become in using them on their own.

3. **Have a plan for addressing peer conflict during discussion.** Here are some guidelines:

   • Acknowledge the strong feelings in the room.

- Take a break, and have students quickly write down or draw what they may be currently feeling, thinking, and or experiencing.

- Reorient students to the class norms and skills you have discussed, such as showing respect and empathy and engaging in responsible listening. Help students use these tools to communicate their experiences in a way that encourages understanding.

4. **Explore format variations.** Once your students get the hang of Yes-No-Maybe, don't hesitate to mix it up. Here are some variations we've seen:

   - Students write their ideas *before* stating each side of the Yes-No-Maybe.

   - Students revisit their position in writing after each or all sides of the Yes-No-Maybe.

   - Students keep a Yes-No-Maybe notebook, journal, or electronic folder where they keep track of how their ideas have changed as a function of having discussions with their peers during the activity.

   - The teacher gives the Yes-No-Maybe before starting a new lesson to get students involved; another Yes-No-Maybe can take place in the middle or end of the lesson to check in with students about whether their opinions changed.

5. **Keep generating new topics, questions, and discussions.** Here are some guidelines:

   - **Selecting relevant topics:** Choose Yes-No-Maybe topics based on historical content and questions you are teaching or on current events that relate to what you are teaching and for which there might not be a clear answer or solution.

   - **Creating unbiased questions:** As adults, we have our own opinions about many issues. The point of the Yes-No-Maybe is not for the students to arrive at a particular position but for them to learn how to reason, listen, and weigh options. So it's important to frame the questions in a neutral, unbiased way. For instance, a Yes-No-Maybe prompt that says, *"Gangs contribute to much of the drug use, violence, and crime within our society"* can be made more neutral by rephrasing it as *"There is a link between gangs and drugs, violence, and crime."* The former prompt assumes that gangs are directly responsible for drug use, violence, and crime. It has a restrictive connotation, claiming from the start that there *is* a link between gangs and drugs, violence, and crime rather than leaving space for students to formulate their own stance.

6. **Explore optional lesson extensions.** The lessons available on this book's companion website, **https://www.secdlab.org/stat/book**, include extensions for further enrichment of the skills and content. These align with research-based practices vetted by Rutgers Social-Emotional and Character Development Lab to advance academic content and civic discourse skills. Reach out to the lab staff at **secdlab@gmail.com** if you have any questions or want to share your success stories.

7. **Explore possible digital applications.** The lessons available at **https://www.secdlab.org/stat/book** include digital platforms you might integrate into the lesson to promote digital literacy and digital citizenship and gather daily formative feedback that can drive your follow-up planning. Consult with your technology coach if you need support around applications tailored to these lessons. If you don't have access to these applications, feel free to substitute an alternative digital or paper-based approach.

Teaching Tips for RESPECTFUL DEBATE

1. **Collaborating with a mental health professional in your school:** Debates or any similar open-ended exchanges of opinions could elicit some strong feelings from some students. This is good and correlates with deep learning, but it can also bring about some discomfort. If you have any hesitation, speak to a school mental health professional either in advance or as a debrief, or ask that person to attend, colead, or even model an activity to help you feel more comfortable.

2. **Taking an interdisciplinary approach:** Consider introducing and modeling activities like Respectful Debates during advisory time. In addition, given that students are arranged in teams in many middle schools, seek opportunities to implement Respectful Debates into all content areas, taking a team-based approach. The more exposure students have to the strategies, the more effective they will become in using them on their own.

3. **Addressing peer conflict:** *What happens if there's a conflict in discussion?* Here are some tools to use:

   - Acknowledge emotions, review class norms, and problem solve.

   - Acknowledge the feeling in the room.

   - Take a break and have students quickly write down or draw what they are currently feeling, thinking, or experiencing.

   - Reorient students to the class norms and skills, including respectful interaction, empathy, and responsible listening. Help students use the tools to communicate their experiences in a way that encourages understanding.

   - Help students focus on solutions, not problems.

   - *Note:* If a student attacks another student's *character* (an *ad hominem* argument) rather than the argument itself, point this out, clarify the difference, and redirect the focus of the debate.

4. **Tweaking materials:** *Can I create variations in this activity?* By all means, yes! Just document them for us. Here are some examples we've seen:

   - Students write down their ideas before starting each side of the debate.

   - Students revisit their position in writing after each or both sides of the debate.

   - Students keep a Respectful Debate notebook, journal, or electronic folder where they keep track of how their ideas have changed as a result of having discussions with their peers in the debate format.

5. **Generating debate topics and questions:** *What are some tips for generating fruitful debate topics, questions, and discussions?*

- **Create unbiased questions:** As adults, we have our own opinions about many issues. The point of the debate is not for students to arrive at a particular position but to learn how to reason, listen, and weigh options. So it's important to frame the debate questions in a neutral and an unbiased way. For instance, take the debate prompt *"Should the government limit gun owners' liberties by putting 'safety' locks on new guns?"* You can make it more neutral by saying, *"Should guns be required to have technology that would only allow their registered owners to use them?"* The former question assumes without question that gun owners' liberties will be "limited"—which has a restrictive connotation—rather than leaving that point up for debate, and the quotation marks around "safety" suggest that such measures are inconvenient at best. The latter question doesn't make any assumptions about whether such technology is helpful, and it doesn't assume that freedoms or rights are at risk of being taken away. This question leaves those topics up for debate.

- **Create pro/con-structured questions:** When structuring the debate questions, start with a statement or question that leads to two clear sides (pro/con), such as *"Only the police should be able to have and use guns"* or *"Should police be the only people allowed to have and use guns?"* rather than starting with an open-ended question, such as *"Who should be able to own guns?"* This latter question can generate many answers, and it will be difficult to create two clear sides. However, open-ended questions related to the debate topic can be a great option for do-nows or for introductory activities as students get settled at the start of class.

6. **Guiding the debate:** Students will likely benefit from having some form of graphic organizer that lists potential themes that can focus and guide the debate. For instance, most debates on historical and current events touch on ethical, legal, scientific, and economic considerations. See the Debate Theme Considerations Exercise at https://docs.google.com/document/d/1_NdQs7AMrOEt_eGXkp2mEJCRdi0ejdI_VLwuUm-5nXU/edit for an activity that looks at those four considerations.

7. **Optional lesson extensions:** Throughout the lessons, we've included lesson extensions for further enrichment of the skills and content. These align with research-based practices vetted by Rutgers Social-Emotional and Character Development Lab to advance academic content and civic discourse skills. Some extensions surrounding Audience-Focused Communication align directly with authentic assessment practices and citizenship skills. Reach out to lab staff at **secdlab@gmail.com** if you have any questions or want to share your success stories.

8. **Digital application suggestions:** We recognize the need for students to be digital democratic citizens. We've included digital platforms that you can integrate into the lesson to help students engage in digital literacy and digital citizenship and to assist teachers in using daily formative feedback from students to drive their planning. Consult with your technology coach if you need support with applications tailored to these lessons. If you don't have access to these applications, feel free to substitute an alternative digital or paper-based approach.

Teaching Tips for PLAN

1. **Alternative problem-solving strategy:** If you or other teachers in your grade are currently using a different problem-solving strategy, that's excellent. You may want to use that as a framework (instead of PLAN) for the sake of consistency for the students. Exercise your judgment to explore the elements of PLAN that

might complement your school- or grade-based problem-solving strategy.

2. **General considerations for PLAN Steps:**
   - **About the problem:** Students may identify multiple problems. A PLAN project might only address one or some of those problems as opposed to assuming there's only one problem that needs to be addressed.

   - **About the goals:** Each of the problems identified may have different goals, although some goals may overlap and address multiple problems.

   - **About listing options:** Students should list as many solution options as possible. With problem solving, people tend to stop listing options too soon, which can prevent them from thinking beyond their usual solutions.

   - **About weighing pros and cons:** Students weigh the pros and cons of each solution option. You might create a 2 x 2 matrix to chart the relative impact of the solution's goal (low or high) and the relative likelihood of carrying out the solution (low or high).The hope is that students would choose an option that falls in the top right-hand box of the matrix (high impact/high likelihood of success).

3. **Using graphic organizers:** The graphic organizers help students capture their ideas and organize their thoughts. You can distribute graphic organizers at the beginning of the lesson (for students to use as a guide throughout the problem-solving process) or at the end of the lesson (for students to summarize their answers). You can pass out hard copies of the organizers or make them available to download to a computer or tablet.

4. **Organizing student groups:** Feel free to assign roles within groups, such as *note taker, timekeeper, devil's advocate, motivator,* and *organizer.*

5. **Collaborating with mental health professionals in your school:** Open-ended exchanges of opinions may result in strong feelings from some students. If you have any concerns or hesitation, speak

with a school mental health professional. They may help you prepare the lesson, observe your lesson, colead a lesson, or model an activity to help you feel more comfortable.

6. **Interdisciplinary approach:** Consider exploring how to apply the PLAN problem-solving framework during advisory time (identify the **P**roblem, **L**ist options, create an **A**ction plan, and **N**otice successes). In addition, given that students are arranged in teams in many middle schools, seek opportunities for students to explore the problem through the lens of more than one content area. Given that students conduct research with this approach, the PLAN strategy also supports media literacy and digital citizenship skills. Consider consulting or partnering with the media center specialist in your school to enhance the implementation of PLAN.

7. **Involving relevant stakeholders:** This strategy contains rich opportunities to involve guidance counselors, faculty, community members, and school leaders. We encourage teachers to actively involve additional stakeholders to make connections beyond the classroom where the content allows. This is particularly the case for topics involving sensitive material or issues that generate controversy in the community.

8. **Aligning with standards:** PLAN integrates with specific curricular content indicators in state standards. For example, the PLAN activity about Elizabeth Cady Stanton and the Seneca Falls Convention aligns with New Jersey Social Studies Standard 6.1: U.S. History's demand for background knowledge of the Declaration of Independence and of women's rights during the early 1800s, and it calls upon critical thinking skills to evaluate the extent to which the ideals of the Declaration of Independence were fulfilled for women. PLAN also integrates instructional strategies that meet the global aims of active social studies learning in which students practice and apply the behaviors, habits, and skills required for democracy, such as those stipulated in New Jersey Social Studies Standard 6.3: Active Citizenship, and in the National Council for Social Studies Standard V (Individuals, Groups, and Institutions); Standard VI (Power, Authority, and Governance); and Standard X (Civic Ideals and Practices). You

can find additional standards connections in the separate STAT Standards Alignment Document.

PLAN instructional strategies include problem-based learning, activating prior knowledge, collaborative learning, small- and whole-group discussion, accountable talk and listening, modeling, flexible and strategic grouping, peer coaching and collaboration, and goal setting for student self-assessment and recognition.

9. **Classroom structure:** You can teach all aspects of the PLAN framework during whole-group or small-group instruction. When students are more familiar with PLAN, they can work independently or collaboratively in small groups.

10. **Alternating steps in Part II of the lesson:** You can reverse the hypothetical list options activity by having students analyze the actual decision that was made in history.

11. **Timing for teaching and implementing PLAN:** There are no guidelines for how long it takes to teach the PLAN framework or how often you should use it. The framework is flexible, so it can fit within your existing curriculum. You may use the framework in one lesson or break it up over the course of a week. Feel free to use it at your own discretion.

A Weeklong PLAN Lesson Format

Day 1	Day 2	Day 3	Day 4	Day 5
Problem Description	List Options	Action Planning	Present Action Plans	Notice Successes

Appendix D: Resources for Further Reading and Learning

Education Books

- *Building Better Citizens: A New Civics Education for All* (2019) by Holly Korbey
- *Educating for Civic Dialogue in an Age of Uncivil Discourse* (2020) by Dennis Gunn
- *Education and Democracy in the 21st Century* (2013) by Nel Noddings
- *Experience and Education* (1997) by John Dewey
- *Pedagogy of the Oppressed* (2005) by Paulo Freire
- *School's Over: How to Have Freedom and Democracy in Education* (2017) by Jerry Mintz
- *Teaching to Transgress: Education as the Practice of Freedom* (1994) by bell hooks

Social Issues Books

Race

- *How to Be an Antiracist* (2019) by Ibram X. Kendi
- *The New Jim Crow: Mass Incarceration in the Age of Colorblindness* (2012) by Michelle Alexander
- *Stamped from the Beginning* (2016) by Ibram X. Kendi

- *The Sum of Us: What Racism Costs Everyone and How We Can Prosper Together* (2021) by Heather McGhee
- *White Fragility: Why It's So Hard for White People to Talk About Racism* (2018) by Robin DiAngelo

Gender

- *The Gender Creative Child: Pathways for Nurturing and Supporting Children Who Live Outside Gender Boxes* (2016) by Diane Ehrensaft
- *Teaching the Teacher: LGBTQ Issues in Teacher Education* (2020) by Cathy A. R. Brant and Lara Willox (Eds.)
- *Transgender 101: A Simple Guide to a Complex Issue* (2012) by Nicholas M. Teich
- *The Verso Book of Feminism: Revolutionary Words from Four Millenia of Rebellion* (2020) by Jessie Kindig (Ed.)

Socioeconomic Status

- *Class and Schools: Using Social, Economic, and Educational Reform to Close the Black–White Achievement Gap* (2004) by Richard Rothstein
- *The New Human Rights Movement: Reinventing the Economy to End Oppression* (2017) by Peter Joseph
- *Poor Participation: Fighting the Wars on Poverty and Impoverished Citizenship (Democratic Dilemmas and Policy Responsiveness)* (2019) by Thomas A. Byer and Sofia Prysmakova-Rivera
- *The Poverty Problem: How Education Can Promote Resilience and Counter Poverty's Impact on Brain Development and Functioning* (2021) by Horacio Sanchez
- *Prisoners of the American Dream: Politics and Economy in the History of the Working Class* (1986) by Mike Davis

Neuro-abilities

- *Being Heumann: An Unrepentant Memoir of a Disability Activist* (2020) by Judith Heumann and Kristen Joiner
- *Care Work: Dreaming Disability Justice* (2018) by Leah Lakshmi Piepzna-Samarasinha

- *Disability and Human Rights: Global Perspectives* (2015) by Edurne Garcia Iriarte, Roy McConkey, and Robbie Gilligan (Eds.)
- *Disability Visibility: First-Person Stories from the Twenty-First Century* (2020) by Alice Wong (Ed.)

Podcasts

- *This American Life* (https://www.thisamericanlife.org/listen): A great resource for teachers to obtain background sources for STAT lessons on historical and current events.
- *The Cult of Pedagogy* (https://www.cultofpedagogy.com/pod): Advice for educators on how to make their practice more effective based on interviews with educators, students, administrators, and parents.
- *Embedded* (https://www.npr.org/podcasts/510311/embedded): Another resource for teachers to obtain background sources for STAT lessons on current events.
- *Inclusive Activism* (https://inclusiveactivism.com): A podcast for students and teachers that offers advice on finding our voices and emerging as leaders to debunk stereotypes and create an inclusive society.
- *On Being with Krista Tippert* (onbeing.org/series/podcast): This Peabody Award–winning program explores what it means to be human.
- *Pod Save the People* (https://crooked.com/podcast-series/pod-save-the-people): Keeps teachers up to speed on the latest social justice issues and provides inspiration for STAT lessons.
- *Pushing the Edge* (https://pushingtheedge.org/pushing-the-edge-podcast): Provides educators with stories of other educators who have challenged systemic inequities through social justice initiatives like STAT.
- *Queer America* (https://www.learningforjustice.org/podcasts/queer-america): Offers teachers background on the history of gender identity in the United States.
- *The Science of Happiness* (https://podcasts.apple.com/us/podcast/the-science-of-happiness/id1340505607): Offers educators research-based strategies that promote happiness, compassion, gratitude, and mindfulness in the classroom.

- *Teaching Hard History* (https://www.learningforjustice.org/podcasts/teaching-hard-history): A great resource for teachers to obtain background sources for history lessons and STAT lessons on current events.

- *Unlocking Us* (https://brenebrown.com/podcast/introducing-unlocking-us): Through discussions with many well-known scholars, artists, and authors, Brené Brown tackles universal issues of the human experience.

Websites

- ACLU: LGBTQ Youth & Schools Resource Library (https://www.aclu.org/library-lgbt-youth-schools-resources-and-links): Provides information about the rights of LGBTQIA+ students and how to make schools more inclusive spaces.

- Cult of Pedagogy (https://www.cultofpedagogy.com/social-justice-resources): A resource for educators that includes blog posts and videos that illustrate innovative teaching practices and offer classroom management tips and general advice for becoming more effective in your practice.

- EduColor (https://educolor.org): A hub of resources (books, websites, and articles) for teachers and students on issues of equity, agency, and justice, as well as opportunities to engage your students in taking social action.

- EdSurge (https://www.edsurge.com): A virtual community of teachers, administrators, and entrepreneurs that also offers many articles on educational technology.

- *Edutopia* (https://www.edutopia.org): A resource for teachers who are looking to improve their practice; *Edutopia* provides topical articles and blog posts by K–12 educators.

- *EdWeek* (https://www.edweek.org): A credible source of the latest news in education, as well as a font of suggestions about innovative teaching tools and strategies.

- Facing History and Ourselves (facinghistory.org): Offers social studies teachers lesson plans, articles, and professional development resources that are excellent for STAT lessons on historical and current events.

- Global Oneness Project (https://www.globalonenessproject.org): Offers teachers and students inspiration by presenting stories in the form of films, photo essays, interviews, essays, and virtual reality about people who have taken action in their community.

- GLSEN (the Gay, Lesbian, and Straight Education Network) (https://www.glsen.org): Offers educators support in the form of educator guides, webinars, lesson plans, and safe space kits to ensure that K–12 schools are inclusive spaces for all LGBTQIA+ students.

- Greater Good Science Center (https://greatergood.berkeley.edu): Through podcasts, videos, and articles, Greater Good provides science-based advice to teachers to improve their practice.

- IIRP Restorative Practices (https://www.iirp.edu/restorative-practices/what-is-restorative-practices): Gives teachers instructional support in implementing listening and restorative circles in their classrooms.

- Learning for Justice (learningforjustice.org): Offers a plethora of resources (lesson plans, background sources, film kits, student tasks, and so on) for teachers on the topics of race, ability, class, gender, and immigration.

- LiberatED (https://linktr.ee/liberated_sel): Dena Simmons's website offers educators resources on issues of human rights and strategies for navigating these issues with students.

- Open Circle (https://www.open-circle.org): This legacy website for the Open Circle program, which ran from 1997 to 2021, features links to a number of useful resources, including a library of children's literature that supports the development of core SEL competencies.

- Racial Equity Tools (https://www.racialequitytools.org): Offers tools, tips, research, and lesson plans for teachers interested in combating racial inequity and leading their schools as anti-racist educators.

- Rethinking Schools (https://www.racialequitytools.org): Another credible source of the latest news in education and of upcoming events that educators can attend hosted by several well-known educational organizations.

- Zinn Education Project (https://www.zinnedproject.org/materials/learning-for-justice): A great resource for obtaining background sources for STAT lessons in history for students in grades 5–12.

Related ASCD Resources

- *Building Learning Communities with Character: How to Integrate Academic, Social, and Emotional Learning* (2002) by Bernard Novick, Jeffrey S. Kress, and Maurice J. Elias

- *The Equity & Social Justice Education 50: Critical Questions for Improving Opportunities and Outcomes for Black Students* (2021) by Baruti K. Kafele

- *Neurodiversity in the Classroom: Strength-Based Strategies to Help Students with Special Needs Succeed in School and Life* (2012) by Thomas Armstrong

- "A Positive Classroom Climate, Even from a Distance" (*ASCD Express*) (2020) by Nancy Frey, Dominique Smith, and Douglas Fisher

- *Project Based Teaching: How to Create Rigorous and Engaging Learning Experiences* (2018) by Suzie Boss and John Larmer

- *Promoting Social and Emotional Learning: Guidelines for Educators* (1997) by Maurice J. Elias, Joseph Zins, and Roger P. Weissberg

- *Setting the Standard for Project Based Learning* (2015) by John Larmer, John Mergendoller, and Suzie Boss

- "Social Justice in the Suburbs" (*Educational Leadership*) (2009) by Scott Seider

- "Stirring Up Justice" (*ASCD Inservice*) (2009) by Laurel Schmidt

- *Teaching the Core Skills of Listening and Speaking* (2014) by Erik Palmer

Appendix E: STAT Elevator Pitches to Key Stakeholders

All key stakeholders in education—teachers, parents, special services/school mental health professionals, and administrators—are concerned with students becoming cynical about their schools, communities, and democracy. Too often, the national narrative of public education is shaped by forces beyond public education that claim that education is broken. That narrative says that educational stakeholders don't hold shared interests and that we are more divided than united when we discuss the desired outcomes for student learning.

We began this book by countering this narrative. Stakeholders have powerful common interests and hopes for students to exercise their voice and become agents of social action and social justice. And that's exactly what Students Taking Action Together (STAT) accomplishes. Stakeholders can use STAT to strengthen the purpose of public schools so they become laboratories for connecting knowledge, social-emotional competence, and democracy.

Talking About STAT to a Teacher

Given the unexpected demands that many educators are facing these days, you may feel overwhelmed about the prospect of meeting all your students' needs. You may wonder how you can teach all necessary content and, at the same time, attend to your students' social-emotional needs. The answer is Students Taking Action Together (STAT)—five teaching strategies that you can integrate in existing academic curricula and use to address school-based issues while meeting national and state instructional standards, particularly in social studies. The time you invest in STAT will be invaluable because it helps students develop the skills of critically examining issues from multiple perspectives, empathizing with people of diverse backgrounds, and collaboratively solving problems that affect their school, their community, and the wider world.

Now more than ever, students need to have the skills for civility and democratic action. STAT enables students to address unexpected events that happen in society—from an assault on the U.S. Capitol building, to a global pandemic, to racial unrest—and dig deep to analyze the underlying issues of power, privilege, and patriarchy that sustain social injustice. STAT provides teachers of all disciplines with the tools to empower students to become agents of social change; students learn how to reflect on their own beliefs, courageously stand up for them, and develop action plans to make those beliefs a reality.

Talking About STAT to a Parent

The question of what we want for our children in the future is ever-present in the minds of parents and educators. Together, we want students to possess the skills and character needed for success in school and life. You and your children's schools are partners in the process of empowering students to have a voice in their classroom, their school, and their community.

Students Taking Action Together (STAT) gives youth opportunities to reach their fullest potential, to become better humans to serve the common good. In the classroom, educators help students look at multiple sides of an issue, arrive at solutions to problems, and collaborate with others to put those solutions into action. Acquiring knowledge is not enough in the dynamics of the 21st century global economy and in a democratic society. STAT enables students to rehearse the skills they need for active civic engagement and constructive social change.

Talking About STAT to Special Services/School-Based Mental Health Personnel

School-based mental health personnel serve the important role of supporting teachers and students in acquiring social-emotional skills and developing character. It can be quite the balancing act to provide the necessary in-class and out-of-class support within an already jam-packed school day. That's where Students Taking Action Together (STAT) comes into play. STAT is a set of intuitive teaching strategies that give students opportunities to build the skills of emotional regulation, respectful listening, empathy, perspective-taking, and social problem solving in nonstigmatizing and supportive contexts.

School counselors have seen the benefits of STAT in the classroom, as well as in individual sessions. You will find that students start to grasp the concept of perspective-taking; they come to understand other points of view even if they don't agree with them, and they show mutual respect. The STAT strategies provide opportunities for consistent language and skill building across school settings, which enable students to gain mastery in these social-emotional skills and character virtues. The strategies empower students to successfully resolve conflicts, stay calm during stressful situations, and collaborate with a range of different personalities with confidence. STAT helps you, as a mental health professional, meet your goals in positive and enhancing ways.

Talking About STAT to an Administrator

As a school leader, you can't transform the culture of your school on your own. Supporting faculty to integrate transformational learning experiences is an all-hands-on-deck team effort. At the heart of school leadership are love, justice, equality, and a desire to help your school become a leader in student voice and engagement—not for some students or special students, but for *all* students.

What if you could put your school on the map as a center of constructive social action in the community by making it a place of student voice? What if it were possible to bring social-emotional learning (SEL) to your classrooms in a way that fully integrates it with academics, particularly social studies; English language arts; science, technology, engineering, and mathematics (STEM); and the visual and performing arts (VPA)? Students Taking Action Together (STAT) can transform your school into a school of social-emotional competence, civic engagement, and character—and have it formally recognized as such. Social-emotional learning is essential to achieve all valued learning outcomes in schools, and STAT builds this learning within the existing curriculum.

Nelson Mandela once stated that "an educated, informed, and enlightened populace is the surest way to ensure a healthy democracy." Indeed, our democracy needs to be nurtured by guided civil discourse and social justice learning in our public schools. With STAT, schools can provide a forum for teaching students the skills to critically examine issues from multiple perspectives, empathize with people of diverse backgrounds, and effectively solve the problems that plague their communities and the wider world. STAT's five instructional strategies satisfy these hopes, desires, and needs for active meaningful student learning. Ready-to-go lesson plans incorporating Norms, Yes-No-Maybe, Respectful Debate, PLAN, and Audience-Focused Communication offer a feasible and integrative path forward. STAT works with existing academic content related to history, social studies, and current events, and can also be employed to address issues and problems specific to schools. When you bring STAT into your school, you will see it's not an add-on, but rather an engine of synergy that will turn your "better" into "best."

References

Addams, J., Stanton, E. C., Harper, I. H., Shaw, A. H., Gage, M., Anthony, S. B., & Blatch, H. S. (2018). *Votes for women: Complete history of the women's suffrage movement in the U.S.* Madison & Adams. Kindle Edition.

Alsubaie, M. A. (2015). Hidden curriculum as one of the current issues of curriculum. *Journal of Education and Practice, 6,* 125–128.

Anderson, C. (2016). *TED Talks: The official TED guide to public speaking.* Houghton Mifflin Harcourt.

Armstrong, T. (2012). *Neurodiversity in the classroom: Strength-based strategies to help students with special needs in school and life.* ASCD.

Aungst, G. (2014, September 4). Using Webb's depth of knowledge to increase rigor. *Edutopia.* www.edutopia.org/blog/webbs-depth-knowledge-increase-rigor-gerald-aungst

Bahnson, A., Wilcox, J., Kruse, J. W., & Schou, T. (2020). Moving from surviving to thriving: Teaching social emotional learning alongside the NGSS. *Science Teacher, 87*(6), 28–34.

Baldwin, J. (1962, January 14). As much truth as one can bear. *New York Times.* https://www.nytimes.com/1962/01/14/archives/as-much-truth-as-one-can-bear-to-speak-out-about-the-world-as-it-is.html

Battelle for Kids. (2019). Framework for 21st century learning. http://static.battelleforkids.org/documents/p21/P21_Framework_Brief.pdf

Beeman, R. R. (n.d.). Perspectives on the Constitution: A republic, if you can keep it. *National Constitution Center.* https://constitutioncenter.org/learn/educational-resources/historical-documents/perspectives-on-the-constitution-a-republic-if-you-can-keep-it

Benne, K. D., & Sheats, P. (1948). Functional roles of group members. *Journal of Social Issues, 4*(2), 41–49.

Bond, L. F., Elias, M. J., & Nayman, S. J. (2021, January 25). Empowering students for social action in social studies. *Phi Delta Kappan.* https://kappanonline.org/empowering-students-social-action-social-studies-bond-elias-nayman/

Boss, S., & Larmer, J. (2018). *Project based teaching: How to create rigorous and engaging learning experiences*. ASCD.

Brown, B. (Host). (2020, October 21). Brené with Joe Biden on empathy, unity, and courage. [Audio podcast episode]. *Unlocking Us with Brené Brown*. https://brenebrown.com/podcast/brene-with-joe-biden-on-empathy-unity-and-courage/

Buck Institute for Education: PBL Works. (n.d.). Gold standard PBL: Essential project design elements. https://www.pblworks.org/what-is-pbl/gold-standard-project-design

Budesheim, T. L., & Lundquist, A. R. (1999). Consider the opposite: Opening minds through in-class debates on course-related controversies. *Teaching of Psychology, 26*(2), 106.

Burke, M. (2010). Overcoming challenges of the technological age by teaching information literacy skills. *Community & Junior College Libraries, 16*(4), 247–254.

Cartledge, G., & Milburn, J. F. (1995). *Teaching social skills to children and youth: Innovative approaches* (3rd ed.). Allyn & Bacon.

Cedano, S., (2021), *Assessing obstacles for "Students Taking Action Together" in lower-income school districts*. STAT Evaluation Report, Rutgers SECD Lab.

Centers for Disease Control and Prevention. (2018). CDC: 1 in 4 adults live with a disability. http://cdc.gov/media/releases/2018/p0816-disability.html

Chibana, N. (2015, December 5). 10 TED Talks by brilliant kids. *Visme*. https://visme.co/blog/ted-talks-kids/

Cohen, R. K., Opatosky, D. K., Savage, J., Stevens, S. O., & Darrah, E. P. (2021). *The metacognitive student: How to teach academic, social, and emotional intelligence in every content area*. Solution Tree.

Collaborative for Academic, Social, and Emotional Learning (CASEL). (2021). Guide to schoolwide SEL. https://schoolguide.casel.org/focus-area-2/learn/reflecting-on-personal-sel-skills/

Collaborative for Academic, Social, and Emotional Learning (CASEL). (n.d.). *FAQs*. https://casel.org/faq/

Common Core State Standards. (n.d.). *Standards for mathematical practice*. http://corestandards.org/Math/Practice

Cook, D. A. (2013). The engaged dialogue: Reflections on preparing African American teachers for diverse classrooms, *Multicultural Perspectives, 15*(1), 46–51.

Dart Center for Journalism & Trauma. (2005, December 1). Covering trauma: Impact on the public. https://dartcenter.org/content/trauma-coverage-impact-on-public#.UW2l-ivzbOV

Dean, C., & Brookhart, S. M. (2013/2014, December/January). Mathematical practices for deep understanding. *Educational Leadership, 71*(4). https://www.ascd.org/el/articles/mathematical-practices-for-deep-understanding

Desh. (n.d.) Change management: Kotter's 8-step change model. Project Pundit. https://projectpundit.com/change-management-kotters-8-step-change-model/

Dewey, J. (1938). *Experience and education*. Kappa Delta Pi. Macmillan.

Dewey, J. (2018). *Democracy and education*. Myers Education Press.

Draper, S. H. (2010). *Out of my mind*. Atheneum Books for Young Readers.

Durlak, J. A., Domitrovich, C. E., Weissberg, R. P., Gullotta, T. P., & Comer, J. (Eds.). (2015). *Handbook of social and emotional learning: Research and practice*. Guilford.

EdSurge. (2016, March 11). How can Edtech boost social emotional learning? https://www.edsurge.com/news/2016-03-11-how-can-edtech-promote-sel-a-new-report-answers-this-question

Edutopia. (2015, November 10). Empowering kids to be part of the solution. https://www.edutopia.org/practice/real-world-problem-solving-project-based-solutions

Elias, M. J. (2004). The connection between social-emotional learning and learning disabilities: Implications for intervention. *Learning Disability Quarterly, 27*(1), 53–63.

Elias, M. J. (2017, July 3). Helping your students identify their values. *Edutopia.* www.edutopia.org/blog/helping-your-students-identify-their-values-maurice-elias

Elias, M. J., & Butler, L. B. (2005). *Social decision making/Social problem solving for middle school students.* Research Press.

Elias, M. J., & Schwab, Y. (2006). From compliance to responsibility: Social and emotional learning and classroom management. In C. M. Evertson & C. S. Weinstein (Eds.), *Handbook of classroom management* (pp. 94–115). Lawrence Erlbaum Associates.

Elias, M. J., & Yuan, M. (2020). Creating coherent conceptualization and communication among character education kinfolk: Averting a "Tower of Babel." *Journal of Character Education, 16*(2), 19–26.

Emmons, M., Keefe, E. B., Moore, V. M., Sanchez, R. M., Mals, M. M., & Neely, T. Y. (2009). Teaching information literacy skills to prepare teachers who can bridge the research-to-practice gap. *Reference & User Services Quarterly, 49*(2), 140–150.

Evans, A. L., Evans, V., Kanra, A. L. Lami, & Jones, O. S. L. (2004). Public speaking in a democracy. *Journal of Instructional Psychology, 31*(4), 325–329.

Fine Acts. (n.d.). Fine Acts is a playground for social change. https://fineacts.co/about

Freire, P. (1968). *Pedagogy of the oppressed.* Seabury Press.

Freire, P. (2005). *Pedagogy of the oppressed: 30th anniversary edition.* Continuum International.

Fullmer, L., & Bond, L. (2021, March 29). Three strategies for helping students discuss controversial issues. *Greater Good.* https://greatergood.berkeley.edu/article/item/tips_for_resilience_in_the_face_of_horror

Garner, P. W., Gabitova, N., Gupta, A., & Wood, T. (2018). Innovations in science education: Infusing social emotional principles into early STEM learning. *Cultural Studies of Science Education, 13*(4), 889–903.

Goleman, D. (1994). *Emotional intelligence: Why it can matter more than IQ.* Bantam Books.

Goleman, D., Boyatzis, R., & McKee, A. (2002). *Primal leadership: Realizing the power of emotional intelligence: Tapping into your team's emotional intelligence.* Harvard Business School Press.

Goodloe, M. (2021). *Kingmaker: Applying Dr. Martin Luther King Jr.'s leadership lessons in working with athletes and entertainers.* Dream Life Loud.

Hackman, H. W. (2005). Five essential components for social justice education. *Equity & Excellence in Education, 38,* 103–109.

Hatchimonji, D. R., Linsky, A. C. V., DeMarchena, S., Nayman, S. J., Kim, S., & Elias, M. J. (2017): Building a culture of engagement through participatory feedback processes. *The Clearing House: A Journal of Educational Strategies, Issues and Ideas.* https://doi.org/10.1080/00098655.2017.1386000

Heim, J. (2021, March 1). Massive investment in social studies and civics education proposed to address eroding trust in democratic institutions. *Washington Post.* https://www.washingtonpost.com/education/civics-social-studies-education-plan/2021/03/01/e245e34a-747f-11eb-9537-496158cc5fd9_story.html

Heumann, J., & Wodatch, J. (2020, July 26). We're 20 percent of America, and we're still invisible. *New York Times.* https://www.nytimes.com/2020/07/26/opinion/Americans-with-disabilities-act.html

hooks, b. (1994). *Teaching to transgress: Education as the practice of freedom.* Routledge.

Hunt, L. M. (2015). *Fish in a tree.* Puffin Books.

Husband, T. (2012). "I don't see color": Challenging assumptions about discussing race with young children. *Early Childhood Education Journal, 39*(6), 365–371.

Inside Mathematics. (n.d.) Mathematical practice standards. https://www.insidemathematics.org/common-core-resources/mathematical-practice-standards

Jagger, S. (2013). Affective learning and the classroom debate. *Innovations in Education & Teaching International, 50*(1), 38–50.

Kaufman, M., & Belber, S. (2001). *The Laramie project: A play.* Vintage Books.

Kello, K. (2016). Sensitive and controversial issues in the classroom: Teaching history in a divided society. *Teachers and Teaching Theory and Practice, 22*(1), 35–53.

Kluth, P., & Schwarz, P. (2008). *Just give him the whale: 20 ways to use fascinations, areas of expertise, and strengths to support students with autism.* Paul H. Brookes.

Kotter, J. P., & Cohen, D. S. (2012). *The heart of change.* Harvard Business Press.

Kotter, J. P., & Schlesinger, L. A. (2008, July–August). Choosing strategies for change. *Harvard Business Review.* https://hbr.org/2008/07/choosing-strategies-for-change

Land, S. L. (2017). Effective teaching practices for students in inclusive classrooms. William & Mary School of Education. http://education.wm.edu/centers/ttac/resources/articles/inclusion/effectiveteach/

Larmer, J., Mergendoller, J., & Boss, S. (2015). *Setting the standard for project based learning.* ASCD.

Lee, L. (2020, March 5). 4 strategies to improve group work. *Edutopia.* https://www.edutopia.org/article/4-strategies-improve-group-work

Library of Congress. (2019). H.R. 849, Civics Learning Act of 2019. https://www.congress.gov/bill/116th-congress/house-bill/849/text

Lickona, T. (2004). *Character matters: How to help our children develop good judgment, integrity, and other essential virtues.* Touchstone Press.

Linsky, A. C. V., Hatchimonji, D. R., Kruzik, C. L., Kifer, S., Franza, M., McClain, K., Nayman, S. J., & Elias, M. J. (2018). Students taking action together: Social action in urban middle schools, *Middle School Journal, 49* (4), 4–14.

Lopez, S. J., & Louis, M. C. (2009). The principles of strengths-based education. *Journal of College and Character, 10*(4), 1–8.

Lord, C. G., Lepper, M. R., & Preston, E. (1984). Considering the opposite: A corrective strategy for social judgment. *Journal of Personality and Social Psychology, 47,* 1241–1243.

Ludstrom, K., Diekema, A. R., Leary, H., Haderlie, S., & Holliday, W. (2015). Teaching and learning information synthesis: An intervention and rubric based assessment. *Communications in Information Literacy, 9*(1), 60–82.

Marsh, J. (2013, April 16). Tips for resilience in the face of horror. *Greater Good.* https://greatergood.berkeley.edu/article/item/tips_for_resilience_in_the_face_of_horror

Marteney, J. (2020). *Arguing using critical thinking*. Academic Senate for California Community Colleges.

Martinson, D. L. (2005). Building a tolerance for disagreement. *Clearing House, 78*(3), 118–122.

Mayer, J., Salovey, P., & Caruso, D. (2004). Emotional intelligence: Theory, findings, and implications. *Psychological Inquiry, 15*(3), 197–215.

McCauley, D. (2015, November 10). Empowering kids to be part of the solution. *Edutopia*. https://www.edutopia.org/practice/real-world-problem-solving-project-based-solutions

McConaughy, S. H. (1986). Social competence and behavioral problems of learning-disabled boys aged 12–16. *Journal of Learning Disabilities, 19*(2), 101–106.

Moore, D. W., Bean, T. W., Birdyshaw, D., & Rycik, J. A. (1999). Adolescent literacy. [Position statement]. Commission on Adolescent Literacy of the International Reading Association.

Murphy, M. (2016, June). The tug of war between change and resistance. *Educational Leadership, 73*(9), 66–70.

National Art Education Association (NAEA). (2018, March). NAEA position statement on visual arts education and social justice. https://www.arteducators.org/advocacy-policy/articles/545-naea-position-statement-on-visual-arts-education-and-social-justice

National Council for the Social Studies. (n.d.-a). *Guide to civil discourse for students*. www.socialstudies.org/sites/default/files/guide_to_civil_discourse_student_version.pdf

National Council for the Social Studies. (n.d.-b). *National curriculum standards for social studies*. https://www.socialstudies.org/standards/national-curriculum-standards-social-studies-introduction

Nayman, S. J. (2019). *Students Taking Action Together: Final report, 2019*. Rutgers SECD Lab.

Newton, D., & Wolf, M. (2017, March). The change journey: Facing terminal illness. *Virginia Satir Global Network*. https://satirglobal.org/wp-content/uploads/2017/03/Change_Journey_Companion_Guide.pdf

Niemiec, R. M., Shogren, K. A., & Wehmeyer, M. L. (2017). Character strengths and intellectual and developmental disability: A strengths-based approach from positive psychology. *Education and Training in Autism and Developmental Disabilities, 52*, 13–25.

Noguera, P. (2019, July 8). Equity isn't just a slogan. It should transform the way we educate kids. *The Holdsworth Center: Insight*. https://holdsworthcenter.org/blog/equity-isnt-just-a-slogan/

Ontario Ministry of Education. (2006). *A guide to effective literacy instruction, grades 4 to 6, Volume Two: Assessment*. http://www.eworkshop.on.ca/edu/resources/guides/Guide_Lit_456_Vol_2_Assessement.pdf

Palacio, R. J. (2012). *Wonder*. Knopf.

Palmer, E. (2011). *Well spoken: Teaching speaking to all students*. Stenhouse.

Palmer, E. (2014a, November). Now presenting…. *Educational Leadership, 72*(3), 24–29.

Palmer, E. (2014b). *Teaching the core skills of listening and speaking*. ASCD.

Paul, M. (2015). *One plastic bag: Isatou Ceesay and the recycling women of the Gambia*. Millbrook Press.

Postman, N. (1996). *The end of education: Redefining the value of school*. Vintage Books.

Rashawn, R. (2020, July 23). Five things John Lewis taught us about getting in "good trouble." https://www.brookings.edu/blog/how-we-rise/2020/07/23/five-things-john-lewis-taught-us-about-getting-in-good-trouble/

Sawchuk, S. (2020, September 17). $1 billion for civics education? Bipartisan bill eyes dramatic federal investment. *EdWeek*. https://www.edweek.org/education/1-billion-for-civics-education-bipartisan-bill-eyes-dramatic-federal-investment/2020/09

Schermerhorn, J. R., Hunt, J. G., & Osborn, R. N. (2005). *Organization behavior* (9th ed.). Wiley.

Science Buddies. (n.d.). The engineering design process. https://www.sciencebuddies .org/science-fair-projects/engineering-design-process/engineering-design-process-steps

Sholette, G., Bass, C., & Social Practice Queens. (2018). *Art as social action: An introduction to the principles and practices of teaching social practice art*. Allworth Press.

SmartFocus on Social and Emotional Learning: A SmartBrief Update. (2019, Summer). Civility and society: How to boost civil discourse in K–12 classrooms. https:// static1.squarespace.com/static/5b5882f8b98a78554648ca48/t/5d976fe4c5f7cb7b66 7f73ee/1570205669752/Rutgers+SECD+Lab+SmartFocus+Civility+and+SECD+final .pdf

Sneider, C. (2018 November 28). Social emotional learning: Using collaboration in science. [Blog post]. Houghton Mifflin Harcourt. https://www.hmhco.com/blog/ social-emotional-learning-using-collaboration-in-science

Stanton, E. C. (1848). Seneca Falls keynote speech. https://susanb.org/wp-content/ uploads/2018/12/Elizabeth-Cady-Stanton-Seneca-Falls-1848.pdf

State of New Jersey Department of Education. (2020). *New Jersey student learning standards: Social studies*. https://www.state.nj.us/education/aps/cccs/ss/

Stevens, R. J., & Slavin, R. E. (1995). Effects of a cooperative learning approach in reading and writing on academically handicapped and nonhandicapped students. *Elementary School Journal, 95*(3), 241–262.

Svoboda, E. (2017, June 27). Why is it so hard to change people's minds? *Greater Good*. https://greatergood.berkeley.edu/article/item/why_is_it_so_hard_to_change_ peoples_minds

Tavarez, Y. (2021). *Culturally affirming youth programs: Students Taking Action Together (STAT) program assessment and feedback analysis*. STAT Evaluation Report, Rutgers SECD Lab.

Teaching Tolerance. (2019). *Let's talk! Facilitating critical conversations with students*. Southern Poverty Law Center.

Thomas, C. M. (2020). Society and the classroom: Teaching truths and bridging diversity in a discordant era. *Education Studies, 56*(1), 83–94.

Tomlinson, C. A. (2017). *How to differentiate instruction in academically diverse classrooms* (3rd ed.). ASCD.

Tyson, K., Hintz, A., & Hernandez, K. (2014, November). How to foster deep listening. *Educational Leadership, 72*(3). https://www.ascd.org/el/articles/how-to-foster-deep-listening

Vacca, R. T. (1998). Let's not marginalize adolescent literacy. *Journal of Adult and Adolescent Literacy, 8*, 604–609.

Washington University in St. Louis: Center for Teaching and Learning. (2020). *Using roles in group work.* https://ctl.wustl.edu/resources/using-roles-in-group-work/#:~:text=Group%20roles%20encourage%20individual%20accountability,less%20confident%20in%20volunteering%20for

Webster, S. (2019). Understanding lack of development in early career teachers' practical knowledge of teaching speaking skills. *System, 80,* 154–164.

Welter, B. (1966). The cult of true womanhood: 1820 to 1860. *American Quarterly, 18*(2), 151–174.

Westbrook, B. E. (2002). Debating both sides: What nineteenth-century college literary societies can teach us about critical pedagogies. *Rhetoric Review, 21*(4), 339–356.

Williams, R. (2002). *Multiple intelligences for differentiated learning (in a Nutshell Series).* Corwin.

Woodson, J. (2001) *The other side.* Putnam.

Yu, J. (2015). Analysis of critical reading strategies and its effect on college English reading. *Theory and Practice in Language Studies, 5,* 134–138.

Zins, J. E., Weissberg, R. P., Wang, M. C., & Walberg, H. J. (Eds.). (2004). *Building academic success on social and emotional learning: What does the research say?* Teachers College Press.

Index

The letter *f* following a page number denotes a figure.

About the Authors

 **Lauren M. Fullmer, EdD,** is a 5th grade teacher in Summit, New Jersey; an instructor for the Academy for Social-Emotional Learning in Schools, a partnership between Rutgers University and St. Elizabeth University an adjunct professor at St. Elizabeth University, an adjunct professor in the doctoral program at the University of Dayton; and a consulting field expert for the Rutgers Social-Emotional Character Development (SECD) Lab. Her firsthand experiences working with students in grades 1–5, coupled with four years of supporting pre-service teachers in their clinical internships at the higher education level, offer her a unique perspective on the pressing need for social justice education in grades 5–12. Her primary research areas focus on trauma-informed practices to meet the needs of at-risk learners in the K–12 classroom and on integrating social-emotional learning and social justice practices into content-area instruction. She lives in Whippany, New Jersey, with her husband, Dave, and sons, Cade and Rhys. She enjoys spending time outdoors with her family. Her hobbies include reading, doing puzzles, and cooking. You can reach her at lauren.m.fullmer@gmail.com.

Laura F. Bond, MEd, is an educational leader in central New Jersey and has taught secondary social studies for 19 years. She has served as a high school and an elementary school assistant principal and, recently, as a K–5 curriculum supervisor. She is passionate about whole child education and disrupting the hidden curriculum in schools and classrooms through equity-driven social-emotional learning and inclusivity measures. She is a member of the executive board of New Jersey ASCD and sits on the board of Mercer Street Friends in Trenton, New Jersey. She has served on a PK–6 public school board as the curriculum chairperson and as the head clerk of a Quaker school committee. Laura resides in Central New Jersey with her educator husband and two children. She enjoys hiking, biking, and spending time exploring and discussing the possibilities of our shared humanity and the world with her family.

Crystal N. Molyneaux, PsyD, is a New Jersey–Certified School Psychologist and graduate of the Graduate School of Applied and Professional Psychology (GSAPP) at Rutgers University. Crystal works in Maurice Elias's SECD Lab on the Students Taking Action Together (STAT) project, which has developed materials embodying social action pedagogy and social-emotional character development for integration into middle and high schools throughout New Jersey. Crystal is passionate about social-emotional learning (SEL), restorative justice (RJ), empowering women and girls, decreasing systemic racism and oppression, amplifying student voice, and creating and maintaining student support systems while also using evidenced-based methods to build confidence. Her ultimate goal is for the work done with students and staff within the school to have a positive impact on families and communities as a whole. Crystal works with students in group and individual settings to assist in self-awareness, self-efficacy, and self-management in hostile or adverse situations. In an effort to keep youth who are disproportionately represented in juvenile justice systems out of the school-to-prison pipeline, Crystal helps youth of minority backgrounds to discover new and more adaptive ways to cope and express themselves. Outside her work, you can find Crystal with her family, attending basketball games, hosting movie night, and attending concerts and the theater.

 **Samuel J. Nayman, PhD,** a postdoctoral fellow in clinical child/pediatric psychology at Mayo Clinic, served as the Students Taking Action Together (STAT) project director in the Rutgers Social-Emotional Character Development (SECD) Lab. Sam is committed to creating greater opportunities for people to achieve their potential by way of policies and SECD interventions. In this pursuit, he has designed and consulted on school-based SECD programs, as well as published peer-reviewed articles and a book chapter on this subject. Sam is a graduate of Rutgers University's clinical psychology doctoral program and Yale School of Medicine's doctoral internship in clinical and community psychology. He also enjoys participating with family in the annual JDRF bike ride (which funds research for type 1 diabetes), singing karaoke with friends, and listening to podcasts.

 **Maurice J. Elias, PhD,** is a professor in the psychology department of Rutgers University and director of the SECD Lab. He is codirector of the Rutgers-based Academy for SEL in Schools (SELinSchools.org), which offers online certificates in social-emotional learning instruction and school leadership, and he is a member of the leadership team for SEL4NJ (https://sel4nj.org) and SEL4US (www.SEL4US.org).

He received the Joseph E. Zins Memorial Senior Scholar Award for Social-Emotional Learning from CASEL, the Sanford McDonnell Award for Lifetime Achievement in Character Education, and the Jane Bostrum Service to School Psychology Award. Maurice is a past winner of the Lela Rowland Prevention Award, of the Ernest McMahon Class of 1930 Award for service to New Jersey, and of the American Psychological Association/Society for Community Research and Action's Distinguished Contribution to Practice and Ethnic Minority Mentoring awards. Most recently, he is the coauthor of *Social-Emotional Learning Lab: A Comprehensive SEL Resource Kit* (2021), *Nurturing Students' Character: Everyday Teaching Activities for Social-Emotional Learning* (2020), and *Boost Emotional Intelligence in Students: 30 Flexible Research-Based Lessons to Build EQ Skills* (2018); he also writes a blog on social-emotional and character development for *Edutopia* (www.edutopia.org/profile/maurice-j-elias). Maurice is a licensed psychologist and lives in New Jersey with his wife, Ellen, near their two children and two grandsons, Harry and Isaac. He enjoys doing everything with his grandsons, especially sports, reading, imaginative play, music, building, and being silly. His hobbies include racquetball and pinochle. He can be reached at secdlab@gmail.com. His Twitter handles are @SELinSchools and @SECDLab.

Related ASCD Resources

At the time of publication, the following resources were available (ASCD stock numbers in parentheses):

Demystifying Discussion How to Foster Academic Talk for Radical Student Growth, K–5 by Jennifer Orr (#122003)

Improve Every Lesson Plan with SEL by Jeffrey Benson (# 121057)

Literacy Is Liberation: Working Toward Justice Through Culturally Relevant Teaching by Kimberly N. Parker (#122024)

Making Curriculum Matter: How to Build SEL, Equity, and Other Priorities into Daily Instruction by Angela Di Michele Lalor (#122007)

Media Literacy in Every Classroom (Quick Reference Guide) by Faith Rogow and Cyndy Scheibe (#QRG117107)

The Power of Place: Authentic Learning Through Place-Based Education by Tom Vander Ark, Emily Liebtag, and Nate McClennen (#120017)

The Power of Voice in Schools: Listening, Learning, and Leading Together by Russ Quaglia, Kristine Fox, Lisa Lande, and Deborah Young (#120021)

Project Based Teaching: How to Create Rigorous and Engaging Learning Experiences by Suzie Boss and John Larmer (#118047)

Questioning for Classroom Discussion: Purposeful Speaking, Engaged Listening, Deep Thinking by Jackie Acree Walsh and Beth Dankert Sattes (#115012)

Setting the Standard for Project-Based Learning: A Proven Approach to Rigorous Classroom Instruction by John Larmer, John Mergendoller, and Suzie Boss (#114017)

Teaching the Core Skills of Listening and Speaking by Erik Palmer (#114012)

Teaching Students to Decode the World: Medial Literacy and Critical Thinking Across the Curriculum by Chris Sperry & Cyndy Scheibe (#122006)

Teaching to Empower: Taking Action to Foster Student Agency, Self-Confidence, and Collaboration by Debbie Zacarian and Michael Silverstone (#120006)

For up-to-date information about ASCD resources, go to www.ascd.org. You can search the complete archives of *Educational Leadership* at www.ascd.org/el.

For more information, send an email to member@ascd.org; call 1-800-933-2723 or 703-578-9600; send a fax to 703-575-5400; or write to Information Services, ASCD, 1703 N. Beauregard St., Alexandria, VA 22311-1714 USA.

WHOLE CHILD
TENETS

1 HEALTHY
Each student enters school healthy and learns about and practices a healthy lifestyle.

2 SAFE
Each student learns in an environment that is physically and emotionally safe for students and adults.

3 ENGAGED
Each student is actively engaged in learning and is connected to the school and broader community.

4 SUPPORTED
Each student has access to personalized learning and is supported by qualified, caring adults.

5 CHALLENGED
Each student is challenged academically and prepared for success in college or further study and for employment and participation in a global environment.

ascd
whole child

The ASCD Whole Child approach is an effort to transition from a focus on narrowly defined academic achievement to one that promotes the long-term development and success of all children. Through this approach, ASCD supports educators, families, community members, and policymakers as they move from a vision about educating the whole child to sustainable, collaborative actions.

Students Taking Action Together relates to the **engaged** and **challenged** tenets.

For more about the ASCD Whole Child approach, visit **www .ascd.org/wholechild.**

Become an ASCD member today!
Go to www.ascd.org/joinascd
or call toll-free: 800-933-ASCD (2723)

ascd